THE DIPLOMACY OF HOPE

The Diplomacy of Hope

THE UNITED NATIONS SINCE THE COLD WAR

Newton R. Bowles

Published in 2004 by I.B.Tauris & Co. Ltd
6 Salem Road, London W2 4BU
175 Fifth Avenue, New York, NY 10010
www.ibtauris.com

In the United States of America and Canada distributed by Palgrave Macmillan, a division of St Martin's Press, 175 Fifth Avenue, New York, NY 10010

Copyright © 2004 Newton R. Bowles

The right of Newton R. Bowles to be identified as the author of this work has been asserted by the author in accordance with the Copyright, Designs and Patents Act 1988.

All rights reserved. Except for brief quotations in a review, this book, or any part thereof, may not be reproduced, stored in or introduced into a retrieval system, or transmitted, in any form or by any means, electronic, mechanical, photocopying, recording or otherwise, without the prior written permission of the publisher.

ISBN: 1 85043 458 1
EAN: 978 1 85043 458 0

A full CIP record for this book is available from the British Library
A full CIP record for this book is available from the Library of Congress

Library of Congress catalog card: available

Typeset in Garamond by A. & D. Worthington, Newmarket, Suffolk
Printed and bound in Great Britain by MPG Books Ltd, Bodmin

Contents

	Abbreviations	vi
	Acknowledgements	x
	Foreword	xi
	Introduction	xiii
1.	The Great Thaw?	1
2.	Human Insecurity: Ten Years and More	5
3.	Disarm: Life or Death?	25
4.	Who Owns Terror?	38
5.	No Hiding Place: War Criminals	42
6.	Human Rights, Human Wrecks	56
7.	Women: The Whole World in Their Hands?	67
8.	Children: The Future is Now	77
9.	Humanitarian Rescue and On	90
10.	People and Poverty	97
11.	The World Around Us: The Environment	109
12.	Nature's Terror: HIV/AIDS	115
13.	'We the Peoples': Civil Society	119
14.	Mapping, Management, Money	128
15.	The Millennium	141
16.	Into the Twenty-First Century	157
17.	Yes, We Can	168
	Notes	170
	Bibliography	175
	Index	183

Abbreviations

ABM	Anti-Ballistic Missile Treaty
ASEAN	Association of South-East Asian Nations
Bretton Woods	This is where the international financial institutions, the IBRD and IMF, were negotiated.
CHR	Commission on Human Rights
CIS	Commonwealth of Independent States
CSW	UN Commission on the Status of Women
CTBT	Comprehensive Test Ban Treaty
DRC	Democratic Republic of the Congo
ECOSOC	Economic and Social Council
ECOWAS	Economic Community of West African States
EU	European Union
FAO	Food and Agriculture Organization
G7	Group of 7 (industrialized countries)
G77	Group of 77 (developing countries)
GA	General Assembly (of the United Nations)
IAEA	International Atomic Energy Agency
IASC	Inter-Agency Standing Committee
IBRD	International Bank for Reconstruction and Development (World Bank)
ICC	International Criminal Court
ICFTU	International Confederation of Free Trade Unions
ICJ	International Court of Justice
ICRC	International Committee of the Red Cross
IFOR	Implementation Force (for Dayton Agreements)
ILO	International Labour Organization
IMF	International Monetary Fund

INTERPOL	International Criminal Police Organization
NAM	Non-Aligned Movement (developing countries)
NATO	North Atlantic Treaty Organization
NGO	Non-Governmental Organization
NORDICS	Denmark, Finland, Norway and Sweden
'NORTH'–'SOUTH'	'North' in quotes means the economically advanced countries; and 'South' means the developing countries.
NPT	Non-Proliferation Treaty (for nuclear weapons)
OAS	Organization of American States
OAU	Organization of African Unity
ODA	Official Development Assistance
OECD (DAC)	Organization for Economic Co-operation and Development (Development Assistance Committee)
OIC	Organization of the Islamic Conference
OIOS	Office of Internal Oversight Services
OSCE	Organization for Security and Co-operation in Europe
PERM 5	Permanent 5 members of the Security Council
SC	Security Council (of the United Nations)
SG	Secretary-General (of the United Nations)
TNC	Transnational corporation
UNCED	UN Conference on the Environment and Development
UNCTAD	UN Conference on Trade and Development
UNDAF	UN Development Assistance Framework
UNDP	UN Development Programme
UNEP	UN Environment Programme
UNESCO	UN Educational, Scientific and Cultural Organization
UNFPA	UN Population Fund
UNHCR	UN High Commissioner for Refugees
UNICEF	UN Children's Fund
UNIFEM	UN Development Fund for Women
UNPROFOR	UN Protection Force (Yugoslavia)
UNRRA	UN Relief and Rehabilitation Administration

UNRWA	UN Relief and Works Agency (for displaced Palestinians)
WFP	World Food Programme
WHO	World Health Organization
WILPF	Women's International League for Peace and Freedom
WMD	Weapons of Mass Destruction
WTO	World Trade Organization

To Jean
aka Pres
Death does not part

Acknowledgements

Is there a new way to say thanks? And to apportion credit or blame? Some thank their cats, others thank their mothers. Having neither cat nor mother, I lay it all on you, friends and colleagues. Some will rejoice in anonymity. Others flinch at being named: Rachel Brett, Phyllis Lee, Roy Lee, Randy Rydell, Margaret (Peg) Snyder, whose brains I borrowed. For their inerrant ferreting of glitches, disjunctures and opacities, my obeisance to Frances Allee, Vicky Balcomb and Gene Brewer. For her meticulous index finger, my great thanks to Christina Richards. For her infectious bibliomania, I salute Diana Ayton-Shenker. And for meticulous endnotes, my thanks to Jenny Acton and Leslie Morris.

Special thanks also to Denise Yuspeh Hidalgo for her assistance with proofreading and document preparation, to David Worthington for his keen editorial eye, and to Stephanie Paradiso whose hand behind the scenes kept this show on the road.

Better than I can, Jim Sutterlin speaks for himself.

Foreword

Beginning in 1978, Secretary-General Javier Pérez de Cuéllar perceived a growing commonality of interests among the five permanent members of the Security Council in resolving regional conflicts and dealing with global issues. 'It was as if,' he wrote in his 1987 Annual Report to the General Assembly, 'the sails of a small ship, in which all the people of the earth are gathered, had caught again, in the midst of a perilous sea, a light but favourable wind.' In the ensuing years the small wind gained greatly in strength, and nowhere did it have more impact than on the United Nations. The Security Council, enjoying a new solidarity, took the lead in ending the long war between Iraq and Iran, in resolving conflicts in Cambodia and Central America, in guiding Namibia to independence and in repelling the Iraqi invasion of Kuwait. The first President Bush and Russian President Mikhail Gorbachev were both moved to declare the birth of a new world order grounded in an effective Security Council, competent to meet its responsibility for maintaining peace and international security.

But the favourable winds of the post-Cold War era proved inconstant. There have been further notable achievements in resolving regional conflicts and in building peace based on democratic governance. There have also been dismal failures of will even in a united Security Council and, at times, an alarming lack of competence on the part of the UN peacekeeping establishment. Secretary-General Boutros Boutros-Ghali, after being the first to define the concept of peace enforcement, quickly concluded that when major military enforcement action was required, the Security Council had best ask member states to act on its behalf. Most of the conflicts with which the Security Council has been concerned in these years have been internal in nature, which has led to a major change in the understanding of 'security'. No longer could the UN be concerned only with the security of states, as the founders had expected. Its responsibility grew to include the security of peoples within states and in countries where the state had failed. The logic of concern for the security of persons within states led inevitably to the need for humanitarian intervention, a concept that while never authoritatively defined, has prompted remarkable achievements for human well being and has led to divisive controversy as to the limits of national sovereignty.

In this sympathetic history of the United Nations since the end of the Cold War, Newton Bowles brings these developments into clear perspective, conveying a sense of the excitement and turmoil that have characterized the post-Cold War years. He does not limit himself to the security issues that dominate the headlines, but goes fully into the activities of UN programmes, the specialized agencies, and even associated non-governmental organizations that provide the very basic elements of human security – nourishment, shelter, health, human rights, sustainable development and the protection of children and women. His pallet encompasses the whole panoply of the UN family. One recognizes very quickly that the author is a member of this family, joined to it by affection and long association but, as any intimate family member, well aware of its flaws and weaknesses. This is a very personal book that lets the reader appreciate the humour and wisdom of the author as well as the importance of the events he describes. The title of the book, *The Diplomacy of Hope*, is apt. The author's hope in the UN as the first among multilateral institutions was severely challenged by the action of the United States and the United Kingdom in mounting a pre-emptive war against Iraq without the authorization of the Security Council. In touching on this event, the author lets us feel his despair. 'What we need is the anatomy of failure,' he writes, 'not the anatomy of hope.' Yet, he can blame the UN for what has happened only insofar as it reflects the reality of the world. From all that he writes, it emerges that in so many ways the UN remains of vital importance to world security in the broadest sense of the meaning of security. As emerges clearly from this book, the UN remains alive and relevant across the extent of its Charter responsibilities. The hope that has long been placed in multilateral diplomacy remains justified if it is tempered by a realistic appreciation of the tendency of states to pursue national interests at will through unilateral action and of the consequent imperfection of multilateral institutions.

James S. Sutterlin

Introduction

As the son of a Protestant pastor, I was reared in Semitic mythology, fables of hope and despair, of escape from evil, of a new life. For those who bore the burden of hope, the Red Sea would open and we would walk into the Promised Land where all is peace. In these dark days as we walk into a new century, who can live without such a vision? In the dungeons of hate, where is the vision?

'We the peoples' who keep hope alive have learned the bitter lesson. The Red Sea will not open up. There is no other Promised Land. This is the Promised Land, to do with as we can.

We live by our myths. We make myths to give meaning to our lives. The United Nations is a myth. Only 'we the peoples' can make it real. We are the Red Sea, the blood of life, the blood of hope.

This book is a sort of diary. It tells of work in progress, reclaiming good ground from the pit of despair. The work has begun. There is joy in the mending. 'Better is a poor and wise child than an old and foolish king who will no more be admonished' (*Ecclesiastes* 4, Verse 13).

I begin this diary by confronting despair, by engaging in a dialogue with the dark. Then I walk on to paths of hope, of good things we have done to stem violence, to vanquish disease, to save, protect and nourish the mothers and children of our old new world. It is we who write this diary.

Every end has a beginning. So let me begin with the end. This book ends with war, cynicism, despair. Iraq and terrorists have shown that the UN cannot work. The UN Millennium celebrations, ushering in the twenty-first century, were a sham. After all the talk, it is power that decides. The UN has failed. What we need is the anatomy of failure, not the anatomy of hope.

I say *need*, and that is the give-away. *Need* means we want to know why. And that also implies understanding failure. What is failure? The UN is the world. Has the world failed?

Mesmerized by TV – if you are – you can see the UN dead. And looking back just 50-odd years, you can see that the UN was still-born. But here's the catch. If still-born, why is it dying now? What kind of death is this?

War, cynicism, despair. What kind of despair is this? The poet Nadezhda Mandelstam wrote about despair in her book, *Hope Against Hope*, on the tragic political entrapment and death of Russia's great poet, her husband Osip Mandelstam. Her name, Nadezhda, means hope. Her suffering is life itself, a poet's alchemy. How many children these days are named 'Hope'?

But what has this to do with the United Nations? Nadezhda was one person against *the state*. Isn't that precisely our problem? We have codes of behaviour, moral codes for individuals, and most people on the whole follow the rules. We have something called a conscience that keeps us on track. But people in groups, in nations, seem to revert to a kind of jungle behaviour. Put them all together and what can you expect?

We have touched on a profound and perplexing problem. What is it that determines national behaviour? Is there such a thing as national, and hence international, morality? The historical record is pretty bad. Yet along with all the bloodshed, in the last century or so, serious measures and codes have emerged to regulate and mitigate international violence. There is some kind of tenuous group morality. Without it there would be no United Nations. The UN is an experiment. Its idea is for states to co-operate, not to fight. States have their national legal systems for defining acceptable behaviour, for settling disputes. The UN is to do that for the world, to make laws for international behaviour, and to be a place where diplomacy – talk, compromise, accommodation – will be the road to peace.

Instead, since the UN was born, there have been dozens of wars killing millions of people. True, especially since the Cold War, since 1989, most of these have been domestic affairs, wars at home, not wars between states. But war is war.

And now, in 2003, the USA has given up on the multilateral process (seeking a common international approach to Iraq's intransigence) and has turned its gigantic military machine against Baghdad. The USA was not alone in this: with it were the UK, Spain and most of Eastern Europe. Still, this was not the UN. Most UN members have not supported US action. It was preceded by a strenuous, at times bitter, UN debate. President Bush, speaking at the General Assembly on 12 September 2002, in effect put the UN on notice. He seemed to be saying: The UN either goes with us or it will be irrelevant. So now the USA is installing a new government in Iraq, with the UN relegated to providing humanitarian aid or political façade. Is that what has become of the UN, a housekeeper for the great?

In Iraq, for now, so it seems; although the dust is still settling. More dust lies ahead. How will a US-sponsored government go down in Iraq and in the region? Even if Israel and Palestine find a way to live together, can Iraq be stable without UN legitimacy? The USA has found making peace much harder than making war.

The showdown over Iraq was a heavy blow to the UN, not the first but certainly the worst yet. The crisis showed how desperately the world needs the UN as the bulwark against anarchy, terrorism and war. The crisis gave conviction and passion to rhetorical support at the General Assembly. And this drama was played out at the UN.

Not only at the UN. 'We the peoples' took to the streets. Millions marched for peace, not war, on the streets, in great cities and towns, in the media and on the Internet. Thousands had protested, in Seattle (2001) and Genoa (2002), against inequities of globalization. But 2003 was new, and around 15 million citizens, families young and old, many first-time protesters, said no to war, yes to peace, yes to the UN. There lies hope.

With the UN in jeopardy, why have I anchored my ship in hope? I have anchored it in experience. In 1998 I wrote an analytic history of the United Nations Inter-Agency Task Force for Child Survival and Development. From 1984 to 1998 this Task Force, in which I had a part, was the nerve centre for strategic action to promote child health, especially the remarkable immunizations that continue today. Thinking about what had given life to that complex process, I decided to call my study *Hope as Energy: An Experiment*. Coming five years later to this analytic history of life at the UN, could I turn that title around: Energy as Hope? Maybe energy, at its best, is hope. My good friend Maynard Gertler handed me the right way to say it: The Diplomacy of Hope. Whatever else it is, the United Nations is the symbol and vector of hope.

The United Nations is itself a product of hope, a hope that was generated in despair, in a desperate world war. In 1965 the UNICEF representative in Egypt was Dr Olga Makeyeva, a prominent Moscow paediatrician. My work had taken me to Egypt. 'Before you leave, there is something you must see,' said Olga. Our driver took us west into the desert, beyond Alexandria, to El Alamein, scene of the epic battle where the British stopped the German advance into the Middle East. Stark in the desert were three vast graveyards: German, Italian and British. Two hundred thousand dead. That I could see. 'Never again,' said Olga. Stark in the windswept desert, 200,000, I see it still. Never again.

The name 'United Nations' came from Franklin Delano Roosevelt, to signal a break from the sad League of Nations that limped between two world wars. The UN was grounded in the victors' wartime alliance (China, France, United Kingdom, USA, USSR), reincarnated in the five permanent members (PERM 5) of the Security Council. It is this Council that has power to act, and its decisions are binding on all members. Even so, the UN hardly made it up to the moment of its birth in San Francisco in June 1945. Without the veto power of any one of the PERM 5 to block action, neither the USA nor the USSR would have embraced the UN. The General Assembly's full membership could talk, the Security Council with luck could act. That was the political compromise that launched the UN. Cold War clouds were already creeping over San Francisco Bay. It took 40 years for the clouds to dissipate. The UN and hope survived. (For more on the UN system, see pages 128–30.)

Investment in hope is risky. The collapse of the USSR released a lot of hope. From teetering on the brink of a nuclear holocaust, Washington, Moscow and satellites could plant the fields of peace. From trudging along the sidelines, the United Nations could be the staging ground for a new world. Trimming the military would produce a peace dividend. No more war. Naïve? This was indeed the US–Russian pitch at the UN in 1990, in the recorded voices of George Bush senior (President) and Eduard Shevardnadze (Russian Minister of Foreign Affairs). That is where my story begins.

That is not where it ends. The story is much more complicated than any had foreseen, with plots and subplots and a shifting swarm of characters. The real world had always been there, but for 40 years it had been obscured, distorted through Cold War binoculars, the artifice of confrontation, not one world but two. Now the world was one, *and there was no peace dividend.*

My book traces the bizarre story, from *perestroika* through the UN Millennium Summit to the crisis over Iraq. It has been quite a journey.

Let's begin with some numbers. The world's population was 2.5 billion in 1945, 5.3 billion in 1990 and 6.2 billion in 2003. There were 51 states in the UN in 1945, 159 in 1990, and 191 in 2003.

Core staff of the UN was 9,000 in 1990 and 9,000 in 2002. The UN regular budget was US$1.2 billion in 1990 and US$1.3 billion in 2003. There were no UN peace operations in 1945, but there were 36 in the 1990s and 15 still ongoing in 2003. Peacekeeping was budgeted at $1.4 billion in 1992 and at around $2.3 billion in 2003. Over 1,800 peacekeepers have been killed and over 200 unarmed humanitarian workers have given their lives in UN service.

Following Iraq's invasion of Kuwait in 1990, there were no old-fashioned wars between countries in the 1990s, but there were 50 armed conflicts inside countries. Five million civilians were killed in these wars, of whom 2 million were children. As for poverty, the number of people in the world surviving on something like $1 a day stands at about 1.2 billion, most of them in South Asia and sub-Saharan Africa.

Apart from what is implied in its peace operations, where does the UN come into this picture? Here are a few more numbers.

- In 1990 nearly 13 million toddlers under the age of 5 died of preventable disease. In 2002 the number of deaths had dropped to 10 million.
- Immunization has brought polio cases down from 300,000 in 1988 to under 5,000 in 2002. Polio eradication is within sight.
- In 1990 iodized salt, which prevents serious brain damage, was available to only 20 per cent of the people in developing countries. By 2002 70 per cent of them had iodized salt, protecting the annual crop of 20 million babies.
- Births per woman have fallen from nearly 6 before 1990 to half that number in 2002. At the same time, women's literacy has doubled to around 60 per cent.
- Those having access to clean water rose from 4.1 billion in 1990 to over 5 billion in 2002.

Just a few indicative figures. Do numbers speak for themselves? They say something. But numbers, of course, are only part of the story.

My lead story is about trust, respect, compromise and sharing. It is about peace, justice and equity. It is about national interest that transcends borders. It is about the whole process of multilateral give and take that is this hopeful, fearful, fragile United Nations. It is about the only live forum where impoverished nations speak up to the rich and strong, where, for example, little Timor-Leste (formerly East Timor) could stand up to Indonesia. It is a club of sovereign governments, of big politicians, of intrigue, of lust, of compassion.

But these are not the only actors in this forum. Especially now, ever present are 'the peoples', citizen organizations, advocates, watchdogs, and the media, prying and prodding.

For peace and security, the UN has done a lot of quiet mediation to head off conflict, something that cannot be publicized. At the same time, in visible operations the UN approach has been maturing, from military peacekeeping towards peacemaking and peacebuilding. After Iraq's invasion of Kuwait, all wars were domestic affairs. The UN was called in to defuse and mediate many of these civil wars: everywhere peace rests on social, not military stability – human security. In these new engagements, unforeseen in the Charter, the UN Security Council fumbled tragically in Srebrenica and Rwanda. Critiques of these tragedies led to serious and practical improvements in UN capacity. UN military operations are becoming more and more one phase of nation-building, as in Kosovo, Timor-Leste and Sierra Leone. Under the UN banner there have been 54 peace operations, over 30 initiated since 1990. The number of persons serving in these operations – military, police, civilians – peaked at 78,000 in 1994, but declined to 43,000 in 2003. From the beginning, more than 750,000 persons from 90 countries have served in these UN operations, and, as already noted, over 1,800 have given their lives in the cause of peace.

As for disarmament, the UN is where all negotiators can be found. Treaties are in place to regulate and eliminate biological and chemical weapons. For nuclear weapons, the Non-Proliferation Treaty (states ratifying the Treaty are bound not to go nuclear) was renewed in 1995, but India and Pakistan went nuclear in 1998. Although critical nuclear negotiations between the United States and Russia moved ahead a little in 2002, the US posture on nuclear weapons remains most troubling. A treaty to formalize forever the existing moratorium on nuclear tests was blocked by the US Senate in 1999. Although most states fear 'missile defence' as a step towards weaponizing outer space, the US government has initiated a missile defence system. For other (conventional) weapons, UN guidelines to prevent weapons pouring into troubled regions are largely ignored. The UN Register of Conventional Weapons tracks the weapons trade, but as a base of regulation it is hardly noticed. The use of some weapons most dangerous to civilians is restricted in one existing treaty, and many states have joined the Ottawa Treaty to eliminate land mines. Principles have been adopted for controlling the black market trade in small arms. In a world bristling with armaments, the forces for ploughshares look to the UN.

Progress towards a world ordered by law is manifest in human rights, now identified and given legal status in wide-ranging treaties. Most were adopted before 1990, including the Convention on the Rights of the Child (1989). Although most states have formally accepted these treaties, none like their delinquencies exposed, while many in the 'South' maintain that here is a neo-colonial export. The issue was joined at the World Conference on Human Rights (Vienna 1993) where all states reconfirmed their formal allegiance to universal rights. Vienna also led to the establishment of a new office, the UN High Commissioner for Human Rights. Following Vienna, the UN adopted a declaration to protect human rights defenders, an endangered species. Also adopted were protocols strengthening the Convention to eliminate discrimination against women and the Convention on the Rights of the Child. On the legal frontier the 1990s saw important rights advances.

For most human rights, however, the only enforcement has been exposure before the conscience of the world, at the UN Commission on Human Rights and the General Assembly. UN monitoring is mightily reinforced by independent citizens' organizations (NGOs) like Amnesty International and Human Rights Watch. But now the UN is growing judicial teeth, already evident in the war crimes tribunals for Yugoslavia and Rwanda, as well as the permanent International Criminal Court (ICC) which came into being in 2002. The tribunals are ad hoc systems to prosecute the worst butchers, to break the spell of impunity and to help the Balkans and Rwanda escape their bloody history. As practical exemplars of objective justice, the tribunals have provided good experience for the permanent ICC. The Court will be able to prosecute individuals in countries that have agreed to join it, but only if national courts can't or won't do it. Neither the tribunals nor the permanent ICC have their own police; they rely on states to catch indicted suspects. The International Court of Justice (ICJ) deals only with disputes between states.

As for poverty, equity, social and economic progress, discourse at the UN keeps the moral and political issues alive. Without a universal doctrine about the brave new world, the UN consensus is that globalization so far has benefited the rich at the expense of the poor. Globalization has to be taken in hand somehow so as to get the neglected into the mainstream. Corrupt autocracies will never make it. The poor of Africa cry out for help. These issues continue to obsess the UN.

The 1990s were studded with richly productive conferences on major aspects of human development – rights, population, women, children, the environment, slums – their findings converging in a comprehensive UN report, an *Agenda for Development*. Support for national development must put the poorest countries first. Poverty is a breeding ground for violence and war, and so attacking poverty converges with the Security Council's search for ways to forestall conflict.

In house, fresh air has come since Kofi Annan took over as Secretary-General in 1997. His international team, drawn from over 160 countries, has begun to enjoy a new sense of direction and of responsibility. His Deputy, Louise Frechette, is the co-pilot who gets things done. Staff morale is now tested by the Iraq crisis.

As his last act for the UN, Richard Holbrooke, US Ambassador to the UN under President Clinton, managed to free up the log-jam on the US contribution to the UN. Not only US money but a more positive US engagement is desperately needed. Following Iraq, the USA is, at best, ambivalent.

At the start of a new century in 2000, the Millennium Summit of 147 heads of state gave a sense of direction to the UN. The Summit Declaration was not only an affirmation of faith, but was also a plan of action for the UN and for member states.

Secretary-General Kofi Annan keeps a steady hand at the helm. Here, in part, is what he said as the 2002 General Assembly began:

> All States have a clear interest, as well as a clear responsibility, to uphold international law and maintain international order.

> Our founding fathers, the statesmen of 1945, had learned that lesson from the bitter experience of two world wars and a great depression. They recognised that international security is not a zero-sum game. Peace, security and freedom are not finite commodities, like land, oil or gold, which one State can acquire at another's expense. On the contrary, the more peace, security and freedom any one State has, the more its neighbours are likely to have. And they recognised that, by agreeing to exercise sovereignty together, they could gain a hold over problems that would defeat any one of them acting separately. If those lessons were clear in 1945, should they not be much more so today, in the age of globalization?
>
> On almost no item on our agenda does anyone seriously contend that each nation can fend for itself. Even the most powerful countries know that they need to work with others, in multilateral institutions, to achieve their aims. ...
>
> That applies even more to the prevention of terrorism.[1]

Referring then to urgent demands for international solutions – Israel/Palestine, Iraq, Afghanistan – he said:

> Let me conclude by reminding Members of their pledge two years ago, at the Millennium Summit, to make the United Nations a more effective instrument in the service of the world's people. Today, I ask them to honour that pledge. Let us all recognise from now on – in each capital, in every nation, large and small – that the global interest is our national interest.

Postscript

Today as I write it is 11 September 2003. Two years ago today terrorists flew hijacked planes into New York's World Trade Towers and into the Pentagon in Washington. The United Nations is based in New York, and so I live here. Today, like two years ago, is a clear sunny day. In my taxi on the way to work, I asked my driver where he had been on that fateful day. 'I was there,' he said. 'My passenger died.'

On 19 August 2003 a truck bomb demolished the United Nations Office in Baghdad. Nineteen UN people died, including Sergio Vieira de Mello, senior representative of UN Secretary-General Kofi Annan.

Such terrorism strikes the UN at its base. This is random violence confronting UN ideals and norms. Terrorists succeeded in putting the US military into Afghanistan and Iraq. The UN was consulted but not embraced.

Speaking to the press on 8 September 2003, a week before the annual UN General Assembly was to convene, the Secretary-General said:

> Events have shaken the international system. ... Member States have been sharply divided about some of the most fundamental issues that the Organization was set up to deal with.

> We all agree that there are new threats. ... But we don't seem to agree what exactly they are, or how to respond, or even whether the response should be a collective one. ...

> And last month, in Baghdad, the United Nations itself suffered the most direct and damaging attack in its history.

This is indeed a critical hour in humanity's desperate struggle towards a sane international order. The UN emerged from world war. Will it survive?

CHAPTER 1

The Great Thaw?

The year 2000 marks a turning-point, beginning not only the turn of the decade, not only the turn of the century, but also the turn of the millennium.[1]

Which devout millenarian came up with this profound observation? It was the elder George Bush, President George Herbert Walker Bush, speaking at the General Assembly on 1 October 1990.

So what was this all about? The war was over, the Cold War that is; Reagan and Gorbachev had their love feast; nations united! Bush continued: 'The founding of the United Nations embodied our deepest hopes for a peaceful world. And during the past year, we have come closer than ever before to realizing those hopes.' Also: 'On a personal note I want to say that ... I have never been prouder to have once served within your ranks [he was US Ambassador to the UN 1971–73] and never been prouder that the United States is the host country for the United Nations.'

As the world keeps rushing by, I find it hard to take myself back even a decade or so. What was it like in 1990? What was it that turned him on? Since 1988 the European East – Poland, Czechoslovakia, Hungary, Romania and all – had come tumbling down. The Warsaw Pact was dead. The Berlin Wall had crashed, its debris picked up as souvenirs. Speaking on 1 October Bush knew that two days later the impossible would happen: East and West Germany would unite. And just two months earlier, on 2 August, Saddam Hussein had marched into Kuwait, seizing its oil and everyone, diplomats and all, who happened to be there. For once, the UN Security Council promptly and with one voice denounced Iraq and said, if you don't get out by 15 January you'll be sorry. This was the new UN embraced by the US President.

President Bush was not alone in his euphoria. Eduard Shevardnadze, Foreign Minister of the still extant USSR, said a few days earlier: 'Politically, this has been not just a calendar year but a light-year in the history of the world. The Cold War, with its accompanying stress, psychoses and anticipation of disaster, is no longer a part of our life.' Continuing, he said, 'The United Nations, too, is being reborn.' Citing his President Gorbachev, he said: 'The central concepts of today's politics are co-operation, interaction and partnership.' He saw Iraq's invasion of Kuwait as a dark cloud on the sunny worldscape, 'a blow ... against all that mankind has recently achieved.' What he said after that had a touch of compassion and humility, qualities that are taboo in UN jousting: 'From this rostrum, we should like to appeal once again to the leaders of Iraq. We are making this appeal as their old friends and as a country that has found the courage to condemn its own wrong-doings against certain States in the past.'[2]

What signals came from the other three permanent members of the Security Council (the PERM 5, the Second World War allies)? None were as exuberant as the old Cold Warriors, the USA and the USSR. UK Foreign Secretary Douglas Hurd said, 'We can be enthusiastic about the real progress which has been made in the world, provided that we are sober about the tasks still to be accomplished.'[3]

France's President François Mitterand entered on a high plateau: 'The end of the East–West conflict should be hailed as the triumph of reason and of a sense of responsibility. ... However, I would refrain from engaging in premature optimism.' Now a little dig at the Anglos: 'With the North Atlantic Treaty Organization paralysed, the United Nations ... is coming into its own.' (Douglas Hurd told the Assembly that at a July 1990 summit in London, 'we decided that NATO should remain.') But, as for Iraq, Mitterand found himself in the same boat as Shevardnadze. 'France has long had friendly relations with Iraq,' he said. 'But France is first and foremost in the service of the law as defined by this arbiter between nations: the [UN] Organization. ... Our policy is the policy of the United Nations.'[4] (Interlarded was reference to France's support for Iraq's massive eight-year invasion of Iran, an aggression in which Western powers were complicit.)

Foreign Minister Quan Quichen maintained China's careful stance, a little aloof, a circumspect sovereign member of the UN. 'Reviewing the 1980s, we can see that the world has taken an uncommon course. ... Thanks to the efforts of people of all countries, military confrontation has been reduced and the factors for peace have increased. ... However, power politics continue. Political, economic and ethnic strains have become increasingly evident.' No blanket endorsement of the UN; yet 'we are pleased to note that in the past year, the United Nations has continued to play an active part in maintaining world peace and security and in resolving a number of urgent problems facing mankind.' The UN should play a more important role in the future 'so that it will not let down the high expectations of the people of the world.' There was no equivocation in condemning Iraq's invasion of Kuwait, 'an action that, in China's view, constitutes a violation of the United Nations Charter and a gross trampling on the accepted norms governing international relations. ... The Chinese government supports a political settlement of the Gulf crisis.' International relations should be based on mutual respect for sovereignty, non-interference in internal affairs and peaceful coexistence. Every country is entitled to choose its own political system.[5]

The Canadian Foreign Minister Joe Clark joined the chorus: 'Never before has the opportunity for this body to exercise its intended mission been greater, and never before have the risks and challenges been so daunting.' He continued: 'Walls of the mind and real walls' have come tumbling down. We had been seeing the world 'through the prism of the Cold War. ... That prism was a prison, and it has now been shattered.' Looking over the ills of the world – poverty, pollution, armaments – he said: 'This is not the picture of a planet in promise: it is the picture of a planet in pain.' Canada advocates 'co-operative security,' he said, encompassing social and economic well being, disarmament, democracy, trust and respect. 'Let us behave as United Nations.'[6]

To clear the decks for my survey, I turn back to the General Assembly on 1 October 1990, and to President George H.W. Bush:

> There are ten more years until the century is out – ten more years to put the struggles of the twentieth century permanently behind us; ten more years to help to launch a new partnership of nations. Throughout those years, and beginning now, the United Nations has a new and vital role in building toward that partnership.[7]

No more war: out of the blue?

Who chose blue for the UN? It stands for peace and hope, yes, but also for despair. Our desperate hope, the UN.

It was the night of 2 November 1956. In my office in the UN I had been working late. My normal discipline was to shut out political shenanigans and give my all to UNICEF. This night was different, a crisis, the General Assembly in special session. Following border skirmishes that summer, on 29 October Israel had invaded Egyptian Sinai. In July President Nasser had seized the Suez Canal. Now the British and French, colluding with Israel, had troopships afloat to take back the Canal. Moscow supported Nasser. I walked into the General Assembly hall, standing beside the podium. The Security Council had told the British and French to call it off. On that November night, I saw empire go down and the UN come up. Canada's Foreign Minister, Lester Pearson, sold the General Assembly on the idea of a UN peacekeeping force to secure a Suez ceasefire, soon accepted by all. This was a completely new idea, not to be found in the 1945 Charter. In the Suez crisis it worked, and opened a new window for the Security Council from then on. Lester Pearson got the Nobel Peace Prize.

Keeping world peace, at the cost of 50 million lives, was the top concern of the Second World War Allies, led by Roosevelt and Churchill, in creating the UN. Its Charter begins on a high and solemn note:

> We the peoples of the United Nations determined to save succeeding generations from the scourge of war, which twice in our lifetime has brought untold sorrow to mankind. ...

The whole Preamble to the Charter exudes power and dignity. It should be read, along with received sacred script, in private and public devotions.

CHAPTER 2

Human Insecurity: Ten Years and More

The Cold War was waged outside the UN, keeping most action away from the Security Council. After Gorbachev, and released into 'cold peace', the Council became the dumping ground for Cold War leavings, contaminating many a new drama of domestic violence.

Things change. The 1990s turned out to be the decade when UN peace operations matured from standing between enemies to repairing countries after war, from restraining warriors to protecting women and children, from fire-fighting to seeking the sources of violent conflict. This was the decade when wars were wars at home, domestic wars among their own people. It was the decade that heard the cries of innocents, women and children, caught in the cross-fire of greed and lust for power. It was the decade when the Security Council was stuck over how and when the UN should try to end domestic conflict. It was a decade of sparse diet, peacekeeping on short rations. Entering the twenty-first century, little has changed.

As the years went by, although there was no progress in updating its membership, the Security Council opened its doors to the General Assembly (GA) and to advocates of war's victims. The Council also made its words come alive by fielding its own missions to such hot spots as Kosovo, the Democratic Republic of the Congo (DRC), Sierra Leone and East Timor/Indonesia. The Council also dug into dirt in Angola and the Democratic Congo, fielding its own emissaries to get at the facts. It was an interlude when brilliant success was overshadowed by failure. Late in these years, serious analyses of two tragedies – Srebrenica and Rwanda – led to a searching review of UN peace operations by an expert group chaired by UN veteran Lakhdar Brahimi. It was an interlude of hope, unique in witnessing two summit meetings of the Security Council (involving heads of state) in 1992 and 2000.

Peace walk

To help us understand where the UN is today, let us walk through the critical 1990s and into our new century, beginning with a glance at 1945.

In 1945 the responsibility for keeping the peace was put in the hands of the Security Council, the five wartime allies as its permanent core, with a few more members (originally six, increased in 1965 to ten) elected biennially by the General Assembly. The Cold War hobbled the Council; its action in the Suez crisis was exceptional, bridging the Washington–Moscow chasm. In 1987, even before the USSR had split up, Gorbachev's about-face, embracing the UN, took all by surprise. Armageddon no more? Smooth sailing? Wind in the Council's sails?

Yet it was not just rhetorical wind that fanned UN optimism. In 1988 the UN had helped the USSR to get its bloodied troops out of Afghanistan, and that same year the UN had arranged the peace between Iran and Iraq. The UN also helped Fidel Castro get his bewildered soldiers out of Angola. Central American presidents in 1987 agreed on a common approach to political stability and economic growth, a framework for the UN to monitor a ceasefire and free elections in Nicaragua in 1990 (the first UN presence in national elections). There followed the UN-mediated reconciliation in El Salvador and the first steps towards peace in Guatemala. Cambodia was coming out of its nightmare in 1990 as bloodied hands signed on to a peace accord. After 20 years' gestation, the UN delivered independent Namibia in 1990, and in that year South Africa, with the UN looking on, moved formally to end apartheid. How easy it has been to forget that UN Peacekeeping was awarded the Nobel Peace Prize in 1988. All this set the stage for the first summit meeting of the Security Council in January 1992.

On 31 January 1992, for the first time ever, heads of government took over: an impressive array, with Prime Minister John Major of the UK presiding over George Bush, Boris Yeltsin, François Mitterand, Li Peng and nine other heads of government. This Summit wound up with a universal affirmation of the central role of the UN in maintaining peace, the need to strengthen the UN in its new peacekeeping functions, the urgency of disarmament and the imperative of eradicating poverty as an underlying cause of war. With one voice they declared 'the world now has the best chance of achieving international peace and security since the foundation of the United Nations.'[1]

Agenda for peace

More than three decades of peacekeeping appeared to be getting results. Until then, it had been all ad hoc action as crises arrived on the UN doorstep. Now was the time to anticipate, at least to set some guidelines on, where and when the UN might get involved. The Council asked Secretary-General Boutros-Ghali, just elected in December, to give them some ideas to think about. Dr Boutros-Ghali was a bright and seasoned diplomat who, after extensive consultations with leading institutions and persons outside the UN, in June produced his comprehensive report, *Agenda for Peace*, a splendid achievement. Although initiated by the Security Council, the *Agenda* would define policy for all, so that it was put before the General Assembly as well as the Council. Developing countries, dominant in the GA, were ever on their guard against creeping imperialism under the guise of the Security Council. Nevertheless the Assembly approved most of Boutros-Ghali's proposals, specifically anticipating and preventing armed conflict by:

- More diplomatic missions by the Secretary-General and his representatives.
- Better early warning of impending conflict.
- More active fact-finding missions where trouble is brewing.
- Doing more to inspire trust and confidence between contenders.
- Providing adequate humanitarian assistance.
- Preventive deployment of UN troops where trouble is brewing.
- Peacebuilding and mending societies damaged by war.

To enable the UN to move a bit faster, a 'peacekeeping reserve fund', a token $150 million, was approved. UN peace operations, like all else, were chronically starved. This 'fund' was not real money – it was a window at the bank waiting for deposits, i.e. in this case, special contributions for peacekeeping.[2]

That is not the end of the peace agenda story, not quite. Experience – Somalia, Yugoslavia, Rwanda – led to elaboration and clarification in the form of a supplement to the *Agenda* in January 1995. A second summit had been planned, but that had to wait another five years.

To summarize the supplement:

- Don't mix up peacekeeping and peace enforcement. Peacekeeping, cooling off, mediating, demands strict neutrality and impartiality. Peacekeeping forces are lightly armed solely for the purpose of self-defence.
- In the long run, the UN should be given the means to enforce peace, as foreseen in the Charter (i.e. a UN stand-by force). Right now, the UN is resource starved and hard pressed to handle peacekeeping and peacemaking. The UN could consider peace enforcement only in a small way. Any big peace enforcement operation would have to be entrusted by the Security Council to member states, with all the attendant political risks.
- The stand-by arrangement whereby national units are on call to serve the UN is not so good because governments may not answer a UN call. Rwanda is a flagrant case.
- The main obstacle to preventive diplomacy and peacemaking is that warring parties don't want to make peace. Can we create the international ethos where UN mediation is the norm? Meantime, the UN faces practical problems: few senior diplomats are available to take on UN assignments, and the UN does not have money for even small backup staff in the field.
- Small arms and land mines are the killers and destroyers in today's conflicts. Disarmament energies have addressed mass weapons but neglected small arms. These weapons are everywhere and represent about one-third, by value, of the international arms trade. A recent UN mission to Mali confirmed the extreme difficulty of controlling the flow of small arms. Control is hard but it must be achieved.
- Sanctions must be designed to hit the powers that are running wars, not the ordinary people. Peripheral states – trading partners suffering collateral damage from sanctions – should get some relief. This would involve the UN-related international financial institutions (the IMF and World Bank) as well as major bilateral aid.[3]

Sanctions were popular with the Council in the 1990s. Before then, they had been imposed only twice (Rhodesia in 1966 and South

Africa in 1977). In the 1990s the Council imposed sanctions on Iraq, former Yugoslavia, Libya, Liberia, Somalia, Cambodia, Angola, Rwanda, Sudan, Sierra Leone and Afghanistan. Sanctions were appealing as an alternative to forceful intervention. They seldom worked as intended, and sometimes caused great suffering among the ordinary people (e.g. in Haiti and Iraq). Yet it was only towards the end of the decade that the Council began to think twice about old and new sanctions.

A painful problem that was not fully analysed in the supplement was how to accommodate humanitarian aid in peacekeeping operations. In today's civil wars, civilians are the targets. Starving people on the other side is a common weapon. Taking food across the lines, therefore, is seen as taking sides in the conflict.

Also touched on lightly but not elaborated by the Secretary-General was the somersault trick of turning young soldiers trained to kill into disciplined and skilled peacekeepers whose loyalty to the UN transcended national loyalty. The problem is immensely complicated by the mix of many different national contingents assigned to peacekeeping in alien environments.

Foreign ministers of the PERM 5 met with the Secretary-General on 29 September 1994 and issued a joint statement reviewing 'the world situation', UN peacekeeping and the many conflicts on the UN agenda. They affirmed their support for UN action in the framework of the *Agenda for Peace*, noting the need to improve political direction, military command and operational efficiency. Any new operation should be undertaken only after careful study of objectives, duration, the means available and the safety of UN personnel. They said that they were determined 'to ensure that the principles and provisions of humanitarian law are fully complied with. ... Peace and development are interrelated and inseparable,' they declared. In all this, the key words were 'careful study'. The big powers, in uneasy alliance and licking many a self-inflicted wound, were already pulling back.

So what was this all about, the *Agenda for Peace*? Big states, the powerful, especially the founding fathers, had never known what to do with their UN. For them, the Cold War put that dilemma on hold. Now they should decide. Here we had a historic moment when top national leaders, seeing that collaboration through the UN had worked, sought to put some order in their handling of the warring world. What Boutros-Ghali gave them seemed right for that time, guidelines drawn from experience, pragmatic, not doctrinaire or theoretical.

We need to remind ourselves that the UN and its Security Council are not legislative bodies. While the *Agenda for Peace* and its supplement on the whole have been accepted by the Security Council, this means only that here are some guidelines, a sort of pragmatic arrangement, but nothing legally binding. True, the UN Charter is a formal treaty, so that joining the UN means accepting commitments. How the Security Council decides, or agrees, to do its work can be seen as an elaboration of Charter commitments, but this is only a working agreement to be tested in practice. The Security Council proceeds case by case, creating a body of common law, with the difference that no precedent is binding. At the UN, governments may criticize and scold, but there is no provision in the Charter to 'lock up' a bad government. A delinquent can be excommunicated, but there is no world prison, certainly no death penalty. In case of war, of course, there are ways for the Security Council to affect the course of events, if it decides to do so. A mix of political and mundane considerations – resources, money, manpower – determine the Council's decisions and indecisions.

Storms and shoals

In my old house on Grand Manan Island, in the Bay of Fundy off Canada's east coast, I have a map of the many shipwrecks round about, bespeaking fog, treacherous currents and wild storms. The seas into which the UN was sailing were far wilder, and the UN helmsman had neither meteorological service nor charts to warn of hidden shoals.

What were the shoals on which the UN might founder? Most common and threatening was the changed theatre of warfare: instead of neighbours clobbering neighbours, it was domestic violence, something not foreseen in the UN Charter. The UN was intended to maintain international peace, to prevent or stop conflict between nations. The Charter is a compact among sovereign states: no interference in internal affairs. But when does trouble at home rock the international boat? Who was to decide and on what grounds? This was totally new to the UN; what could it do to pacify and stabilize – what kinds of intervention in sacred domestic affairs would be feasible and effective?

Another and even more treacherous shoal was human rights: does a national government, presenting itself as 'the State', have the right to harass, torture and slaughter its own people? When may the UN sail into such bloodied waters? What limits to sovereignty go along with joining the UN? These questions were not answered in the *Agenda for Peace*. Not foreseen, of course, was the stateless terrorism that erupted in 2001.

The Cold War not only put a lid on many a seething cauldron, it also created savage conflicts within and among its proxies. Stranger still was that global epidemic, mass complicity in mass murder, celebrated by fanatic governments, right and left. Ambient evil is hard to see.

The fair weather of 1990 did not last long. Just off the radar screen, storm clouds were gathering in Iraq, Somalia, Yugoslavia and Rwanda. Fair weather friends would soon fall away.

First, Iraq. Putting Saddam Hussein in his place seemed a straightforward affair, the four-day Desert Storm defeat of Iraq's army (February 1991) leading to surrender to the mighty US Army, supported by 28 other armies, all under the UN flag.

Iraq's invasion of Iran in 1980, and the ensuing deadly eight-year war, came to the UN only when exhaustion needed the international hand to write peace. In fact, major Western states, notably the USA and France, were complicit in supporting Iraq against Iran. But for Saddam Hussein to swallow Kuwait and its oil was a gross miscalculation: the price of military defeat was a strict engagement, spelled out in detail by the Security Council, to eliminate Iraq's military arsenal ('weapons of mass destruction') except for a minimum of conventional forces. Unprecedented was the imposition of intrusive hands-on inspection to ensure compliance. How this led to a major crisis for the UN is the climax of this book. Meanwhile, in summary, from 1991 to 1998, despite evasive tactics by Iraq, UN inspectors made a good start in their disarmament mission. The to-and-fro between Baghdad and the Security Council is a complicated and fascinating story, documented in a full-length book, *The United Nations and Iraq*, by Jean E. Krasno and James S. Sutterlin. After ejecting UN inspectors in 1998, Iraq opened its gates once more in 2002 to a reinforced UN inspectorate. Why? Because the USA, invoking the Security Council, threatened. Renewed UN inspection was well under way early in 2003, with frequent reporting to the Security Council. A majority in the Council and in the General Assembly felt that the inspection process should go forward, that more time was needed to do the job. The USA and its allies, notably the UK and Spain, were convinced that only immediate military intervention would eliminate Iraq's weapons of mass destruction. In March 2003 US and UK forces invaded Iraq. The results are now being played out at the UN and throughout the Middle East.

Turning back to 1992, after Iraq, Somalia looked easy, a handful of petty warlords hijacking humanitarian aid and colluding with famine. Television had opened the floodgates for food to pour into Ethiopia in 1984, and again gave popular support for humanitarian intervention in Somalia. With UN approval and TV cameras at the ready, 20,000 US Marines hit the Mogadishu beaches in December 1992. Their mission was to reinforce the UN presence, military and humanitarian, so that food could flow. At first the UN refused to disarm the petty brigands, but then became embroiled in the local strife. In Mogadishu, Mohammed Aidid defied the UN and killed 26 Pakistani troops as they tried to establish UN control of the airport. The Security Council labelled Aidid as Enemy Number One, and in October 1993 a US Marine contingent went after him. They failed. Instead 18 Marines fell into the deadly hands of Aidid's mob. TV showed a mutilated Marine body dragged through the streets. The US Army pulled out and the UN was blamed for it all. What began as a humanitarian operation had drifted into tinkering in local politics with the implied aim of putting in place a national government. Blundering and obfuscation: a defining moment in the US retreat from UN peace operations. Despite sustained efforts to establish a national government, greed and guns have kept Somalia in fractious disarray.

Yugoslavia was an even more complicated story. The ambivalent UN–US–European entanglement in former Yugoslavia from 1992 onwards is hard to grasp. The whole mess was stirred up by Germany's 1991 blunder, recognizing the breakaway Croatia. As four more states fell away, hungry political leaders exploited old ethnic and religious passions, culminating in Serbia's campaign under Slobodan Milošević to create an ethnically pure 'greater Serbia'. Genocidal encroachment on Muslims in Bosnia looked like a return of the Nazis.

In 1992 a joint UN–European Union plan would have stabilized the situation, fixing borders – a feasible compromise. The plan was threatened by Russia's support for its Serbian brothers, and finally scuppered by President Clinton and his new team. What a tragedy! The killing could have been stopped then, but instead it continued for three more years. Effecting a political solution would have meant massive military intervention with US participation.

While this was on hold (1993–95) the UN was sent in to do the impossible, to provide huge humanitarian aid under the military protection of Blue Helmets. Although this enormous humanitarian programme, carried out under very difficult and dangerous conditions, saved thousands of lives, the UN became the scapegoat for European and US dithering.

Failing to enforce a political solution, the UN had a minimal military presence on the ground, to protect humanitarian assistance. With Milošević on the rampage, the Security Council blundered into creating so-called 'safe havens' without the military strength to make them safe. Little UN contingents, like the handful of Dutch soldiers at Srebrenica, were hostage to the Serbs. And so the UN was humiliated by the massacre of men and boys at 'safe haven' Srebrenica, and by the shattering of Sarajevo, formerly a sophisticated and tolerant city.

In 1995 the USA finally went it alone. Using the threat of force, US negotiator Richard Holbrooke pushed through the Dayton Accords along the lines of the 1992 plan, but actually giving more to Serbia. Milošević had signed on, but three years later he defied Dayton and set about a military and political suppression of the Albanian majority in semi-autonomous Kosovo. Ethnic cleansing followed.

Megalomaniacs are not forever. The Security Council told Milošević to desist, but when he did not the Council was split on UN military intervention. The West invoked NATO and the 1999 bombing of Serbia. After 78 days, many civilian deaths and severe damage to the economy, Milošević pulled back. He is now (2004) on trial for war crimes, in The Hague.

NATO could drop bombs but it could not pick up the pieces. The UN was handed the much more difficult job of constructing a stable multi-ethnic Kosovo, from the ground up, leaving undecided its eventual relations with Serbia. By 2002 the UN had succeeded in establishing a provisional self-government in Kosovo, still under UN supervision, while in Bosnia-Herzegovina the UN had trained and fielded a modern professional police force. Along with Milošević, many warmongers have faced justice at the UN Tribunal in The Hague.

Out of the Yugoslav conflicts, two good things were accomplished. One was the sending of a small UN military group to Macedonia to keep the war from spreading into that little country and beyond. The other was the setting up of the UN War Crimes Tribunal, for Yugoslavia as a whole, created by the Security Council in what looked like a face-saving device for want of decisive political action. Yet this Tribunal, later extended to Rwanda, would contribute greatly to the formation by 2002 of a permanent International Criminal Court.

This brings us to the nightmare of Rwanda, a tale twice told. In 1994, intent on stabilizing this little country, the Security Council installed a small UN military presence in the capital city, Kigali, commanded by Canadian General Romeo Dallaire. A national government was in place, bringing together Hutus and Tutsis, long in contention. When the Hutu president was killed in a plane crash – was it an accident? – a crazy Hutu faction took over and launched a well-planned genocidal slaughter of Tutsis. In 100 days between April and July, around 800,000 men, women and children were killed. General Dallaire had warned UN headquarters of the impending disaster, but no one wanted to get involved. Following the massacre a Tutsi military force, trained in Uganda, took over in Kigali. Under French military protection, Hutus fled, mostly to the Democratic Republic of the Congo (DRC), where their refugee camps were dominated by the Hutu killers, the militia. This whole disaster might have been prevented if the Security Council had promptly deployed the 5,000 peacekeepers requested by General Dallaire. Now, in 2003, the government in Kigali has set out on the difficult road to national healing. In neighbouring Democratic Congo, the struggle to achieve a degree of stability has been further complicated by the lingering on of Hutu militia.

Why take the trouble to regurgitate these painful experiences? Though once familiar on paper and on screen, how easily forgotten they are. Look again and see how clearly they displayed the worst side of the Security Council, the sophistry and stumbling of the PERM 5 and followers, hardened cynics and timid pilgrims, wandering into the great unknown.

Peace missions worldwide

But these are only four of the many ongoing UN peace operations. The UN has been present in all regions. In the vast Eurasian land mass, the UN has lent a hand in mediating conflict in Georgia and Tajikistan. In Asia, besides a major peacebuilding mission in Cambodia, the UN has been essential in holding the Kashmir line between India and Pakistan, and has been relentless in the pursuit of peace in Afghanistan.

Around the Mediterranean, the UN presence was important in facilitating the Israeli withdrawal from Lebanon, and in advancing a carefully crafted plan (the 'road map') to make peace between Israel and the Palestinians. On Cyprus, although the UN plan for a marriage of convenience between Greeks and Turks has foundered, yet it is the UN that for many years staunched the haemorrhage.

In the Americas, although volatile Haiti has yet to end its pervasive violence in some sort of political stability, the UN has been patiently trying to create a decent police force. Nearly three years of quiet UN mediation have helped Guatemala to end the brutal suppression of its indigenous majority, although the pervasive culture of violence is slow to die.

In tormented Africa the promise of UN-monitored elections in Angola (1992) was revived by the death in 2002 of Jonas Savimbi. His refusal to accept electoral defeat had prolonged civil conflict. Now the UN is helping Angola's recovery, getting thousands of soldiers into civil society and investing in basic social needs. Now, also, the UN is deeply involved in peace and national reconstruction in fragile Sierra Leone. The Security Council has joined African states in mediating conflict in the Democratic Congo now that, in March 2003, warriors have agreed to talk. Ethiopia and Eritrea called a halt, after two lethal years, in a border war over some rocky terrain; in 2000 UN peacekeepers were deployed and a settlement is in the works.

The mere naming of these peace operations tells us how desperately the world needs the UN. Every one of those names carries a story of life and death.

Down and up: from keeping to building

Numbers tell part of the story. From the beginning there have been 54 UN peace operations; out of 36 operations in the 1990s, only eight were active in 1991. In the year 2003, 15 were ongoing. More than 750,000 men and women from 90 countries have served in UN peace missions, and over 1,800 have given their lives in the cause of peace. In 1989 there were 10,000 military peacekeepers in the field.

The number peaked at 78,000 in 1994, dropped to 14,000 in 1998 and climbed back to 43,000 in 2003. Along with uniformed personnel in 2003 there were over 5,300 police officers and 12,000 civilian staff (4,000 international, 8,000 local). Five ongoing peace operations were in Europe, four in Africa, four in the Middle East and two in Asia. The UN was also supporting peace through its liaison offices in the Balkans, Central America, Colombia, Africa and Asia. Even less known are the sensitive UN diplomatic missions, 13 in all in 2002, aimed at defusing potential conflict and constructing peace.

The rapid expansion of civilian participation marks a radical advance in UN peace operations, from military buffer to phased military–civilian missions. Even in simple peacekeeping, the UN military got involved in practical assistance like repairing bridges and roads, and occasionally protecting women and children from criminal exploitation. This was not planned, it just happened. But now the UN peacemaker has matured. The UN Security Council has been moving from state security to human security. That means peace and freedom for people, with access to basics that sustain a decent life.

With shifting concerns among the PERM 5, the Security Council has had its ups and downs, beginning high in 1992 and falling down in 1994. As the 1990s drew to a close, what got the Security Council moving? Probably it was Africa that made heads turn. Boutros-Ghali had sounded off: you love Europe, you disdain Africa. Guilt over Rwanda was there. When in 1998 President Clinton made a symbolic visit to Africa, it meant something. And in 1997 US Secretary of State Madeleine Albright, at the Security Council, initiated a formal request to Kofi Annan to do a think-piece on Africa. He did. It was a new kind of presentation: direct, clear in identifying sensitive problems (e.g. corruption, the pervasive black market in small arms) and in balancing international and national responsibility. As an African, Kofi Annan was able to tell African leaders to shape up. His report broke the diplomatic etiquette that somehow made government leaders immune from criticism. This opened the way in 1999 for the Security Council to do a thorough investigation of diamond trading in Angola – naming names as never before – that financed the Savimbi troops and kept the war going. More than diamonds were involved: the Security Council made a meticulous and dogged investigation into how traders and governments subverted sanctions against Savimbi. The Council went on to expose the exploitation of Democratic Congo's rich natural resources as the fuel that sustained violent conflict in that ravaged land. This was a tougher Security Council. It also blew open the diamond trade, from Sierra Leone to Charles Taylor's Liberia, as the fuel that fired brutal conflict in Sierra Leone. So-called civil war was exposed as venal power, a free market for greed. This has shaken up the international trade in diamonds, with some controls begun to block tainted gems.

The UN challenged: Kosovo, East Timor, Afghanistan

Two crude acts of defiance confronted the UN in 1998–99: Milošević's suppression of Kosovo, and the Indonesian militia running amok in East Timor. Kosovo is formally a part of Serbia, so that China and Russia blocked UN forceful intervention into a sovereign state. With the Security Council paralysed, the West called in NATO. Prolonged NATO bombing of Serbia from 15,000 feet inevitably killed civilians, missed targets and occasionally hit the wrong targets, famously the Chinese Embassy. Nevertheless NATO brought Milošević to his knees, acting outside the UN Security Council. How bad was the damage to Security Council authority? This issue came next with Iraq, in 2003.

East Timor was different because Indonesia's occupation of this former Portuguese colony had not been accepted by the UN. The Security Council quickly condemned the scorched earth violence of Indonesia's militia, in their effort to sabotage East Timor's vote for independence. Australian troops were at the ready and, under the UN flag, moved in at once. Indonesia is now faced with the war crimes of its military. A UN success, crowned by creating a new state, Timor-Leste, joining the UN in 2002.

Afghanistan, wild and rugged, where both nineteenth-century Britain and twentieth-century Russia met ignominious defeats, came to the UN emergency ward in 2002. This followed the UN–US military operation aimed at the Taliban regime and the Al-Qaeda terrorist network, triggered by the 2001 terror attack on New York and Washington. The Taliban government collapsed and Al-Qaeda went missing. Extensive political negotiations, both among concerned governments and among Afghanistan's ethnic fiefdoms, led in 2002 to the establishment of an interim national government in Kabul. While a serious start has been made at giving central national authority to Kabul, regional warlords are slow to come under central control. The UN has brought substantial humanitarian reconstruction to the country, but massive long-term international aid will be essential for the survival of this embryonic government. So far, substantial aid has been promised but not much has been delivered.

Building the broken

History is yesterday, and it seems only yesterday that the UN was thrust into Kosovo, Timor-Leste, Sierra Leone and Afghanistan to pick up the post-war debris and start social reconstruction. For social and political construction, there was practically no debris. Only Sierra Leone had any memory of putative democracy. What experience was there to guide these social architects? The UN had brought peace to Namibia through local leadership and international support. Massive UN resources had introduced Cambodia, an authoritarian culture and still in profound shock, to the idea of democracy. The fragile structure collapsed when the UN walked away, but the seeds of democracy had been planted. Angola, after Savimbi's death in 2002, was limping towards recovery. Mozambique, severely wounded, showed an astonishing capacity to forgive and heal, welcoming international assistance. Kosovo, in contrast, hot with hatred between returning Albanians and remaining Serbs, had to be coaxed into the structures and the will to build tolerant democracy. For Kosovo, the first UN Administrator, Dr Bernard Kouchner, had an imperial UN mandate without imperial riches: he had to make do, keeping the banners of tolerance flying. Following him, Michael Steiner in 2002 continued the patient work of policing and persuasion that is leading Kosovo towards reconciliation and peace. Vieira de Mello (before his 2003 death for the UN in Baghdad) had a similar mandate in Timor-Leste, an infant nation recovering from the slash-and-burn of retreating Indonesia, and at last entering the UN company of nations in 2002. Sierra Leone, with the battered remnants of democratic government, finally got its diamond mafia under control and began the process of healing and reconstruction. The UN peace mission itself had been saved by British troops, giving the country back to the shaky new government. Poor Sierra Leone: can it be forgiven and given some sort of life? With international support, a Truth and Reconciliation Commission was set up, and to buttress this Commission a mixed national plus UN War Crimes Tribunal has begun. This hybrid arrangement is new and unique, a model for similar situations in the future. Not only is Liberia's Charles Taylor involved; Sierra Leone is the nub of a regional malaise, yet to be addressed.

No pain, no gain: the Brahmini analysis

The two disasters of Rwanda and Srebrenica received straight treatment in two 1999 studies of UN failure. Both were done at Kofi Annan's request. Rwanda was studied by an independent group led by Ingvar Carlsson, former Prime Minister of Sweden. The Srebrenica study was done by the UN itself, and was no less frank.[4] Both showed that the cowardice and temporizing of the Security Council, abetted by weakness in the military chain of command and bungling in the Secretariat, together were a recipe for tragedy. In their wake Kofi Annan assembled a strong team, headed by that well-tempered UN veteran, Lakhdar Brahmini (subsequently saddled with Afghanistan), to make a full diagnosis of UN peacekeeping. The study revealed systemic faults originating in the Security Council and running through the implementing machinery.[5] The Security Council had not quite left behind the notion that UN peace missions must always be neutral, never aggressive, only lightly armed for self-defence. This doesn't fit many home-grown wars where peace agreements are flouted by the contenders and where innocents are being slaughtered. So the 'mandate' as it is called, the design of a UN peace operation, must be clear about its objective. Peace missions should integrate military and civilian functions, such as political analysis, human rights, humanitarian aid and civilian police. And the mandate, the design of any peace operation, must be clear in specifying the command structure (since several national contingents may be involved) and the 'rules of engagement' (the situations in which force may be used). It is essential also that the whole operation, from headquarters to the field, is strong enough to do the job. No operation can succeed unless adequate resources – money, military and civilian personnel – are provided.

Sensible things are cited, like bringing together the top brass of a new mission to get acquainted and agree on how to do the job. The UN intelligence, planning and support staff must be greatly strengthened. For example, as of mid-year 2000, there were only 32 officers to provide military planning and guidance to 27,000 troops in the field. It is strange to read in this Brahmini study that the backup staff had been treated as temporary in the UN budget: no wonder people were leaving.

This is from the introduction to the report:

Without significant institutional change, increased financial support, and renewed commitment on the part of the Member States, the United Nations will not be capable of executing the critical peacekeeping and peace-building tasks that the Member States assign it in the coming months and years. There are many tasks which the United Nations peacekeeping forces should not be asked to undertake, and many places they should not go. But when the United Nations does send its forces to uphold the peace, they must be prepared to confront the lingering forces of war and violence with the ability and determination to defeat them.

So here are the two essentials for successful peace operations: a clear mandate (what to do and why) and the ability to act (money, headquarters' leadership and support, a full complement of military and civilian personnel in a hurry). The last sentence quoted above marks the radical change from buffer (standing between fighters during ceasefire) to enforcer, protector (fighting when necessary to contain violence and to consolidate peace). Objectives defined by the Security Council (in the mandate) not only give focus to action but also tell whether and when an operation is over. As for ability and capacity, there are two aspects. One is inside the UN house, the other outside. In house, for peace operations the UN has needed many more people and better organization. Peace operations now touch on nation-building, and that means that planning the operation and assembling the personnel must go well beyond the military, to take in, for example, judicial systems (laws and courts) within which police can perform. Steps taken in-house include hiring over 180 more professionals, made possible when the GA approved funding for that. Better briefing of heads of individual operations – they come from many countries – is being done. Standard training and rules of conduct have been hammered out. A stockpile of basic supplies has been established.

Outside the UN house lies the substance, the life blood: that is, the troops, the police, the civilian professionals, now including specialists concerned with women and children. There is no international army, no standing UN peace corps. Each UN expedition has to be assembled anew. As you can imagine, this is an enormous complication both in getting quick action and in achieving a standard international military and civilian culture. A big effort has gone into persuading those governments having good military and civilian resources to streamline their on-call readiness. It is surprising to find that hitherto most troops have come to the UN from developing countries. This is not so good politically; there needs to be a fair mix from rich and poor. The fact that the UN reimburses contributing countries has no doubt been one reason for poorer countries participating. But it can't be the only reason. Some contributors are backing off. The volatile international situation has its way of inhibiting the UN. How encouraging that the UN continues to attract first-class committed professionals. The 2003 crisis in the Middle East must not obscure the worldwide demand for the pacific hand of the United Nations. UN peace operations are unique and will be as good as the UN members want them to be.

The face of peace: what's new?

'Freedom from fear': this is how Kofi Annan sees peacemaking, as summarized in nine pages of his *Millennium Report*: 'The 1990s saw an upsurge in our peacekeeping and in our peacemaking activities: three times more peace agreements were negotiated and signed during that decade than in the previous three combined.'[6]

Looking back over the years since the Cold War, he reminds us that ending wars between states was not the end of war, but rather its resurgence in brutal internal conflicts killing more than 5 million people, mostly civilians. This makes us think of security in a new way, as protecting people. Continuing, he says prevention of conflict has to be our fundamental goal, and that means reducing poverty, establishing 'political arrangements in which all groups are represented', promoting human rights, protecting the innocents (women and children) and stopping the dirty commerce that fuels war. He recalls his brave challenge to the General Assembly in 1999: What about UN 'intervention'; how should this club of governments act when one of its members, in a row at home, and clobbering its own, upsets and insults the club, the international community? Kofi Annan says that, of course, we should first try talk and persuasion, then try economic pressure (sanctions that hit the perpetrators, not the victims), and only as a last resort break down the doors and march in to bring an end to the violence. Intervention is a perennial source of contention in the UN club, still unresolved.

Fragile peace: climbing and stumbling

When a state joins the UN, it promises not to use force except in self-defence or in the common good. This is a legal commitment you make when you accept the UN Charter. *Legal* means a formal treaty, a commitment between states, international law. You give the Security Council the authority to decide, on your behalf, when force shall be used for the common good. Exceptionally, if the Security Council, in a specific case, has given up trying to decide what to do, all UN members gathered in the General Assembly can take over and decide, by default.

So how has this arrangement worked? Looking back over millennia of wars, the UN record is pretty good. What can we expect? If we define peace as absence of armed conflict, in all recorded history peacetimes have been few and short. And war isn't what it used to be. The nation state is able to mobilize enormous resources to fight. And along with that comes science and technology with 'kill skills' that can destroy states in short order or, indeed, destroy all life on earth. Even for bloody-minded humanity bent on orgies of mass murder, this is a bit much.

Following the First World War came the League of Nations, the first attempt to bring all nations together in a peace compact. The League had no empowered executive, no focus of authority to enforce peace. Out of the Second World War came the United Nations and its Security Council. The wartime allies were barely able to agree on even this United Nations. The price of its birth was the Security Council, perpetuating that wartime alliance. This marriage of convenience, obsolete from the start, remains today the only enduring authority in this dysfunctional family of nations. Everyone agrees that the Council needs fresh blood: it should be bigger, more representative and should not be so tied to the will of the five permanent members, each of which can say no to all the rest. Nearly ten years of struggle over exactly how to remake this Council have gone nowhere. The reason is political. To be at all decisive, the Council has to stay small, adding only five or six new members. The regional groupings at the UN have been unable to agree on which state among them should join the Council. None of the present PERM 5 will step down. And why permanent versus fixed-term members? So for now, this old Council is all we've got: an imperfect instrument entrusted with our peace.

At this primitive stage in planetary civilization, nation states pretend to a quasi-religious sovereign independence. In reality their independence is nibbled away through many formal and informal happenings: formal treaties regulating, inter alia, commerce, travel, communications, disease, crime, even the conduct of war and terror, and through informal transnational phenomena like economic globalization, migration, ideas, information, radio, TV, the Internet. But there is no UN army or police to enforce treaties, to enforce international standards of behaviour. The UN Charter embodies basic principles and objectives to guide the Security Council. But the Council is political, not judicial, responding to political concerns and acting ad hoc from case to case. The presence of China and Russia among the PERM 5 tempers the Western three, and the geographical diversity of the elected ten can leaven perceptions and decisions.

Although there is no logical progression in the Council's decisions, there are major trends, omissions and commissions. During the Cold War only a few inter-state conflicts reached the Security Council, and of these, only two (Suez and Korea) implicated Washington and Moscow. Just to remind, the Suez crisis pitted Egypt (backed by the USSR) against a coalition of the UK, France and Israel. The issue was control of the Suez Canal, seized by Egypt. It was the UN, Washington in the lead, that intervened, and in the process initiated UN peacekeeping. Korea was UN war against invasive North Korea (backed by China, linked to the USSR), resulting in the unresolved and still divided North–South peninsula of today. Evading Armageddon elsewhere, Cold Warrior proxies wrestled in confusing disarray, competing for dystopia. China had its skirmish with India, the USA got entangled in Vietnam, Iraq invaded Iran, the USSR invaded Afghanistan. None of these went to the Security Council. India and Pakistan, not directly in the Cold War, took their dispute over Kashmir to the Council: there the fighting stopped but, like Korea, the dispute remains. Cyprus is a similar situation, where the Security Council brokered a truce between Greeks and Turks, not yet resolved. This is by no means a complete inventory of Cold War conflicts, but enough to show the limited uses of the Security Council during that perilous time.

How curious it is that the Security Council took on new life after 1989, when the USSR fell apart. This was a new life not foreseen in the UN Charter, taking the Security Council into an ill-defined role as umpire or mediator in domestic conflicts. At first the rationale for infringing on national sovereignty was the threat to international peace: civil wars could spill over, involve neighbours, export hordes of refugees. But then along came a radical new imperative for breaching national sovereignty: upholding human rights together with providing humanitarian aid to victims of conflict. The Cold War had suppressed or obscured much domestic tension. Now it was out in the open, with local warlords and politicians vying for wealth and power, playing on old grievances or ethnic rivalries. With few exceptions (like Somalia), states have national governments, and nearly all governments have committed themselves to treaties affirming human rights. No state has a perfect rights record, but some do dreadful things to their people, while survival needs are not met. Bad governments precipitate civil strife and lay themselves open to UN intervention. But such intervention is still exceptional, restrained by the cult of sovereignty embedded in the UN Charter. Where the UN does go in, however, the Security Council mandate can extend to nation-building with special attention to human rights, to women and children. This is a huge enrichment of Security Council responsibility.

And now, in our new century, next to Iraq, terrorism tops the Security Council's agenda, with explicit instructions to all UN members and active monitoring on what is being done. This is an accepted vigorous intervention into every state, conferring power and authority on the Security Council.

Finally there is more and more talk at the Security Council and throughout the UN on getting at the causes of war, the 'root causes'. At this level of discourse war and terrorism are conflated, all mixed together, as though there is one cure for all. Despite this simplistic verbalizing, it is a good thing that the Security Council wants to go beyond fire-fighting to promoting peace and making people happy. In 2000 and 2001, even before the terrorists hit the USA, the Security Council held open discussions – open to all member states and to civil society – on preventing violent conflict. To help the Council, in June 2001, the Secretary-General delivered a comprehensive analysis of what can be done. Thus the Council has at least touched on the essentials for peace; for example, in culture (in the mind, education), in economic life (poverty) and in security (disarmament, small arms).

CHAPTER 3

Disarm: Life or Death?

Lawrence Keeley, anthropologist, in his book *War Before Civilization*, has dug up history (archaic history, archaeology) to show that war has always been with us. What good is it, then, to say: get rid of the weapons? The good is obvious: a rocket is not a rock, a nuclear weapon is not a hex. War ain't what it used to be. Tackling weapons nowadays is tackling war. So here at the United Nations we see disarmament as essential to everything the UN says and does.

The UN idea implied a downturn in arsenals, in a world at peace under the Security Council. But that is not what happened. Instead there came the Cold War, Washington and Moscow in a deadly struggle that set off an arms race. That science and technology would fuel this race was clear from 6 August 1945 when the USA dropped an atomic bomb on Hiroshima. From the start, the political meaning of nuclear weapons was evident, and already in 1946 the General Assembly moved to bring nuclear arms under international control. But the Cold War killed that, and scientific war marches on. The atomic bomb has been eclipsed by the far more devastating hydrogen bomb. Sophisticated targeting and delivery systems, by land, sea and air, make modern war a sci-fi nightmare. Meanwhile, little killers, small arms, feed conflict worldwide. That is where we are today. That was not what the UN set out to do.

Nowhere does the UN Charter suggest that all weaponry must be abolished. The Charter invites the General Assembly to think about how to approach the whole issue of disarmament. To the Security Council it gives the job of creating a system for the regulation of armaments. It accepts that force exists, that it may be used by states in self-defence, and it implies that the Security Council has the exclusive right to use force against any state that breaks international peace. In practice the Council has left disarmament to the General Assembly and its spin-offs: the First Committee (a committee of the whole UN membership), the Disarmament Commission (open to all), and to the everlasting Conference on Disarmament, a self-sustaining affair of 66 governments that sits in Geneva. The General Assembly and offspring are supposed to sort things out, to work on political issues, to seek general agreement on principles or guidelines, while the Conference on Disarmament does the tough work of drafting treaties to curb or prohibit this or that. And outside the UN (same member governments, of course) there are important disarmament talks and treaties, bilateral (especially Washington–Moscow) and regional. While there is ritual obeisance to 'general and complete disarmament', no one in the big game is looking seriously at that. Weaponry is being tackled in chunks, major categories, amidst a welter of institutions and negotiations. The radical difference between weapons of mass destruction and small arms presents very different technical and political problems. Nevertheless, without an overall momentum to disarm and to eventually abolish war, there will be little political energy to reduce any category of weapon. Among nations, the one place where it all comes together, in concern if not in capacity, is the United Nations. A formidable array of citizens' organizations, professional and popular, discomfits, informs and pervades.

The nerve centre for all this is the UN Department of Disarmament Affairs, restored from hierarchical obscurity by Kofi Annan. As Departmental Director for two years, Jayantha Dhanapala left a legacy of intellectual rigour and moral commitment. The Secretary-General has been loud and clear on disarmament, telling the GA (First Committee) in 1998: 'Disarmament is at the heart of this Organization's efforts to maintain and strengthen international peace and security.'[1] In the lean and underfunded Disarmament Department, besides his own staff, Dhanapala was catalyst and gate-keeper for the Secretary-General's Advisory Board in Disarmament (which gives strategic advice), the UN Institute for Disarmament Research (much practice-oriented study) and three regional disarmament centres (some good regional initiatives). Dhanapala could not tell governments what to do, but he was greatly respected for his grasp of the disarmament agenda and his commitment to the job. He also cajoled his UN colleagues into pulling together in a common drive against weaponry, in getting disarmament into the UN mainstream.

Current work on disarmament was well foreseen by the First Special Session of the GA on Disarmament (SSOD I) in 1978, at which these priorities were laid out:

- Nuclear weapons
- Other mass killers
- Conventional weapons (all the rest)
- Armed forces.

Treating armed forces as a weapon tells us that SSOD I viewed disarmament in the big political context, the military establishment as product and symptom of the Cold War. Since 1980 the UN has invited its members to report their annual military expenditures. By the year 2002, 77 countries were reporting, an odd lot that included the USA (the biggest) but excluded China, India, Pakistan, Indonesia and the bristling Middle East. From other sources, however, we have a pretty complete picture. World military expenditures peaked at around US$1 trillion a year in 1987. The economic burden of the military was certainly one reason why the USSR came tumbling down. From the trillion spent in 1990, the world total dropped to about $700 billion in 1996 and then gradually began to go up again, reaching around $839 billion in 2001. A few big spenders account for the increase: the USA (36 per cent of the world total), Russia (6 per cent), and China, France and the UK (5 per cent each).[2]

Another measure of world military strength is the arms industry: production, buying, selling. Arms production and sales correspond roughly to the overall levels of military expenditure. Concentration through mega-mergers, especially in the USA, and a globalizing trend (many countries accept foreign ownership or licensing to sustain production) are formidable obstacles to regulation, let alone control. Around 90 per cent of world arms production, apart from China, takes place in the USA and Western Europe. China's glorious People's Liberation Army, the PLA, has been into all sorts of lucrative business, and China now has hugely increased its military spending so as to modernize its army, air force and navy.

There is remarkably little attention paid to these monstrous powers in the official UN, although the basic facts are there for all to see. One good move towards getting the facts out is the *UN Register of Conventional Arms*, started up in 1992. The Register covers exports and imports of the big things, including systems that you would use to attack your neighbours, such as tanks, fighter planes, helicopters, warships and missiles. It is curious that the Register excludes small arms, not so curious that it excludes the mass killers (nuclear, chemical, biological). The GA resolution (1991) launching the Register says: please, all members of the UN, send in annual data on imports and exports, and, by the way, while you are at it, why not also tell us what you are buying from home production and which of these big items you already have on hand. Reporting of the conventional arms trade has been remarkably good, with around 120 governments coming in as of 2002. All major exporters (the PERM 5 and Germany) have usually reported, although recently China has held back because Taiwan is in the Register. But the good news is that over 95 per cent of this trade is now on public record. In addition, in 2001, 31 governments gave some information on military stocks on hand, and 29 divulged what they had bought from local production. Overall only about 15 per cent of arms are exported.

What good is this Register? In itself it is not an instrument to regulate anything. Governments are so timid that they have told their hired help, the UN disarmament team, not to think, not to analyse these reports: just record and disseminate. Four so-called Expert Groups have reviewed the Register, but of course they have been just as hamstrung as the Secretariat, unable to say anything about the political uses of this information. Among themselves governments have agreed that arms should not be sold to unstable countries. Yet very few African and Middle Eastern governments have reported, and arms continue to flow to hot spots in Asia and the Middle East. The Register could be a base for regulating the arms trade if ever governments had the guts to do that. What a scandal that there is not a single global treaty on regulating the arms trade.

Calling the weapons 'conventional' is of a piece with our denial of their demonic killing power. No more good old-fashioned wars. So here we have at least some beginnings of restraint. The Convention on Inhumane Weapons (its full title is the Convention on the Prohibitions or Restrictions on the Use of Certain Conventional Weapons, Which May be Deemed to be Excessively Injurious or to Have Indiscriminate Effects) imposes technical restrictions on the use of land mines, booby traps and incendiaries, and bans laser-blinding weapons. The Convention has been in effect, legally, since 1983. It has been ratified by 90 governments by the end of 2002. As a sort of moral restraint it is good, but it has had little effect on curbing the ways we blow each other up. More importantly, both practically and symbolically, is the Ottawa Treaty to Abolish Land Mines which prohibits their production and use and requires their destruction. This Treaty (ratified by 133 countries as of 31 December 2002) came into effect in 1999. Over 100 million land mines have lain hidden away, long after their military use, along footpaths and fields, nearly all in poor countries – sinister sleepers that have crippled more than 250,000 civilians, many of them children.

Two good lessons came to us from this Treaty. One was that action can be taken by consensus outside the formal constraints of the Geneva Conference on Disarmament, where decisions have to be unanimous (one government can block the other 65). The other lesson was that a strong and focused network of NGOs can be decisive in humanitarian negotiations among governments. The splendid work of the NGO Coalition to Ban Land Mines (bringing together a wide range of international civilian organizations) earned it the Nobel Peace Prize in 1997. The Canadian government took the lead in negotiating the Ottawa Treaty and in putting it to work, with a target of clearing most land mines within four years. It will certainly take longer than that unless a much more efficient way of finding and defusing mines is developed. The UN is active in supporting mine clearance. So far both the USA and China stand aside, claiming land mines to be an essential military weapon.

One reason why banning land mines was accepted so fast is that their deployment was seen mainly as a humanitarian issue. Much more difficult in every way are small arms, light weapons that you can sling over your shoulder or move around in a jeep. Years of diligent work by governments (Japan, Germany, Canada and Norway) came to a head in the UN Conference on the illicit trade in small arms, held in New York, on 9–20 July 2001. Citizens' organizations again coalesced, this time to push for small arms control. Their success with land mines inspires, but small arms open up a nastier can of worms. While mass killers (nuclear, chemical and biological) stalk our end-game nightmares, right now millions are dead in broad daylight, most of them women and children, killed by small arms in home-made wars. Small arms are everywhere in abundance, many dumped from Cold War obsolescence, easily smuggled, easy to buy, cheap and enduring – they don't self-destruct. Land mines are not used in civil society nor are they big money, whereas small arms have legitimate uses and make some people very rich. Some of these rich are international criminals, battening on civil wars and drugs. By focusing on the *illicit* trade in small arms, the UN has tried to sidestep the powerful gun lobby, but guns are initially in legal commerce, so the door must open on the whole small-arms trade.

The UN got directly involved in all this through its peacekeeping operations, where disarming of combatants had to be attempted. In 1996 the UN Institute for Disarmament Research teamed up with a General Assembly group to see what was happening on the ground. In his 1995 supplement to the *Agenda for Peace*, Dr Boutros-Ghali deplored the neglect of small arms. This was followed at the Security Council by Kofi Annan's 1997 report on Africa's wars in which he singled out the trade and traders in small arms as big thugs. The decision to hold the 2001 Conference came at the 1998 General Assembly, and at last, in 1999, the Security Council put small arms on its agenda. Some piecemeal moves had been made, including a European code to regulate the trade and a formal OAS treaty to control the illegal flow of small arms in the Americas. In Albania small arms were turned in, in exchange for things to increase production and income. West African states, led by Mali, tightened their border controls.

While the UN – the General Assembly and Security Council – was focusing on small arms as weapons of conflict, another branch of the UN was tackling the black marketing of 'firearms', the legitimate tools of the police. Under the UN Commission on Crime Prevention and Criminal Justice, established as late as 1992, a formal Convention to combat transnational crime was negotiated, a major achievement.

The Convention, adopted by the General Assembly in November 2000, will come into force when 40 states have ratified it. Zeroing in on the black market, in 2001 this Commission went on to develop a Protocol, an add-on to the basic Convention, which would ban all illegal manufacture and trade in firearms. Like the Convention itself, the Protocol becomes law when 40 states ratify it. At the end of 2002, 31 states had ratified the Convention, but the Protocol was lagging behind, with 52 signed but only three ratified. Nevertheless these measures to control firearms contribute powerfully to the ongoing drive to regulate small arms.

That there was any UN Conference on Small Arms, however limited in scope, was already a breakthrough. Not only big money, the gun lobby, was opposed to it, but also involved were sovereign national interests everywhere. Small arms are not that important in modern wars *between* nations. Regulating small arms, even if we look only at the 'black market', takes us into conflict *inside* states. It also makes you think about which uses of small arms are legitimate (police, professional army, citizens) and which are not (thugs, drugs, guerrillas, terrorists). The USA, source of over 50 per cent of overall world trade in arms, is politically in thrall to the gun salesmen: no regulation of small arms can work without US participation. Given these political facts, what came out of this Conference?

What came out, first of all, was the official, open recognition of the worldwide scourge of small arms: over 500 million weapons in circulation, used to kill 500,000 civilians, mostly women and children, every year. The Conference adopted a plan of action that commits nations to criminalize the black market trade, to regulate arms brokers, to regulate exports, to mark weapons so as to be traceable and to keep track of them. States must also make sure that stocks of weapons (for the police and army) are held safely, and, where internal conflict has been settled, surplus stocks of arms are destroyed. The Conference called on the World Customs Union and the International Criminal Police Organization (INTERPOL) for help. That so much was achieved was already a big step forward. Unfortunately the Conference was stuck on two issues. One was whether countries should regulate the owning of small arms. The other, most bizarre, was any limit on sales to 'non-state entities', to guerrillas, even terrorists. It is hard to understand why the USA stood alone in blocking that, but one suspects the influence of the US gun lobby, which opposes any restraint on trade in arms. In any case, the Conference outcome, while politically and technically important, is not yet legally binding in the form of a treaty.

Meanwhile many countries will need technical and financial support to put the Conference findings into practice, and help like this could be given through the UN. INTERPOL also needs strengthening so as to reach out to illicit arms. Crime bosses could also be hauled up before the International Criminal Court.

The General Assembly endorsed the Conference findings and the Security Council has small arms on its agenda as a basic factor in peace and security. A vigorous international NGO network is alive and well. There is to be a follow-up UN Conference no later than 2006.

Well now, which death do you choose? To be shot (small arms), to be poisoned (chemical), to be infected (biological), to be transmuted in the twinkling of an eye (nuclear)? Modern science and political industry offer this lethal smorgasbord. We should poll armament CEOs to get their take.

Having seen the shot and the decapitated in my China childhood, I have a gut aversion to the conventionals, the small arms. The mass killers are to me a horrendous abstraction, as incomprehensible as death itself. Yet I know they are there, demanding every ounce of our energy to put them away forever. Can man undo what he has done?

For chemicals and biologicals ('the poor man's nukes') there is hope. The Chemical Weapons Convention, ten years in the making with industry participation, went into effect in 1993, and by the end of 2002, 147 had ratified. This treaty authorizes spot checks: the USA and Russia, the big bio-chemists, backing away from Cold War poisons, say they are destroying these weapons. Although the use of mustard gas in the First World War was not repeated in the Second, more than one state has used chemical killers since then: Egypt in Yemen, the USA (defoliants, dioxins) in Vietnam, Russia in Afghanistan, and Iraq both against Iran and against its own people (Kurds and Shiites). War is never a pretty game, but these tormented civilian deaths make chemicals most repugnant.

The Convention to control Biological Weapons took effect in 1975, and at the end of 2002 had 144 ratifications. As it stands, the Convention has no provision for monitoring compliance. Years went into preparing an addendum – a Protocol – to the Convention that would authorize inspection, along the lines of the Chemical Convention. Even US negotiators were shocked when, in 2001, the US administration rejected the Protocol. But sober second thoughts have brought these negotiations back to life. In November 2002 the 'states parties' (the ratifying governments) agreed to a three-year work plan addressing step-by-step national and international capacity to deal with biological weapons. Codes of conduct for scientists will be considered. This work includes 'bio-security', how to protect sources of pathogens nationally and internationally. The 2001 anthrax scare in the USA – the distribution of anthrax spores through the mail – makes even the superpower take notice. A biosecurity treaty would run parallel to the omnibus Biological Convention. That these Conventions exist is a good beginning for control, but many countries, especially in the Middle East, remain outside.

So that leaves us with the ultimate destroyer, Kali, the nuclear arsenal. This weapon, still with us, is so fearful that in the popular consciousness it has been relegated to science fiction. When I tell people that today there are still more than 20,000 nuclear weapons, thousands on 20-minute alert, most of them simply blink and walk away. The screaming has died down. Reality has won, we have lost. Almost. At least no nuclear bombs have been dropped in war since Hiroshima and Nagasaki in 1945. Despite elaborate security and intelligence arrangements, scares have happened. Between 1950 and 1980, there were at least 32 serious accidents involving US nuclear weapons, as reported by the Pentagon. As recently as 1995 the Russians initially mistook for a US attack the launch of a weather satellite from Norway. Their automatic alert was stopped just in time. This incident tells us how fragile is our serenity.

Whole industries, vested interests, have sprouted around nuclear arms. One interest seeks to keep and *improve* this weapon: more and more arcane technology is applied to making smaller, more alert bombs. This is mainly in continuation of the US research that made the first nuclear weapons. It takes big money to keep this show going. The other vested interest seeks just the opposite: technical and political ways to control, reduce and, maybe, eventually eliminate all nuclear weapons. I say maybe because, in this group, some say you will always need a few control nukes, while others say that all must go. Internationally the original nuclear states (the permanent five in the Security Council) are formally committed to reduce but not eliminate. Non-nuclear states want such weapons to vanish from the face of the earth. Steps towards reducing existing arsenals are choreographed in uneasy partnership between Washington and Moscow. The UN spectators can look on, heckle and applaud, but not join the dance. We have forgotten that the very first official resolution adopted by the General Assembly in 1946 called for the elimination of nuclear weapons and all other weapons of mass destruction.

The Washington–Moscow negotiations, begun in 1983, after 14 years, yielded START I, the first Strategic Arms Reduction Treaty, which brought nuclear weapons down from around 58,000 in 1982 to over 30,000. The collapse of the USSR left nukes in the Ukraine, Belarus and Kazakhstan. What a relief that all were returned to Russia. In 1994 the USA and Russia agreed to stop aiming nuclear missiles at each other, and subsequently China, France and the UK joined in. But targeting can be restored within minutes.

Every sane person agrees that you can't fight a war with nukes. So what use are they? The current 'doctrine', shared by the USA and Russia, as well as Israel, India and Pakistan, is that they deter. This is, of course, NATO policy too, although not everyone in the NATO club is happy about that. Expanding NATO eastward to Russia's verge is hardly an invitation to dance. And I don't see how you can deter anybody with a weapon that you can't use.

What can break this deadlock? Strangely there is strength in Russia's weakness: will its control systems work, and who is in charge? Are the Russian nukes and their materials (e.g. plutonium) secure? Because its land army is in bad shape, Russia's nuclear weapons are important politically, if not militarily. From any point of view, the dominant USA has good reason to make a deal with Russia, to move on. Already in 1997, when Presidents Clinton and Yeltsin met in Helsinki, the goals of reduction of nuclear warheads to around 2,000 to 2,500 on each side had been foreseen.

So what has happened since the current US administration under President George W. Bush came into this deadly game? On 24 May 2002 Presidents Bush and Putin signed a treaty to bring down their nuclear arsenals to between 1,700 and 2,200 warheads on each side by 2012. This would be a major reduction, but it isn't as good as it sounds. The treaty deals only with *deployed* warheads; it does not say that warheads must be destroyed. Stand-by warheads could easily be reactivated. Along with this halfway cutback is evidence that the mighty Pentagon is actually thinking of using some form of nuclear weapon in war. This mindset, if you can call it that, is related to the fact that there exists no formal treaty constraint on the thousands of battle-ready 'tactical' nuclear weapons held by the USA and Russia. And this latest Washington–Moscow treaty has no arrangements for verification. Things are not so quiet on the nuclear front.

The whole world has a desperate interest in what goes on between Washington and Moscow. Already the 19 states in NATO are formally involved. The UN with 191 members is not just a passive observer. And among the traumatized citizenry there are still the strong and articulate who won't let go – Nobel laureates, military brass, scientists, artists, the clergy crying out: pull back before it happens, end this madness, get rid of nukes!

The nuclear threat was all along the top disarmament worry of the General Assembly. In the 1990s this concern came to a head around the Non-Proliferation Treaty (NPT). Coming into force in 1970, the

Treaty struck a bargain between the nuclear club (the five states officially recognized as having nuclear weapons) and the non-nuclear world. These states agreed not to go nuclear on the condition that the club proceeded to divest itself of the bomb. Article VI of the Treaty is specific and sweeping:

> Each of the Parties to the Treaty undertakes to pursue negotiations in good faith relating to the cessation of the nuclear arms race at an early date and to nuclear disarmament, and on a treaty on general and complete disarmament under strict and effective international control.

Built into the Treaty was also the provision that after 25 years states would decide whether to renew it, and if renewed, for how long: hence the NPT Review Conference at the UN in 1995.

Year after year in the General Assembly's First Committee, the nuclear powers, being reminded and excoriated, simply reacted with annoyed arrogance. Not only in the free-for-all at the Assembly but in the sober Conference on Disarmament were deaf ears: the club, with the USA presiding, showed no inclination to speed things up, to work towards eliminating nuclear weapons, nor to share in 'negotiations in good faith'. The non-nuclear states said, in effect: since the club has not lived up to the NPT bargain, why renew the Treaty? At least, if we agree to renew, let's get some firm commitments from the club. The club and its followers argued that NPT was the one and only framework for nuclear control, that its death would be a disaster and that, in an imperfect world, reducing nuclear weapons from 58,000 to 30,000 was quite an achievement.

It was in this atmosphere that the 1995 NPT Review Conference took place. The outcome was touch and go, right up to the dark night hours of its last day. Under its President, Jayantha Dhanapala (representing Sri Lanka), a last-minute compromise let open-ended renewal go through. The compromise established important conditions ('principles and objectives'), laid out in the legislative record if not in the Treaty text. These principles and objectives committed parties to adopt a Comprehensive Test Ban Treaty by 1996, ban production of weapons-grade fissile materials, eliminate nuclear weapons, support nuclear-free zones and give security assurances for all. There are to be serious quinquennial reviews of compliance. So the NPT survives.

At least one of those conditions was met when the Comprehensive Test Ban Treaty (CTBT) was adopted by the General Assembly in 1996. India's opposition to the Treaty had trapped it in Geneva (the Conference on Disarmament acts only by consensus), so Australia took it to the Assembly. Adoption by the GA does not mean that CTBT is legally in force. Built into this Treaty is the requirement that 44 named states with the technical capacity to make nuclear weapons must ratify before it goes into effect. Many, notably the USA, have yet to ratify. One serious criticism is that the Treaty bans explosions only, leaving open the possibility of other ways to test.

To keep up pressure on the nuclear club, the GA in 1994 asked the UN 'World Court', the International Court of Justice, to say whether the use or threat to use nuclear weapons was legally permissible. In 1996 the Court's majority view was that threat or use 'would generally be contrary to international law', although it might be permissible if a state's very survival was at stake. More important was the Court's unanimous opinion that, in view of existing commitments and the indiscriminate devastation that nuclear war would entail, 'there exists an obligation to pursue in good faith, and bring to a conclusion negotiations leading to nuclear disarmament in all its aspects under strict and effective international control.' The Court's only enforcement power is world opinion.

NPT is to be reviewed every five years, so the year 2000 brought another review conference. The atmosphere was not conducive to any big change, so all were surprised when the Big Five chose this occasion to reaffirm their Treaty commitment to eliminate nuclear weapons. But this glimmer of hope was soon doused as the USA abandoned the ABM (Anti-Ballistic Missile) Treaty and as Washington–Moscow negotiations slipped backwards.

So what has happened outside the international chat rooms? On the plus side, Argentina, Brazil and Libya have abandoned plans to make nuclear weapons, and South Africa has renounced its nuclear programme and has destroyed its few nukes. By formal agreement among states, nuclear-free zones have been established in South America, Africa, Southeast Asia and the South Pacific, and a zone is close to establishment in Central Asia (former USSR). The situation in the Middle East led the 1995 NPT Review Conference to urge (in the form of a 'resolution') movement towards a zone free of all mass weapons in that troubled region. Not so good were tests by China and France soon after NPT's renewal in 1995, although both countries have said they will not do any more. Worse were the 1998 demonstrations by India and Pakistan that they have the bomb – especially worrying when the two came close to war in 2002. In 1999 the US Senate refused to ratify the CTBT.

More ominous yet was the US scrapping in 2002 of the Anti-Ballistic Missile Treaty (ABM), concluded between Washington and Moscow in 1972. This was a major Cold War achievement aimed at stabilizing the nuclear threat. Scrapping the ABM (an obsolete legacy of the Cold War, says President Bush) leaves the USA free to proceed with 'missile defence'. Everyone knows that missile defence cannot work. The USA has already spent billions on failed systems. Nevertheless it is going ahead with Alaska-based interceptor units. What is frightening is that missile defence could very well be the first stage of putting weapons into space. The US Air Force has already begun research in order to do just that. Will the USA abide by the existing international treaty proscribing the weaponization of space? The current US administration, obsessed with terrorism, seems bent on the 'pre-emptive' strategy of hit before they hit you – this would mean abandoning UN principles.

All this makes prospects for disarmament bleak. Ideally we need another special session on disarmament, for a UN overview of where we stand, and to update UN strategy. As things stood in 2003 a special session would only expose intransigence without advancing disarmament in any way.

What lies ahead? In the name of security, are we on the road to mass suicide? No one superpower can by itself achieve security through superarmament, neither security for itself nor for the world. Here is our survival agenda. There must be no weapons in space. For nuclear weapons, we must strengthen control and security of nukes, especially and urgently in Russia, ban the production of fissile materials and safeguard the big stocks on hand. We must move on to deep cuts in nuclear arms and eventually get down to zero. Get everyone into the network of formal treaty controls. Ban all weapons of mass destruction. Regulate small arms. Build trust, not bombs. Link disarmament in a real way to survival, to human security, to justice and peace, to putting our whole selves into fighting poverty worldwide.

CHAPTER 4

Who Owns Terror?

War was on the minds of the UN's founders. Terror was not. Years before the UN existed, in 1937, an International Convention for the Prevention and Punishment of Terrorism was drafted under the auspices of the League of Nations, but was never brought into force. Instead, we had the Second World War.

Terror is one thing, terrorism another. Terror we can define, terrorism we cannot. The 1937 Convention died because there was no consensus on what terrorism was. It is easier to condemn terrorism if you don't say exactly what it is. Thus in 1995, in adopting the Declaration of Measures to Eliminate International Terrorism (resolution 49/60), the General Assembly said that 'criminal acts intended or calculated to provoke a state of terror in the general public, a group of persons, or particular persons for political purposes are in any circumstances unjustifiable, whatever the consideration of a political, philosophical, ideological, racial, ethnic, religious, or other nature may be invoked to justify them.'

Nonetheless, entering the twenty-first century, there is still no common understanding, no United Nations definition of terrorism. Simply naming the act doesn't get us very far. We must back up and ask: who did it and why? Terrorists have their reasons.

In what we call 'the West', terror as a political instrument began during the French Revolution, where terror turned first against perceived enemies outside the revolution, and eventually turned inward against itself. Contemporary totalitarian regimes have all used terror in one way or another to hold power, all the way from Argentina's military to Stalin's paranoid purge of millions. Pol Pot's reign killed one-third of the entire population of Cambodia. In China the so-called 'Cultural Revolution' terrorized professionals and intellectuals when Mao unleashed youth in his cynical drive to keep his own political power. Terror has also been used for political independence, for example by Tamil Tigers in Sri Lanka (now into peace negotiations). In their drive to get out from under British rule and create Israel, the Jewish underground blew up the Shepherds Hotel in Cairo, killing many civilians. Now Palestinians are blowing up Israelis in suicide bombings. Not that there is some sort of moral equilibrium, a balance of terror, between Israelis and Palestinians. It is simply that both have felt justified in the use of terror. So terrorists have their reasons.

Who makes terrorism? Who is responsible? Here is the nub of the definition dilemma. If terrorists were always outside governments, always stateless actors, then most UN members (governments) would have a common starting point. Not a few governments have been using more or less covert terrorism to unseat neighbours, notably in Arab–Israeli relations, or to pursue global goals (e.g. the Islamic fundamentalists' war against secular culture spawned by the Great Satan, the USA).

This is one more case in which logic has not stood in the way of the UN. Nor has history. By the year 2001, work at the UN had yielded 12 conventions on threats of terrorism: in the air, on the sea, with nuclear material, and through financing. In the 1980s, under the General Assembly, the Sixth Committee (Legal) was chewing away at the intractable problem of writing an overall convention on terrorism, accommodating all 12. Still no progress.

Year 2001. The 55th session of the General Assembly was about to begin. On 10 September, the day before that beginning, Kofi Annan announced that 11 September was to be the International Day of Peace. Of that day, he said:

> On this International Day of Peace, let us dare to imagine a world free of conflict and violence. And let us seize the opportunity for peace to take hold, day by day, year by year, until every day is a day of peace.[1]

Just down the way from the slim elegance of the UN building, terrorists flew their human cargo into the World Trade Towers, and then in Washington slammed into the Pentagon. Would the UN itself be next? The entire UN staff was marched down into the lower depths, the basement. A security cordon was thrown around the UN headquarters. Nevertheless work resumed the next day, while big UN events were postponed. Heads of state, about to arrive, were held back until November, the annual policy debate delayed until then.

But already, on 12 September, the Security Council and General Assembly met to confront terrorism in this naked form.

Just as deadly was the huge truck bomb that wrecked the UN office in Baghdad on 19 August 2003. The 23 dead included Sergio Vieira de Mello, personal representative of the Secretary-General. For the UN, this was a new and sinister blow.

Terrorism had been on the UN agenda for a good 30 years, in 1999 leading up to a Security Council resolution (1269) laying out a broad international and national approach. That same year, a GA resolution (54/164) called for a comprehensive attack on terrorism.

Not only the UN has been worried about terrorism. In June 1999 the former USSR states, the Commonwealth of Independent States (CIS), concluded a Treaty on Combating Terrorism. In July 1999 the Organization of African Unity (OAU) adopted a convention on combating terrorism. And foreign ministers of the Organization of the Islamic Conference (OIC) in July 1999 also adopted a similar convention.

Clearly then, the states in the UN were not unprepared for 9/11. But this tragedy called for action here and now. An emergency meeting of the Security Council, is that action? It is as close as our untidy world can get to coalescing, joining hands to do something. On 12 September the Council with one voice condemned the attack and affirmed the Charter right of national self-defence. It took just over two weeks for the Council on 28 September (resolution 1373) to spell out how it sees terrorism and what must be done in and between nations. The Council said that terrorism is yet another challenge to peace and security, a challenge to the whole UN undertaking. Terrorism extends into transnational crime, drugs, money, black-market weapons large and small. The Council specified actions to be taken by each and every state: terrorists are criminals and shall be so prosecuted; all support for terrorism, especially financial, shall be found out and stopped; no hiding place (safe haven) or transit shall be given to terrorists. Internationally, said the Council, states shall co-operate in information exchange, travel and asylum scrutiny (fake documents, etc.) and in ratifying the existing 12 conventions. The Council makes law for all, and in this resolution requires states to tell it what they are doing. By December 2002 the Council's Special Committee on Terrorism had heard from 175 countries and was putting this information on its website. At least this can help to show the weak spots, to plug the holes.

While the Security Council has taken the lead, the General Assembly, where all meet, has an essential role. GA action is anchored in the Millennium Declaration which includes a commitment to joint action against terrorism. Right after 9/11 the Assembly came out in support of the Security Council, in October 2001 devoting a week to a special discussion on terrorism. The issue has been alive all through the Assembly since 2001. The Assembly has stressed the importance of arms control, especially of nuclear and other mass weapons. Also the General Assembly has said that we must look into the social, economic and political conditions that foster terrorists.

Kofi Annan has also pulled his team together to back up the Security Council and the General Assembly. He has been outspoken, along with the UN Human Rights Commissioner, in warning against scary hysteria. Speaking to the Human Rights Commission in 2002, the Secretary-General said, in effect, don't feed terrorists by fuzzy guilt-by-association, maintain judicial process, protect human rights. 'And let us be careful, in defending ourselves, not to play into the enemy's hands or to act as his recruiting sergeant.'

Where does the UN go from here? The 9/11 attacks took the USA to the UN Security Council, calling for international action. And yet, since then, the USA has tended towards action outside the UN in a 'war' led by Washington. The energy is good, but what is the thinking, the strategy?

CHAPTER 5

No Hiding Place: War Criminals

In so many ways do we try to make people behave, to conform to common social practice, but getting out of step is a crime only after there is a law that says so. And with that law comes the whole process of catching, trying and punishing. That is the judicial process that supersedes blood feuds and vendettas, that seeks uniform justice and protection of the innocent. We are not so sure about what to do with the guilty. Is prison punishment, revenge or deterrent? Or is it a factory for making good citizens? That depends, we say: some bad people can change, some cannot. We put enormous social energy into this necessary and imperfect process.

What about war, nations fighting nations, or nations at war with themselves – why do we call them 'civil' wars? In the passions of war, so easily aroused, we seem to leap into a vast loony bin. Killers are heroes. In our guts we know that war is inherently amoral, to win anything goes. Almost anything. In the bloody century just past, we have fumbled, struggled to mitigate the worst excrescences of war, to write some rules for this lethal game. How strange that, in our time, this bloodiest tragic century just past has also done something completely new, producing unprecedented laws of war, laws that extend beyond the battlefield to the treatment of prisoners and to the protection of civilians. War has forced us to go international, so we now have an emergent international judicial system, a system that defines and condemns the worst atrocities while deflecting the victor's revenge. It is a miracle that in 2002 a permanent International Criminal Court arrived.

It didn't happen by accident. A lot of moral outrage and disciplined energy went into this great achievement. We salute the Swiss, new to the UN, we salute the pioneering ICRC (the International Committee of the Red Cross) for its heroic humanizing of war prisons and for shaping the basic laws of war – the Geneva Conventions (1949) accepted by most countries.

The supreme test comes at war's end. The vindictive Versailles Treaty after the First World War included specific clauses for trials of Germans (political, military and industrial), but nothing came of it: there was no international arrangement to conduct trials, although some trials were held in national military courts. Passion for revenge was somewhat dissipated; otherwise this was a lesson in what not to do.

Two decades later the fate of German Nazis and Japan's warriors was far from set. Stalin said: shoot 100,000 of them, and something along those lines happened when the Russians arrived in Manchuria in 1945. Churchill was inclined towards a summary dispatch of the most notorious villains. At first Roosevelt seemed ready to go along with that, but there was a mighty struggle in his core cabinet which yielded the decision to go for proper trials of the selected few. The USA prevailed, Churchill went along, Stalin abstained. The 1945 Charter of the Nuremberg Tribunal said that crimes against peace, war crimes, and crimes against humanity were grounds for prosecuting individuals of whatever rank. If we can recall wartime passion, the Nuremberg Trials of the Nazis were historically exemplary; less so, although remarkably dispassionate, were the Tokyo trials of Japanese war criminals. The tone for Nuremberg was set by the Chief Prosecutor, the American Robert Jackson, as the trials began:

> There is a dramatic disparity between the circumstances of the accusers and the accused that might discredit our work if we should falter, in even minor matters, in being fair and temperate. ... We must summon such detachment and intellectual integrity to our task that this Trial will commend itself to posterity as fulfilling humanity's aspirations to do justice.[1]

Jackson was succeeded by Telford Taylor, who subsequently taught law at Columbia University, fought the abominable US Senator Joe McCarthy and opposed the tragic US blunder into Vietnam. Nuremberg was the first serious attempt to apply strict trial practice, as it had evolved in liberal democracies, to individuals accused of war crimes. While the Nuremberg and Tokyo trials were happening, many accused were getting short shrift in national streets and courts. Considering the alternative, the attempt by the Western Allies to do justice was admirable both for the victors and the vanquished. The Nuremberg principles were endorsed by the UN General Assembly (1950), an important base for the future.

So then what? Remember that the Universal Declaration of Human Rights was adopted by the General Assembly on 10 December 1948. The day before, it adopted the Genocide Convention. On that same day it asked the International Law Commission to set about creating a permanent International Criminal Court. (The Law Commission comprises 34 eminent jurists, elected to five-year terms by the GA and serving as individual experts.) After two years' study, the Commission told the GA that such a court was desirable. The Commission was thinking that an international criminal court would have to be structurally within the UN itself, like the International Court of Justice (ICJ), a Charter body. This approach would require amending the Charter, a formidable process that was enough to freeze the political drive to create this new court. Nevertheless, taking the Commission's work one step further, committees of the GA in 1951 and 1953 produced statutes of a criminal court. Then came the ice age, the Moscow–Washington freeze. At last, in 1990, the GA asked the Law Commission to exhume and revive the draft statutes for a permanent criminal court. What loosened up the technical work this time was a new approach, to establish a court structurally outside the UN by means of a treaty like many other treaties. This made it feasible procedurally and politically to go ahead. In 1993 the GA asked the Law Commission to complete its proposed statutes by 1994. The Commission did that, and proposed that an international diplomatic conference be held to set up a permanent international criminal court. The GA then did its own political work, taking account of government reactions to the Commissioner's text, and by 1997 was able to decide that the definitive diplomatic conference – diplomatic means officials authorized to do the job – would be held in Rome from 15 June to 17 July 1998.

At the helm in Rome was Philippe Kirsch, whom I had come to know and respect when he was counsellor to Canada's UN Mission in 1993. Meticulous preparation, much consultation among governments, strong support from civil society (an international network of NGOs) made for agreement on this complex treaty. Late at night on the last day, 17 July, to applause, the International Criminal Court (ICC), the Rome Statute, was adopted: 120 yes, 7 no, 21 abstentions.

Rome was the blueprint for the Court. To make it real, a minimum of 60 states had to formally ratify. It took 50 years to get to Rome. It took under four years to realize Rome: on 11 April 2002 the number of ratifications reached 66. Rejoicing, Hans Corell, UN Legal

Counsel, said: 'A page in the history of mankind is being turned.' The dream of an international judicial system, ending an era of impunity, had come true. By January 2003 the number of ratifications had reached 87. Altogether 139 states had signed up by then, indicating their intent eventually to ratify. The ICC 'came into force' (legal existence) on 1 July 2002. A formal inauguration, a ritual celebration, was held in The Hague on 11 March 2003.

What can the ICC do? How is it unique? I have been tracing its origins in the experiences of world wars, the agony of transforming revenge into justice, the revision from mass guilt to personal responsibility. On the international plane this is new, indeed new to many societies. By example, the Court will be leavening harsh old ways. No death penalty: exposure of guilt in a fair public trial, incarceration, fines – that is all. By targeting individual persons, the Court will also shatter the wall of impunity that has shielded many villains, especially those at the pinnacle of power. Even if they manage to hide away at home, international arrest warrants will scare them away from tropical paradise. The Court will have jurisdiction over crimes committed within, not just between states, a fact that makes it real in our time when most mass violence is happening in our own back yards. Will fear of arrest deter such psychotic behaviour? Who knows? For all of us, to prosecute is better than to ignore.

Crimes coming under the jurisdiction of the Court are well defined: they are genocide, crimes against humanity and war crimes. (Aggression may also come in whenever there is agreement on what it is.) Genocide is defined in a specific treaty. Crimes against humanity comprise known (deliberate), extensive or systematic attacks on civilians, including such acts as murder, torture, enslavement, any form of sexual violence, group persecution (political, ethnic, religious, gender) and 'other inhumane acts' causing great suffering or serious injury. War crimes include such acts as indiscriminate bombing of defenceless communities, deliberate attacks on civilians, torture and hostage taking.

The Court is meant to complement national action, which means that it will step in only when a state is unwilling or unable to prosecute. You can't get away with a sham trial. The Court's own Prosecutor, a key official in the whole process, may initiate an investigation only after the Court's three-judge pre-trial Chamber has given the go ahead. Alternatively, an individual state or the Security Council may refer a case to the Court. The Prosecutor can go after a suspect under one of two conditions: if the suspect is a citizen of a state that accepts the Court, or if the crime was done in such a state. This means that even if your country has not accepted the Court, you could be picked up in any state that has accepted it. Beyond that, the Security Council has universal authority, so any case initiated by the Security Council would apply anywhere.

The Court must stay out of any situation when the Security Council has moved in. In this context the eventual definition of the crime of aggression is mixed up with the basic relationship between the Court and the Council. The Security Council is a political body, the Court is not.

The other great international court at The Hague, the International Court of Justice (ICJ), had its origins under the defunct League of Nations and was born again in the UN Charter. Its main job is adjudicating disputes between states, although it may render legal opinions on issues referred by a UN entity. It does not prosecute and it cannot touch individual persons. The new Criminal Court already has its own house in The Hague, alongside the International Court of Justice.

The Rome Statute has elaborate ways to make the Court independent and fair. The Prosecutor must be experienced in criminal law and be of high moral character; he or she is elected, by states parties (i.e. states formally committed to the Court), by secret ballot. Review by the pre-trial Chamber avoids any whimsical witch hunt. A Prosecutor can be fired by vote of the states parties. The 18 judges in the Court serve for nine years; they are elected by secret ballot of the states parties, with at least a two-thirds majority. Some must have expertise in criminal law practice, others in international law. There should be a good representation of female judges and of persons with expertise on violence against women and children, and there is to be fair geographical distribution. The same criteria apply to the Prosecutor's staff. Strict practice must be followed to assure fair trials.

A good deal of carpentry had to be done to finish the Rome design, and this was done by a Preparatory Commission, leading up to the convening of the Assembly of States Parties after the Court 'entered into force'. Already in its first two sessions (September 2002 and February 2003), the Assembly moved ahead towards making the Court operational. Elements of crime were defined as well as rules of procedure and evidence, and practical arrangements – administration, financing – were set. A real breakthrough was the successful election of the Court's 18 judges, well balanced among regions and by profession (e.g. civil and common law systems). And a good balance of women and men was achieved with the election of seven female judges. In the future life of the ICC, the arrangement is that one-third of the 18 judges will leave office every three years. To get started, this meant that six judges were elected for three years, six for six years, and six for nine years. The experience of the temporary War Crimes Tribunals (of which more later in this chapter) will be carried over into the ICC through the election for six years of Claude Jorda of France, Presiding Judge of the Yugoslavia Tribunal, and the election, also for six years, of Navanathem Pillay of South Africa, who has presided over the Rwanda Tribunal. The Canadian Philippe Kirsch, prominent from Rome onward, is also in for six years. He was later elected President of the Court. The length of service in each case was determined in the old-fashioned way by drawing lots. It speaks well of the whole ICC warm-up that no one complained of misdemeanours. And now an impeccable Prosecutor, the single most important official of the ICC, has been found in Moreno Ocampo of Argentina. His election was by consensus. The ICC now has its full complement of professional staff and will be operational in 2004.

Not every state loves the ICC, however. Some feel threatened for one reason or another, despite the careful provisions to give precedence to national authorities. Initially the USA wanted the Court to be tied to the Security Council with its veto power. The USA has an obsessive fear, stemming from its military establishment, that its soldiers could be caught up in a politically motivated international court. This fear is unfounded. But don't we know that it is almost impossible for the rational to penetrate the irrational. No state, not just the USA, wants a politicized Court.

The USA, under President Clinton, at the last minute signed (not ratified) the Rome Statute so that the USA could have a hand in the ongoing negotiations about ICC jurisdiction and processes (e.g. who is an ICC criminal, and how do you get him and try him). But in 2002 President Bush's team 'unsigned' (something never done before), and, unilaterally, as well as through the Security Council, sought exception from ICC jurisdiction of the US military.

Failing at first to get any such exemption, on 30 June 2002 the US government vetoed the continuation of UN peace operations in Bosnia. Confronted with opposition by 100 UN states, the USA accepted a compromise Security Council resolution, to suspend for one year any ICC action against citizens of any state outside (not having ratified) the ICC. The USA expects this exemption to be renewed. Meanwhile, aggressively attacking the Court, the USA pressed governments around the world to sign a formal commitment not to surrender US citizens to the ICC.

At the end of 2002, 14 countries (including Israel, Romania, Afghanistan, Timor-Leste and other politically vulnerable states) had signed up with the USA. More since then. This is peculiar indeed. How can the Security Council intrude on the formal legal commitments of states ratifying an international convention? This looks like an attack by the US government on the very concept of international law, although as a political act it has a narrow focus on the ICC. Time will tell how this plays out. Meanwhile the ICC exists, with the strong support of a vast majority of UN states.

While the permanent ICC was in the works, two war crimes courts were already operating. Their history and performance is weird and wonderful, exemplifying the strange ways in which international contentions and indecisions get things done. While the Security Council could not grasp the nettles of Yugoslavia and Rwanda, it somehow managed to open a door for practical justice to be done. Skeletal TV ghosts stood sentinel at that door. Avoiding the tedious process of formal treaty making, in 1993 the Security Council created the Ad Hoc Tribunal on war crimes committed since 1991 in the former Yugoslavia, and in 1994 extended its jurisdiction to crimes committed in 1994 in Rwanda. Building on Nuremberg and the technical preparations for a permanent Criminal Court, these Ad Hoc Tribunals became an inadvertent experiment in turning talk into action. The birth and life of the Tribunals were coloured by the inability of their parent governments (the Security Council) to stop the fighting.

The Tribunals have taken on a life of their own. They began poorly and haphazardly funded, understaffed, administratively inept and politically frustrated. But by doggedly sticking to correct legal practice, these struggling Tribunals are showing that, even in the most dismal situations, justice can be done.

National judicial systems took years to mature, so an unprecedented international system was bound to have growing pains. That these Tribunals in just a few years have taken shape and are working is a heroic achievement. Starting from scratch in every sense – financially, physically, structurally, conceptually, procedurally, humanly — they are a model, embryonic if you like, of fair administration of international criminal law, defence of the accused, protection of witnesses, substantiation of evidence.

They have been lucky in having three outstanding Prosecutors: Richard Goldstone of South Africa, Louise Arbour of Canada and Carla Del Ponte of Switzerland. South Africa has contributed not only Goldstone (a leader in probing political violence) but also Judge Navanathem Pillay, President of the Rwandan Tribunal. She and other prominent women in the Tribunals are assuring proper attention to crimes of rape and related offences. These two Tribunals are truly international, their senior staff, judges and prosecutors coming from at least 20 countries.

Although the Tribunals are ad hoc interim affairs, until 2003 they were what we had, in some ways going beyond the infant ICC. As creatures of the Security Council, they have the political backing, however grudging, of the PERM 5, including the USA and China. There is also the fact that the Security Council's authority is universal. Although some sorts of universal, worldwide crime (e.g. piracy) have long been recognized, it took twentieth-century horror to make war crimes, crimes against humanity, universal: so given formal standing by the General Assembly since 1946 and by the four Geneva Conventions in 1949. Individual persons, not states, are responsible. How many of us realize that these Conventions, ratified by most states in the world, oblige us to prosecute the (alleged) criminals in our own national courts, or, if we are squeamish about that, to deliver the accused to a state that will prosecute? Within their mandates of time and place, these Tribunals have been putting this principle into practice.

What do we know of the Tribunals' work so far? We know a lot about how they have struggled with new legal and institutional practice, creating both concept and capacity, i.e. what is the law and how to apply it. For example, preparing an arrest warrant, a case for prosecution, takes a lot of work. Extending its investigating into Kosovo in 1999 involved the Yugoslav Tribunal in interviewing over 3,000 witnesses. Also in the course of its Kosovo investigations, forensic teams dug up and examined more than 4,000 bodies. For Yugoslavia, cases against more than 200 are in the works.

The political context permits and constricts. The Tribunals can investigate and prosecute, but they can't by themselves lay hands on the accused because there is no international police force. Governments are supposed to do that. For the Rwanda Tribunal, most affected governments have done it, but the Yugoslav story is different: until 2002 not only Balkan governments but even the NATO and UN military would not touch the notorious, even under their noses. Local governments' reluctance is easy to understand: why turn yourself in? But this is changing as the bad guys are gradually being turfed out. The NATO reluctance stemmed in part from having dealt with the devil, bringing Milošević into negotiations. But along with that was the timidity of the dominant USA, afraid of the military casualties that might ensue if they went after the big bosses. The British and French were not much better. The result was that, at first, Rwanda got some top criminals, Yugoslavia mostly lower ranks. A turning point for the Yugoslav Tribunal was the arrest and delivery to The Hague in 2002 of Milošević by his own government.

Why do we bother with these difficult Tribunals? Not just punishment as an end, but as a means: a means to destroy impunity, to deter, and, more importantly, to lead on to sanity, to reconciliation, to some sort of peace in the Balkans and Rwanda. For this, the big bosses, the wicked instigators and commanders of enormous crime, must be brought to justice.

Experience has confirmed what was evident from the start, that these international Tribunals could not, and indeed need not, prosecute the thousands implicated in war crimes. Exposing and healing wounds of war could be advanced by putting only the major criminals on the international stage. The run-of-the-mill mobsters must be dealt with in one way or another (e.g. by truth and reconciliation commissions or judicial systems) in the war-torn countries themselves. In fact this is how the work of the Tribunals has evolved.

It follows that the reason for the Tribunals, what they are doing and how they do it, has to be known by those most directly affected, nationally and locally. The Yugoslav Tribunal has been pushing a remarkable outreach programme involving networks of individuals, NGOs, legal organizations, victims' associations and educational institutions. Basic facts about the Tribunal and information on its current operations have been distributed in the several languages of the region, a comprehensive website is maintained, all public sessions of the Court are broadcast live and in local languages on the Internet, and a weekly TV programme on the Tribunal goes out to the region.

The Yugoslav Tribunal has organized its work so as to wind up around 2012, a span of 18 years or so since its creation. To do this the Court is concentrating on the top political and military leaders. The rest of the accused – mid-level criminals, by no means everyone involved – will be referred to national courts. This referral, however, is conditional on the capacity of the national court to handle the job efficiently and up to international standards of human rights and due process. To assure national capacity within the existing judicial system a special 'chamber' has to be created with specific responsibility for trying serious violations of humanitarian law. To get this started in Bosnia and Herzegovina, international judges would work within this national court at the beginning to assist local judges. This is an ingenious experiment both to speed up the trial process and to strengthen the national judiciary.

Balkans atrocities were bad enough, but Rwanda was something else: 800,000 slaughtered in less than three months. It was a carefully orchestrated massacre instigated and led by a Hutu cabal, the Intrahamwe, bringing down a recently installed government uniting Hutu and Tutsi. Although ethnic lines were blurred, former political dominance by the minority Tutsis was exploited by the vicious Intrahamwe. In the wake of the 1994 slaughter a Tutsi army in waiting crossed over from Uganda, the Intrahamwe and cohorts fled (most into the Democratic Republic of the Congo) and a new Tutsi-led government took over in the capital Kigali. Despite credible warnings of the impending disaster, the international community at the Security Council stood by. In shame, it created the War Crimes Tribunal for Rwanda, tacked on to the existing Tribunal for Yugoslavia. Even more than in the Balkans, it was obvious that any serious attempt to bring Rwanda's war criminals to justice would require both national and international action. The new Rwandan government in Kigali could reasonably suspect any belated action by the Security Council, and since 1994 Kigali has blown cold and hot over the UN Tribunal.

Rwanda happened to be among the non-permanents on the Security Council in 1994 when this Tribunal was established. Rwanda was against and walked out. By 2000 the UN had done its *mea culpa*. At the General Assembly in November 2000 the Rwandan delegate said that his government welcomed the Tribunal as an international presence to avert any suspicion of vengeful justice, to get at criminals hiding outside Rwanda, to affirm international responsibility for crimes against all humanity and to promote national reconciliation. Sad to say, bad vibes came back in 2003. This was due in part to the contrast, in process and speed, between the national and international approaches and also because Carla del Ponte, Chief Prosecutor for both Yugoslavia and Rwanda, had announced her intention to pursue both Tutsi and Hutu suspects. A separate Prosecutor for Rwanda has since been appointed. Judicial impartiality makes enemies.

At its start-up the UN Rwanda Tribunal could not wisely live in volatile Kigali, and instead was set down in Tanzania's unadorned Arusha. The site in itself would hardly attract eminent jurists, and, while on the map it seems close enough to Kigali, there is no easy direct passage between the two towns. Time displayed the practical disadvantages of this separation: difficult toing and froing of the accused and victims, and isolation of court proceedings from the Rwandans who needed to know.

Despite a shaky start, by 2003 the Rwanda Tribunal, with its 16 judges and Prosecutors, had indicted 80 suspects and identified another 136. Accepting its limited capacity and the need to wind up in reasonable time, the Court intends to go for only 24 new indictments and to refer 40 suspects to national jurisdiction on condition that there will be no death penalty. More than 20 were on trial in 2003. The Court is aiming to complete its work by 2008.

The Rwandan government, with thousands of accused on its hands, is impatient and critical of Arusha. Nevertheless, with all the constraints of careful jurisprudence, the Tribunal for Rwanda has made history. It was the first ever to convict a former head of state. Well before Milošević went to The Hague, Prime Minister Jean Kambanda, who presided over the 1994 slaughter, was convicted of genocide. This was also history's first conviction for genocide. In addition, a former mayor of Kigali, a militia commander, a vice-president of the Intrahamwe, a prominent business man and a Belgian journalist have been convicted. A small-town mayor has been convicted of using rape as an instrument of genocide. Eleven former government ministers are in custody. Arrests have been made in 20 countries.

From an international perspective this is an impressive record. But how does it look from Kigali, and what impact can it have within Rwanda? Although the Tribunal has set up an information centre in Kigali and provided press and radio information, the current government gives it a bad name – slow, incompetent.

The government is engulfed by a huge, urgent, relentless problem: what to do with the 120,000 suspects scooped up after the slaughter, crammed into little corrals. By 2003 Rwanda's flimsy courts had actually processed 6,000. But what of the rest? The government has turned the job over to people's courts with locally elected judges in each community. The accused will make their confessions before the entire community. By international standards, this is rough justice, but what is the alternative? How can this communal process make for healing in a society so quickly and violently turned against itself?

Two things will determine the UN Tribunals' contribution to national reconciliation: one is getting hold of the crime bosses, the political and military leaders; the other is doing the job in good time. Carla del Ponte put it straight to the Security Council in November 2000: 'By allowing the main culprits of the Bosnian war to continue to enjoy freedom, a wrong message is sent, both to the people and the politicians of Bosnia: namely, that criminal nationalism and its promoters are and shall remain beyond the reach of justice, and the threatening words of the international communities are just that, words.' She went on to say: 'Milošević must be brought to trial before the international Tribunal. There is no alternative.' Unless those who created the Tribunals have the political courage to corral the wicked leaders, the Tribunals themselves cannot do what they should.

To conclude my sketch of these pioneering Tribunals, I quote the words of the Prosecutor in her year 2000 report to the Security Council and to the General Assembly:

> To achieve a lasting peace and bring an end to the cycles of violence in the Balkans, it will be essential for the ordinary citizens of the region of the former Yugoslavia to be satisfied that justice has been achieved. History has sadly taught that unless a reasonable level of such satisfaction is achieved, ordinary citizens will feel obliged to take justice into their own hands. They will seek justice not otherwise achieved. What is more, any sense of injustice is likely to be transmitted to the next generation and it is possible that injustices of today could be the cause of future conflicts in the Balkans. Here the Tribunal can play an important part in ending such cycles of violence. It is the Prosecutor's firm belief that the conflict in the territory of the former Yugoslavia was sparked and fuelled by greedy and power-hungry politicians who used propaganda and nationalistic sentiments to create an atmosphere of fear and terror, which was then used to motivate ordinary citizens to commit atrocious crimes

against their neighbours. If ordinary citizens can accept that this was the root cause of the conflict, and that they were led into this terrible conflict by deceit and fear, they may be more likely to accept a meaningful reconciliation with their neighbours, who were also led in the same way into the conflict. By prosecuting the leaders, even down to the municipal level, the Tribunal can lay this foundation for reconciliation. Lower-level perpetrators will still have to be dealt with, but this can take many forms, such as local/domestic prosecutions, or even, in the future, some sort of trust and reconciliation process. A lasting and stable peace, however, cannot be achieved unless the Tribunal plays the important role of prosecuting the leaders of all sides to the conflict who were responsible for the commission of crimes falling within its jurisdiction.

Now in 2003 there is good news from wounded Sierra Leone. By formal UN–government agreement, a joint national–international war crimes court has been established to try the worst criminals. Sitting in Freetown in full view, this new hybrid process will work alongside the national Truth and Reconciliation Commission to help the country heal itself.

The situation in Cambodia is fundamentally different. The government would like to have some sort of UN veneer over its killing fields. The fact is that surviving leaders of the Khmer Rouge are living in quiet comfort while everywhere the country is suffused with mistrust and barely suppressed violence. Healing has not begun.

But we can't quite walk away, can we? The nagging, tormenting question is: why only Yugoslavia and Rwanda? And now Sierra Leone? Deep wounds abound. How far back do we go: Europe's Holocaust, USSR/Russia/Chechnya, China's fading myth of Marxist utopia (I was there), the bloodied India/Pakistan, Suharto's Indonesian dead, Nigeria–Biafra, Vietnam? Still in the United Nations' emergency ward are Angola, the Sudan, Somalia, Burundi, Ethiopia-Eritrea, the Congos, Guatemala, Haiti, Afghanistan. Timor-Leste is but a flicker in Indonesia's fires. South Africa shows how reconciliation can be put into play in that nation's lively political theatre.

The Yugoslav and Rwanda Tribunals have broken new ground. The permanent International Criminal Court will carry on. And yet, can all the tears in all the seas cleanse our blood-stained hands?

Transnational crime

Twenty-five years in the making, the Convention against Transnational Organized Crime was adopted by the General Assembly in November 2000, and by the end of the year had been signed by 124 states. It comes into force after 40 have ratified. Sophisticated criminal networks are getting rich smuggling arms, drugs and people, including women and children. The Convention strikes at those crimes and also covers money laundering and international fraud. It defines crimes like these so as to synchronize national laws; it facilitates judicial co-operation and extradition. Two protocols to the Convention are directed against the criminal trade in migrants, women and children. The UN will help countries apply Convention standards in national legislation. The Convention also will bring states together to attack these criminals. This is another first for the UN.

CHAPTER 6

Human Rights, Human Wrecks

We the peoples of the United Nations determined ... to reaffirm faith in fundamental human rights, in the dignity and worth of the human person, in the equal rights of men and women and of nations large and small. ...

Did they really mean it, those 51 governments, on 26 June 1945? How could they know what that might mean in practice? They did have the foresight to build the Commission on Human Rights (CHR) into the ECOSOC structure, the only commission so specified in the Charter. Citizens' organizations lobbied hard for human rights in that great month in San Francisco; from the start they have played a crucial role at the UN. This is one case in which WE THE PEOPLES, not just WE THE GOVERNMENTS, means something.

There was enough push from San Francisco to get the CHR going in 1946 (18 member states at first, now 53), and it plunged right in to the interpretation of the general phrases in the Charter: what are human rights? How lucky that Eleanor Roosevelt was in the chair. The record tells us that the Commission took its responsibility very seriously: fashioning the Universal Declaration of Human Rights took 1,400 rounds of voting. Although in the years that followed, so-called 'hard liners' among developing countries have dubbed this Declaration a sneaky imposition of Western culture, in fact the drafters included China, Chile, Lebanon and the Soviet Union. The hand of Canada's John Humphrey shaped the final text. He became the director of Human Rights in the UN Secretariat.

Finding the definition of human rights so exquisitely difficult, the Commission made a smart decision: first, let us agree on general principles, a Declaration; then let this Declaration be the basis for more detailed formulation of rights in international law, in covenants (or treaties) among states. So that's the way it went. The Declaration was adopted on 10 December 1948 (48 yes, eight abstained – the then socialist states, Saudi Arabia and apartheid South Africa). Thirty-four of the 48 eventually joined the Non-Aligned Movement (NAM), the 'non-aligned' developing countries.

The Declaration is an affirmation of what we should be as persons, as societies, as nations: the worth and dignity of each and every one of us, free to come and go, to think and speak, to marry and divorce, to enjoy health, education and food, to work and form unions, to be protected by a judicial system under a freely elected government. These rights are not conferred on us by the state; they are 'inherent', we have them because we are. The state does not make us, we make the state. How could such a radical Declaration be adopted? If you like it, no problem. If you don't but are afraid to admit it, no problem. The Declaration is not law, it is not legally binding. That is why the next step had to be taken: putting these general principles into legal covenants.

You might think that the whole package of rights in the Declaration would be translated into law in one comprehensive covenant. Not so. Political differences that bedevilled adoption of the Declaration got worse as UN membership grew from 51 to 119 in the mid-1960s. More than half of the new members were former colonies, adding a new dimension to Cold War East–West tension. This group was more concerned with economic and social rights than with the individual liberties and political rights so dear to the West.

In retrospect we can see that these two ways of seeing come together and interpenetrate, but for negotiation it was easier to separate them into two covenants. Even so, the two were not adopted until 1966, and, when enough states had committed themselves, became legal only in 1976, 28 years after the Declaration. These are the two basic legal instruments that turn the Declaration into law: the Covenant on Economic, Social and Cultural Rights, and the Covenant on Civil and Political Rights. Political energies account for the fact that two more covenants were shaped early on: in revulsion against the Nazis, the Convention on the Prevention and Punishment of the Crime of Genocide (adopted 1948, in force 1951), and in opprobrium of apartheid South Africa, the Convention on the Elimination of all Forms of Racial Discrimination (adopted 1966, in force 1969). In the ensuing two decades, this four-square fortress was strengthened by the adoption of four more treaties: on the Elimination of All Forms of Discrimination against Women (adopted 1979, in force 1981), against Torture (adopted 1984, in force 1987), on the Rights of the Child (adopted 1989, in force 1990), and on the Protection of the Rights of All Migrant Workers (adopted 1990; by December 2002, 19 ratifications, just one short of coming into force). These eight treaties cover basic rights on which agreement could be reached. Some important things were put into optional protocols, addenda to the basic treaties, that states may or may not accept. The First Protocol to the Covenant on Civil and Political Rights (adopted 1966, in force 1976) allows individuals to appeal directly to the UN when their rights are violated. The Second Protocol to this Covenant (adopted 1989, in force 1991) aims at the abolition of the death penalty. For children there are also two protocols: one specifies that no child under 18 years of age shall serve in armed conflict (in force 2000), and the other prohibits the sale or prostitution of children (in force 2000). An important Protocol to the Convention for Women lets individuals appeal directly to the UN (in force 2000). So there we have it: these eight treaties and five protocols make up the essential structure of international human rights law.

Was there serious concern for human rights in those early days at the UN? Not much, especially after the falling out of the wartime Allies. The 1948 Genocide Convention provided for the punishment of those found guilty under international law, whether they were constitutionally responsible rulers, public officials or private individuals, but the International Criminal Court envisaged in that Convention was established only in 2002. Even so, complaints of violations kept pouring in by the thousands, especially after the two major Covenants were adopted in 1966. At its very first meeting in January 1947, however, the Commission on Human Rights (CHR) had effectively copped out, saying, 'The Commission recognizes that it has no power to take any action in regard to any complaints concerning human rights.'

But history moved on. Emancipated colonies, after the adoption of the Convention against Racism, saw to it that in 1967 the CHR was told to look into apartheid. This was feasible because, in conjunction with this Convention, a 'Committee of Experts' (independent persons) was established to monitor what countries were doing ('implementation', it is called). This was the very first oversight body for a formal Rights treaty. Two more things happened that same year. Still zeroing in on apartheid, an ad hoc Group of Experts was formed to examine complaints, against the South

African state, of torture. At the same time, a Special Rapporteur (expert inspector) was appointed to see what more the UN could do towards eliminating apartheid. Also in 1967, waking up to the fact that thousands of complaints were being ignored, the CHR took a first step towards doing something about them. Back in 1948 the CHR had appointed what was called a Subcommission of Experts on Prevention of Discrimination and Protection of Minorities. This Subcommission had helped the CHR to produce the Universal Declaration, and now, in 1967, was told to examine 'communications' (complaints) to see where there were 'gross violations'. This fed into the simultaneous activation of the CHR to examine what was going on in countries, so as to identify any 'consistent pattern' of violation. And then at last, in 1970, ECOSOC got real about complaints, setting up a special working group on communications under the Subcommission on Minorities with the specific job of screening complaints. This has resulted in an annual report (via ECOSOC to the General Assembly) for all to see.

So where are we with human rights at the UN at the dawn of the twenty-first century? In Geneva, in the elegance of the Palais des Nations where the Human Rights Commission gathers, do we hear the 1990 euphony of George Herbert Walker Bush and Eduard Shevardnadze? Well, not quite. Eastern Europeans are clearing their emancipated throats, even beginning to turn to the UN for help. In 1992 there was an infusion of ten more countries into the CHR, most of them from the 'South'. Apart from Europe, there is no big change in entrenched battalions at the Commission. The NAM, the non-aligned, had their day in 1986 when the General Assembly adopted the Declaration on the Right to Development (or, as so aptly put by China's late President Deng Xiao Ping, the right to get rich). Shaking hands with the CHR, this Declaration says that 'the human person is the central subject of development and should be the active participant and beneficiary of the right to development'. Then in 1989 the General Assembly decided to convene a World Conference on Human Rights in Vienna in 1993. Is CHR, the Geneva step-child, coming home?

Something was happening. The UN sensor began to notice the annual six-week meetings of the Human Rights Commission. Although only the 53 members (governments) of the CHR can vote, all UN states can attend and speak, and many do. And now they come at the political level, anywhere from two to three dozen top-ranking ministers. The Secretary-General sounds the key note. Civil society, NGOs, are there in force. The media is also present. This is a big show, upwards of 2,500 encamped. Why?

A worldwide information network has begun to get results. There is the formal official network and the informal NGO network, digging out the dirt. The official network has two main operations. One stems from the eight big Rights treaties, each with a monitoring panel of experts and each requiring the 'parties' (committed states) to report on what they are doing. The other operation is the battery of independent but official investigators commissioned by the CHR to visit specific countries, or to study sensitive transnational issues. And then there are the aggressive outspoken NGOs who keep this whole drama alive, feeding information into official ears and speaking bad news to the world audience. Torture, harassment, discrimination, rape, children of poverty for sale: enough information is getting out to make governments squirm. Even the most repressive regimes want to look nice. For all sorts of reasons, including self-defence (all are vulnerable), governments do not like to criticize each other, and that casts a pall of impunity over much public discourse. The Soviet collapse and the increase in relatively democratic status opened official windows a bit, but the hypersensitivity is still there. Meanwhile TV and the Internet are bringing the world into the Palais. That governments care must have some deep meaning. Could it mean that, after all, to look good you have to be good?

Is this whole human rights movement a 'Western' ploy, a sort of neo-colonial culture war? The issue was joined at Vienna in June 1993: 171 states, 800 NGOs, the 'treaty bodies' (the committed states), national institutions, academics, altogether 7,000 participating. By consensus, all agreed in the ensuing Vienna Declaration 'that all human rights derive from the dignity and worth inherent in the human person, and that the human person is the central subject of human rights and fundamental freedoms' (Preamble); and, in Article 1:

> The World Conference on Human Rights reaffirms the solemn commitment of all States to fulfil their obligations to promote universal respect for, and observance and protection of, all human rights and fundamental freedoms for all in accordance with the Charter of the United Nations, other instruments relating to human rights, and international law. The universal nature of these rights and freedoms is beyond question.

In this framework, enhancement of international co-operation in the field of human rights is essential for the full achievement of the purposes of the United Nations.

Human rights and fundamental freedoms are the birthright of all human beings; their protection and promotion is the first responsibility of Governments.[1]

Rights are not West versus East, they are indeed universal.

Vienna gave birth not only to the Declaration, a renewed embrace of human rights like those divorced couples who marry each other again; but also at Vienna the marriage vows were followed by proposals for follow-up action. For immediate action, the most important was the idea of a UN High Commissioner for Human Rights, ranking next to the Secretary-General himself, as advocate and leader. This new post was approved by the General Assembly in that same year. Other actions took up unfinished business. Delinquent states were urged to join, to ratify the Rights Conventions. The UN and the Bretton Woods financial institutions (the IMF and the World Bank) were told to get their act together in supporting human rights. The rights of special groups needed more commitment: minorities, the indigenous, migrant workers, the tortured, disabled, women and children. Many don't know that they have rights – they should be told. And above all, countries should get UN help in creating institutions and practices that put rights into real life.

Vienna should have been the last word, but of course it was not. In human rights there are no last words, but there are plenty of last acts. The CHR carried on in marathon sessions, year after year, fighting old battles over and over. The airing of gross violations in named countries (e.g. Algeria, China, Syria, Turkey) triggered defensive counter-attacks. China's political leaders have managed to avoid the humiliation of exposure in Geneva. Although China blows hot and cold, there are signs of change. While the central government perpetuates the old imperial practice of political control – arbitrary arrest and detention, torture, suppression of any threatening dissent – there is movement towards reform. In November 2000 Beijing signed up for UN help in introducing modern procedures into its judiciary, its courts and prisons, and in re-educating its police. Given the fact that the High Commissioner has been outspoken on China's crackdown on dissidents, accepting UN aid cannot be just window dressing. Old men die and the ranks of the die-hard dwindle – for example, South Africa has moved from villain to exemplar – but even so, the heat has not died down.

Yet there has been real progress. Russia's beatification began in the Conference on Security and Co-operation in Europe, yielding its 'final act' at Helsinki in 1975. Gorbachev wrote the last chapter. In 1977 US President (and now Nobel Peace laureate) Jimmy Carter introduced human rights into US foreign policy, producing another paradox: a useful annual review by the US State Department of rights violations around the world. The appointment of a UN High Commissioner was a critical advance: the first, in 1994, was José Ayola-Lasso of Ecuador, earnest and discreet. He was followed in 1997 by Mary Robinson, long-time human rights lawyer and President of Ireland, and in 2002 by UN veteran Sergio Vieira de Mello, fresh from leading Timor-Leste into independent statehood. Mary Robinson's diplomatic sensibility did much to defuse tired old bombast. She was heard with respect when she told the world about egregious horror, as in Chechnya, Timor-Leste and Sierra Leone. Even the Security Council invited her to speak when, in 1999, they considered the Secretary-General's report on civilians in armed conflict. This was a first, not the last.

Sergio Vieira de Mello followed Mary Robinson in September 2002. He had weathered many a storm for the UN, having had a lot of headquarters and field experience – refugees, humanitarian assistance, peacekeeping – including Kosovo, Cambodia, Sudan, Cyprus, Mozambique and Lebanon, all this before guiding infant Timor-Leste (East Timor) to statehood. Addressing the GA's Third Committee on 4 November 2002, he said: 'I am ... convinced that human rights are not complicated to understand. ... Respect for human life and dignity, which form the basis of our human rights norms, are after all values that are shared by all cultures and religions.' He went on to say that 'the rule of law will form the centrepiece of my approach as Commissioner for Human Rights'.[2]

Sergio hardly had time to catch his breath as Commissioner when he was plucked by the Secretary-General in June 2003 to be the UN Special Representative in Iraq. He was killed in the bombing of the UN office in Baghdad on 19 August 2003. His was a special four-month assignment, to act for the Secretary-General in post-war Iraq. It was in every way a sensitive and risky job, for which he was superbly qualified. As he lay trapped in the blasted rubble, his last words were: 'Don't let them drive the UN out.'

Advocacy linked to action – that is how the UN is promoting human rights. With only a few pennies, the High Commissioner presides over a comprehensive programme of support, inspection and analysis. To help countries do the right thing, the High Commissioner has around two dozen experts in as many countries. Human rights is now a normal part of UN peace operations. Alongside these experts-in-residence, there are more than a dozen peripatetic inspectors mandated to see what is happening in troublesome countries, and more than 20 to examine transnational issues (called themes).

A simple listing shows a staggering range of concerns. Besides those mentioned on page 61, countries covered have included Afghanistan, Bosnia, Croatia, Federal Yugoslavia (Serbia), Burundi, Cambodia, Democratic Congo, Equatorial Guinea, Haiti, Iran, Iraq, Myanmar, Rwanda, Somalia, the Sudan and occupied Palestine. Major issues have included summary or arbitrary executions, enforced involuntary disappearances, torture, arbitrary detention, restitution for victims of grave violations of human rights, the independence of judges and lawyers, freedom of opinion and expression, mercenaries, contemporary forms of racism and xenophobia, religious intolerance, sale of children, child prostitution, child pornography, children in armed conflict, violence against women, internally displaced persons, the disabled, the rights of migrants, and the illicit moving and dumping of toxic wastes. And finally, extreme poverty as deprivation of fundamental rights is identified in the Right to Development.

Besides this formidable array, countries must report every few years to the committees monitoring rights Covenants. Country and issue experts, mandated by the CHR, also produce reports which go all the way up from the CHR to the General Assembly, and these experts are present at the CHR when their reports are discussed. This brings hands-on relevance to the UN.

These Special Rapporteurs are among the unsung heroes of our time. They are paid nothing, they are professional people who take time out from their regular work to serve in this noble cause. There is no blanket agreement that lets them cross borders into countries to be inspected: each entry has to be granted by a reluctant government. Because the UN has little money for human rights, even backup support for these experts is not much. Their reward must be the gratitude of those they serve.

As the new millennium shows an old face, what signs of hope can we see? After 13 years of negotiation (i.e. resistance by repressive regimes), in 1998 the UN adopted the Declaration on Human Rights Defenders, recognizing international responsibility for these brave men and women, so often persecuted or slain for exposing abuse. A Special Representative of the Secretary-General has been appointed to defend the defenders. The Convention on Discrimination against Women was much strengthened by the adoption in 1999 of a protocol that in effect invites individual victims to appeal directly to the UN. In the year 2000 two protocols to the Child Rights Convention were adopted: one raising the permissible age for active military service from 15 to 18, and the other prohibiting the sale or prostitution of children. Also in 2000 a permanent UN Forum for Indigenous People was established. The 2001 World Conference against Racism, Racial Discrimination, Xenophobia and Related Intolerance was a huge and tense affair, but good came out of it. Starting with a look at the sources of racism, actions were identified to dispel this affliction through education, legislation, judicial enforcement and the support of national institutions.

As for such dreads in 2000 as Timor-Leste, Sierra Leone and Chechnya, the High Commissioner was there and witnessing. At the CHR, for the first time a resolution condemning one of the Security Council greats was passed, on Russia's devastation of civilian Chechnya.

It is hard to quantify rights, but we can enumerate ratifications of treaties. Although not everyone is yet on board, the increase in joiners since 1990 is a good sign. Only the Child Rights Convention is nearly universal with 191 ratifications. Among the others from 1990 to December 2002 are: Economic and Social, up from 96 to 146; Civil and Political, from 90 to 149; Genocide, from 100 to 134; Race, from 127 to 165; and Women, from 102 to 170. By December 2002 the Convention against Torture had been ratified by 132 states.

By now it must be apparent that, with all this reporting on so many issues and through so many channels, there is a problem of overload. In what is being reported and in the way that information is extracted there has to be a lot of overlap and intermingle. Besides the thinly staffed UN channels, each treaty body has its own monitoring committee, and although the Committee presidents meet once a year, there is not much they can do except exchange headaches. Streamlining is in the works. Just as important is keeping up the pressure on governments where Rights inspectors have identified serious violations.

Within this reporting complex is another baffling problem: what to do about the thousands of individual complaints about rights violations that come pouring in every year? As mentioned earlier, a Working Group under the Subcommission of the CHR is supposed to screen all these communications, decide which are valid and which show countries with a pattern of serious violations. Then what? CHR airing of the bad countries? Yes, sometimes. But what relief can this bring to the abused individuals? Only Amnesty International has any answer, and that only for the select few: letter-writing to those responsible in government, publicity in some cases.

Then there is the problem of insufficient money – always less than 2 per cent of the regular UN budget going to human rights. And overall the UN income is on a shoestring. Voluntary contributions have helped enormously, amounting to double the regular UN allotment. To give you an idea of how little is going into human rights, the UN regular allotment for the two years 2000–01 was $39 million, but voluntary contributions amounted to $79 million.

Kofi Annan has made a difference. Although his predecessor said the right things, Kofi Annan has done things too. He has not hesitated to speak out about shameful violations. He understands that rights are basic and pervasive in everything the UN means and does. UN peace operations are more and more directed at human security with specific support for human rights. Blue Helmets are being educated about rights. In Kosovo, Timor-Leste and Sierra Leone the UN team includes human rights experts. And national growth – development, we call it – as understood and supported by the UN is now based on human rights. The *Human Development Report* for 2000, emanating from the UNDP, shows how raising national wealth means assuring human rights. Amartya Sen, Nobel laureate and a progenitor of the Human Development Reports, goes one further: see his recent book *Development as Freedom* (or, to paraphrase, development *is* freedom). UN support for development now has a common frame, built on human rights.

For the CHR this is where the right to development comes in. It is not just politically smart to embrace the right to development: it is right. The question here is: what can the human rights approach contribute to this well-ploughed field? The CHR is putting people to work on such issues as the right to democracy, the right to development, extreme poverty, structural adjustment, foreign debt, the right to housing, food and education. Maybe they can put a little more zing into the years of frustrating work already devoted to these problems. For one thing, they might get behind Kofi Annan's global compact with international business which, inter alia, enjoins business to stop violating human rights.

Business is politics, and politics is power. Some people can make a difference: human rights defenders, the eminent volunteers serving the CHR, the persistent NGOs – who remembers that Amnesty International got the Nobel Peace Prize in 1977?

Plunging now into the twenty-first century, where are our precious human rights? What about the Human Rights Commission? The sensitivity of governments about rights has coloured the CHR. Governments shy away from looking too closely into each other's eyes, each other's lies. This is also shown in the practice of 'block voting', where regional groups gang up to cover and dominate. This has weakened but by no means killed the CHR. Mary Robinson, before her departure, suggested that governments elected to the CHR should have fully committed themselves to basic human rights treaties and should have a decent rights record at home.

And what about the big challenges to human rights in the world today? What about terrorism (11 September 2001 and its sequel)? What about Afghanistan? Sierra Leone? Timor-Leste? In all of these the UN and human rights are supremely relevant. Immediately following the 9/11 terror attacks in New York and Washington, Mary Robinson declared these terrorists to be criminals, committing crimes against humanity. Thereafter, however, she warned against hysterical, arbitrary arrest, detention and Star Chamber trials. Acting this way would reward terrorists and only push more unhappy people into terrorism.[3] The UN High Commissioner and his team have also been on the front line in Afghanistan, helping to establish a national Human Rights Commission, and in Sierra Leone and Timor-Leste, assisting their Truth and Reconciliation Commissions. The High Commissioner has also been active in assuring a solid place for human rights in the new International Criminal Court. In these brave pioneering theatres, the banner of human rights flies high.

For human rights, the rules of the game are now set. National behaviour can be judged in the arena of the world. Through the miasma of violence and suffering, can we glimpse a new humanity?

CHAPTER 7

Women: The Whole World in Their Hands?

The story of women at the UN is the story of an ongoing revolution, a celebration of women as the engine of social progress. Here you can see a worldwide women's movement infiltrating the corridors of power, demolishing the macho myth that so often has kept men and women in bondage.

When joining the UN, states make a formal commitment to the UN Charter. The Charter is explicit in affirming the equality of men and women. The Preamble affirms faith in the equal rights of women and men, and Article 55 says that 'the United Nations shall promote ... respect for all without distinction as to race, sex, language or religion.' For the UN itself, Article 8 is even more explicit: 'The United Nations shall place no restrictions on the eligibility of men and women to participate in any capacity and under conditions of equality in its principal and subsidiary organs.'

This formal affirmation of women's standing in the world was no accident. Among the delegates to the UN founding conference, a handful of women from Brazil, the Dominican Republic, Uruguay, China, Canada and the USA together succeeded in getting these catalytic words into the Charter. The voice of women was also heard from 42 NGOs at the conference. Not surprising nevertheless is the fact that among the 160 who signed the Charter only four were women. Of the 51 original states in the UN, only 30 had equal voting rights for women.

These few women at the UN's birth were in the forefront of international women's action going back to the nineteenth century in Europe and North America. At the Hague Peace Conference in 1902, women's organizations pressed for international standards for marriage, divorce and child custody. Women were aghast at the futile bloodshed of the First World War, and out of that came the

Women's International League for Peace and Freedom (WILPF). Jane Addams, the first President of WILPF, got the Nobel Peace Prize. On into the twentieth century, in developing countries heroic women joined the fight for independence from colonial rule, while at the same time struggling for their own emancipation.

We continue to learn that individuals can make a difference. The US delegation at the start-up of the General Assembly in 1946 included Eleanor Roosevelt, widow of the late US President. With 15 other women in attendance, Mrs Roosevelt presented an open letter to the Assembly and to the women of the world, advocating stronger participation of women in international and national life, especially in building peace. She went on to play a key role in the UN adoption of the Universal Declaration of Human Rights in 1948. Yet until today only two women have been elected President of the General Assembly: Vijaya Lakshmi Pandit (sister of Jawaharlal Nehru) of India in 1953, and Angie Brooks of Liberia in 1969. Both women were politically prominent in their own countries.

Fine words and a few outstanding women. But symbols can ignite action. Social and political action must be organized and structured. The UN Charter held no special arrangement for the women's movement, so something had to be created. That something was the UN Commission on the Status of Women (CSW), established in June 1946, a breakout from the Commission on Human Rights. Although human rights are women's rights, anyone could see that the women's cause had to have a distinct and separate push. The CSW was handed an enormous, open-ended task, to inform and advise members of the UN on the whole spectrum of women's rights, social, economic and political. The CSW is mandated to alert the UN to problems facing women and to 'recommend' action nationally and internationally on women's rights. These recommendations should include the need to translate commitments in international treaties into laws and regulations back home.

CSW membership started at 15, rising to 45 in 1989 as overall UN membership grew. The work of the Commission has been enriched by the varied professional qualifications of its members. Early on, the first director of the UN Division of Human Rights, John Humphrey, said: 'More perhaps than in any other UN body, the delegates of the CSW were personally committed to its objectives and acted as a kind of lobby for the women of the world.' Over the years, many women's organizations (now over 600) have made important contributions to the work of the CSW.

When the CSW began, very little objective information was available on the situation of women worldwide. To fix this, one of its first actions was to launch what became an annual survey of the legal status and treatment of women. Initial returns from 74 states in 1947 showed that women had full political rights in fewer than one-third of these countries. Subsequent reports confirmed that illiteracy was much higher among women than men. The data in these annual reports showed up glaring discrimination against women and gave grounds for corrective action.

During its first 15 years, from 1946 onwards, the CSW put this information to work as it set standards for women's rights (e.g. in protection, marriage, education, employment and politics). The Organization of American States (OAS) in 1948 adopted the landmark Inter-American Convention on the Granting of Rights to Women. This was extended worldwide when the UN General Assembly in 1952 adopted the Convention on the Political Rights of Women, providing that women have full rights to vote, to run for election and to serve in any public function. For the first time in human history, universal women's political rights were established in international law. We all know that laws are often ignored, whether national or international; and so, to show up actual practice, the CSW got the UN General Assembly in 1967 to adopt the Declaration on the Elimination of Discrimination against Women.

In the next 20 years, a whole battery of international conventions on human rights came into force. Among these was the Convention on the Elimination of All Forms of Discrimination Against Women, adopted in 1979, turning the 1967 Declaration into law. The Convention defines discrimination as 'any distinction, exclusion or restriction made on the basis of sex' that in any way limits women's rights. Like other human rights conventions, this anti-discrimination Convention is monitored by a committee (23 members) who examine national reports on what is being done to put the Convention into practice. The Committee has focused on the high incidence of violence against women, leading to action by the whole UN General Assembly. The UN Development Fund for Women (UNIFEM) has also swung into action, giving aid to more than 70 countries for specific programmes to curb such violence. Norleen Heyzer, head of

UNIFEM, says: 'We need a world community that is committed to ending violence against women because we know how to do it.'

This Convention was strengthened in 1999 by a Protocol that created a channel for abused women to appeal to an international body. This is at least the beginning of international monitoring of women's rights.

In the 1960s newly independent ex-colonial states infused the UN with a sensitivity to economic and social deprivation in these vast populations. And so the CSW extended its concerns from political to economic, to the advancement of women in poor nations. This outreach of the CSW was energized by the realization that women make a huge contribution to national wealth, not only in the family but also in conventionally recognized production: in agriculture, industry and commerce. These facts were made plain in definitive studies that could not be discounted. Women were everywhere in the marketplace.

The maturing of the CSW was evident when the UN designated 1975 as the Year of the Woman, and went on to make 1976–85 the UN Decade for Women. In 1975 also the UN launched in Mexico City the first World Conference on Women. Delegates from 133 governments came to Mexico, and a parallel citizen's 'Tribune' brought together over 6,000 activists from around the world. A 'Plan of Action' addressed social, economic and political rights. The Conference was a political event that men at the UN could not ignore.

Obviously nation states must do the work of turning international norms into practice. At the core of all this, what could the UN do? Backstopping the CSW was the UN Division for the Advancement of Women, servicing the Commission's work and speaking up for women internationally and inside the UN house. To move out of the house into concrete action, two things were done: the UN Development Fund for Women (UNIFEM) was established in 1976, and at the same time the International Research and Training Institute for the Advancement of Women was conceived. Led by its far-sighted and pragmatic first director, Margaret Snyder, UNIFEM got special staff into UN regional offices, organized training and planning workshops and gave direct aid to women's action in poor communities including the start-up of women's own businesses. It influenced major UN funds such as UNDP and the World Bank, and intergovernmental organizations such as the Southern African Development Community, to include and involve both women and men in all their activities. From this fresh beginning, UNIFEM continues today under Norleen Heyzer with voluntary contributions amounting to about $25 million a year. Working in over 100 countries and with advisers in 40, UNIFEM gives financial and technical support to getting women into political life and getting them out of poverty. UNIFEM works the whole UN system and the NGOs' networks to promote economic and social justice for women.

Problems and aspirations raised at Mexico needed more thought, more probing. Hence three more World Conferences were held: in Copenhagen 1980, in Nairobi in 1985 and in Beijing in 1995. Numbers say something. The 1975 Conference attracted 133 governments and over 6,000 from NGOs; in 1980, 145 governments and over 7,000 NGOs; in 1985, 157 governments and 15,000 from NGOs; and in 1995, 189 governments and 17,000 from NGOs.

Conferences, declarations, strategies, plans. Has anything substantial and practical, nationally and internationally, come out of all these gatherings? Was this anything more than global tourism for NGOs? Let us trace the formal outcomes of these conferences and consider what that says about how the basic issues are understood. Are women in the UN Club or aren't they? And if in, on what conditions? And what does this mean for women desperate in poverty and in war?

At Mexico City, the Conference set a precedent by defining goals in a World Plan of Action for the UN Decade for Women. Major goals were equality, development and peace. The Plan of Action emphasized access to basic services — education, health, nutrition, housing, family planning — all pretty traditional; but, more importantly, it said that women must also become active participants in political life and in social and economic growth.

Five years later at Copenhagen, with the recent adoption of the Convention on Eliminating Discrimination against Women, the big question was: why are women denied their rights? The answer to such a fundamental question, identified at this Conference, seems pretty obvious, but it also tells us why it is necessary to have such a formal legal Convention at all. Women were denied rights for various reasons: little political interest or drive to promote women's standing in society, hardly any women in power establishments, the devaluation of women's manifold contributions to society, weak support services (e.g. day care for tiny tots, financial credit for women entrepreneurs), as well as women's isolation and lack of resources to move ahead. The Convention put pressure on governments to apply international standards in their own legislation which, in most countries, is very weak. Practical measures advocated in the Copenhagen programme included women's rights to own, control and inherit property, their rights to child custody, and their right to a legal national identity. Having to claim those rights tells us a lot about how women have suffered.

At the third conference, in Nairobi in 1985, it was time to make a first assessment of the Decade for Women and to work out an itinerary for the next stretch. The UN had checked around and found that practically nothing was happening to meet the Copenhagen goals. There had to be a shift in direction, in strategy. Getting women and their concerns into the power establishments had to come first, and what that meant had to be spelled out. The Nairobi strategies took another ten-year look, up to the year 2000, beginning with a radical challenge – all rights are women's rights. Nairobi proclaimed that while society must support and protect women, society also needs women, not as objects of charity but as gifted partners in shaping a better world. Women's full partnership must be assured in law and in economic, social and political practice. The Nairobi strategies identified specific areas where women must be involved, including not only social services (e.g. health and education) but also science, the environment, industry, employment and the new realm of communications. Widespread conflict in Africa could hardly be ignored, and Nairobi stressed women's capacity to promote peace.

The Beijing Conference in 1995 took the seminal insight of Nairobi, that women are essential partners in every dimension of national life, and built a new Declaration and Platform for action on that base. Because marginalized, women need specific political support, not as a sort of society unto themselves, but as welcome and gifted celebrants at the head table of life. Women and men will join hands. To carry this transforming approach into social reality, the Platform for Action identified 12 critical issues for women:

- Poverty
- Education and training
- Health
- Violence
- Armed conflict

- The economy
- Power, decision-making
- Institutional support
- Human rights
- The media
- The environment
- Girls' special needs.

The Beijing consensus – women speaking with one voice – was approved that same year by the UN General Assembly. Here was a UN programme for the twenty-first century.[1]

A surge of energy into the women's movement came from UN concerns over population and family planning. For many years the UN has led the world in its demographic statistics and population projections. To assist countries in their population programmes, the UN Population Fund (UNFPA) was created in 1969, supported by voluntary contributions outside the regular UN budget. Following international population conferences in Budapest (1974) and Mexico (1980), the UN convened a major Conference on Population and Development in Cairo in 1994, just one year before the Beijing women's conference.[2] How did these two meetings converge? Cairo, too, formulated a plan. While stressing the link between population and national growth, their plan took the same broad approach to women and their families as Beijing a year later. Women need to be empowered so that they can have a say in running their countries and running their lives; they need jobs and income, they need literacy education, they need maternal and child health services. The 179 states that were at Cairo turned up a year later in Beijing. And all this was funnelled to the General Assembly. How refreshing to get the same advice from different sources! In special sessions, the GA affirmed its continuing commitment to the Cairo plan in 1999, and to the Beijing Platform in 2000.[3]

The five-year review of Beijing was done in New York from 5 to 9 June 2000. The GA was given a detailed report on accomplishments and obstacles. For most of the 12 issues, it is not feasible to set quantitative targets, especially targets that would fit all countries. The review therefore had to be made in general terms, illustrated by specific cases. What emerged was a story of slow advance in most areas, not surprising since fundamental changes in orientation and institutions would have to happen. What we see is work in slow progress.

These declarations and plans of action are expressive of principle (what is right) and of intent (what should be done). They should carry political weight and lead to formal legal and institutional action. Meanwhile there is international law to buttress the women's conferences: the basic human rights conventions, elaborated in the 1979 Convention on the Elimination of All Forms of Discrimination against Women, strengthened by its 1999 Protocol. By the time of the Millennium Summit (September 2000) 166 governments had ratified the Convention and 15 had ratified the Protocol. The Convention is the women's international bill of rights, providing for their equal enjoyment of civil, political, social and cultural rights. What the Protocol does is to establish a way for abused women to appeal to the international committee that checks on countries' behaviour – are they doing what they said they would do when they embraced the Convention? This committee, made up of 23 independent experts from around the world, operates like several other treaty committees: it examines national reports in open meetings, criticizes country performance and identifies general problems, e.g. female genital mutilation (so-called female circumcision), violence against women and women's health. The appeals are likely to give information too disturbing to get into national reports. This is a remarkable way of learning and evaluating what is happening, and then channelling the worst-case findings to the top UN legislative body, the General Assembly. At its 55th Session in the year 2000, for example, the GA took a formal stand, a resolution, expressing deep concern over the persistence of violence and crimes against women throughout the world, urging all states to make such violence a crime punishable by law, and urging states to put an end to these criminal activities.

Wartime is the worst time for women. In today's armed struggles, 90 per cent of casualties are women and children. Sexual exploitation of women, rape as genocide, is high among war crimes under international law. For the first time ever, perpetrators of crimes like these have been prosecuted, convicted and jailed by the War Crimes Tribunals for Yugoslavia and Rwanda. These ad hoc Tribunals will be succeeded by the permanent International Criminal Court. Crimes under the Court's jurisdiction include:

> As war crimes and crimes against humanity, rape, sexual slavery, forced prostitution, forced pregnancy or sterilization.

As genocide, prevention of births in a targeted group.

The International Criminal Court will soon be working. Meanwhile, putting its shoulders behind its Tribunals, the Security Council has opened its doors and its mind to the concerns of women. On 24 and 25 October 2000 the Council held open meetings on Women, Peace and Security. Besides formal presentations by governments and UN organizations, the Council heard from NGOs and citizen organizations in war-torn societies. On 31 October the Council passed a bold and comprehensive resolution, endorsing the Beijing approach, demanding protection of women and girls in armed conflict and urging that women be brought into peacemaking and into UN peace operations. The Security Council said it would keep track of what happens and asked the Secretary-General to report back, specifically on what war does to women and girls, and what women can do to restore and maintain peace.

How are women faring within the UN itself, in the Secretariat? While a lot better than many governments, the UN still has some distance to go in order to reach parity between women and men on its staff. During the 1990s the percentage of women with professional responsibilities rose from 28 to 39, and, within that group, the percentage having managerial responsibilities rose from 7 to 31. In-house, some of the old boys still need reassurance that women won't eat them up. They can be comforted by the cheerful competence and good sense of the Deputy Secretary-General, Louise Frechette.

And then there was the Millennium Summit. In the UN diplomatic community, only 11 ambassadors were women. Although eight governments or states were headed by women, only three were at the Summit: Helen Clark of New Zealand, Vaira Vike-Freiberga of Latvia and Tarja Halonen of Finland. Madam Halonen was co-chair of the Summit. On 5 September 2000 these three women leaders met with UN women executives, including six heads of UN programmes, to agree on what to say to the mostly male Summit. What they said, in sum, was:

- Put more women into peacekeeping and peacebuilding.
- Enable women to fight poverty – give them better education, better health, access to credit.
- Get women into government at all levels.

- Besides raising women to parity with men in the UN staff, governments should place more women as their ambassadors at the UN.

Although what came out of the Summit, the Declaration, was not saturated with gender insight, key references were there:

- In values and principles, 'the equal rights of women and men must be assured'.
- In human rights, combat all forms of violence against women.
- In development and poverty eradication, equal access to all levels of education for girls and boys; also, 'promotion of gender equality and the empowerment of women as effective ways to combat poverty, hunger and disease and to stimulate development that is truly sustainable.'

The words are there, our hope for a richer and more compassionate world.

CHAPTER 8

Children: The Future is Now

Now as I try to hear children through the world's polyglot static, my radio gives me the BBC: West Africa, children for sale in odd lots, carried around by bus. Beyond my emotional reach, abstract statistics in my mind, is the fact that 300,000 children are in the armies of the world and that more than 2 million children have been killed in the last ten years in armed conflicts across the globe. To this burden I add the crime of poverty – more incomprehensible figures, maybe a thousand million, a billion in dire poverty – making children vulnerable to disease and all manner of deprivation. Probably 10 million young children are killed each year by diseases preventable by basic health measures. On top of all this is HIV/AIDS, the dreaded plague of our times. This metastasis can be stopped even though there is no cure.

Where does the United Nations come into this panoply of suffering? The Charter has some words for it: the UN is to save future generations from the scourge of war. That was 1945. Fifty-five years on, the Millennium Summit Declaration identifies children among the victims of 'abject and dehumanising ... dire poverty'. Goals set in the Declaration include full access to primary education for girls and boys, and a two-thirds reduction of under-five child mortality by the year 2015. The Declaration also embraces the Convention on the Rights of the Child with its protocols against child soldiers and against the sale or sexual exploitation of children. Between 1945 and 2000 something important has happened.

The story of United Nations' concern for children begins with the vision of children as victims of war and goes on in the course of time to seeing children as our destiny. How we treat children tells us who we are and who we will be. Investing in children is a moral, social and political imperative. Children not only have special needs, but are young citizens with their own rights. This profound insight matured in the decade just passed. How did all this happen?

As the Second World War drew to a close, the victorious Allies, the USA in the lead, mounted a massive relief and rehabilitation programme, mainly in Europe but also in war-torn China. With the Cold War clouding the horizon, this UN programme lasted little more than two years, leaving much to be done to get civilians back on their feet. Children suffered most. From this unfinished wartime commitment came the drive to create a temporary organization within the new UN, to continue aid to children. So there came into existence, by decision of the General Assembly in December 1946, the infant UNICEF, its mandate to continue emergency assistance to children affected by the great war, and its initial funding of $30 million left over from the big programme. No one expected UNICEF to last more than a few emergency years. Unforeseen was a cry from developing countries: help our children, even worse off than in post-war Europe. And so in 1953 UNICEF was given an open-ended lease of life, to extend its operations into developing countries as long as voluntary contributions kept it going.

How astonishing that UNICEF has taken on a pioneering role in international social development, operating in over 100 countries around the world. While it has not been alone in international concern for children, it has been the catalyst for other UN agencies, for governments and for many private organizations. Thoughtful pragmatism, technical expertise tested against the actual and feasible, and a strong field presence have given UNICEF a special legitimacy. UN concern for children has come to encompass the whole UN system, extending well beyond the institutional history of UNICEF, as the UN has matured along with UNICEF itself. Yet it was pretty much through UNICEF eyes that the conglomerate of internationals began to see not just that children are suffering, but that they are indeed our future.

The evolving UNICEF experience, from the 1950s onward, is a drama with many players. From survival relief, UNICEF more and more invested in building national and community ability to look after themselves. From ad hoc measures like immunization and training midwives, experience led to a sequential process: first, a sort of social diagnosis – what are the main problems of children and what causes them; second, what is the best way to attack those problems (the strategy); third, what to do (plan of action). What to do begins by identifying existing capacity – institutions, people already trained, skills – and then deciding what needs to be done to build on what is there, to fill gaps, to strengthen, to extend in order to reach everyone. Then comes costing: how much is now being put into the system? How much more will this cost? How much can the country afford, what forms of external aid would be useful (professional advisers, training, equipment, transport, drugs, money) and what are the possible sources of external aid (UNICEF being one among many)? Then you have to trim the action to whatever resources you can muster, and trimming means deciding what is most urgent and beneficial. You try to look ahead for several years, you adjust your plan from year to year. If you are smart, you enlist people in helping themselves, an enormous and necessary resource. Since there is never enough money for the ideal, or often even for basic services, there is always a struggle to get what you can from the pot. Decisions are never neat – you make do, you live in a political world.

There, I have given you a short course in social planning. I have put it in the context of children, with which I am most familiar, but the basic approach applies to social development across the board. Even when applied pragmatically, this approach has its obvious limits. Underlying child illness and deprivation may be poverty, ignorance, old customs and traditions, a society at war with itself, vested plutocracy, an economy that feeds exports rather than its own people, population pressures, or other systemic factors that only radical political action can touch. That means child advocacy has to be political, like everything else directed towards social justice. A friend who had a top job in a sister UN agency once told me that, having taken sophisticated training in health planning with mathematical models, he now advocated 'opportunity planning' – you jump when you can.

When the General Assembly kept UNICEF alive in 1953, it did so on the understanding that UNICEF would go to work in that great *terra incognita,* the developing world, much of it still colonized by moribund emperors. Although some relatively benign colonizers had initiated public health measures, with few exceptions no country had anything like a national health service, only a few hospitals in cities. Education, too, was usually for the urban elite, but most people were illiterate. Social statistics hardly existed, but we can be sure that, for example, under-five mortality rates of 200 to 300 deaths per 1,000 live births and maternal mortality ratios well over 500 deaths per 100,000 live births would have been common. Most people lived in rural areas. What was the UN to do? Here is a quick sketch of what happened progressively over 40 years.

The first target was child health: some immunization (BCG against tuberculosis) and midwifery training taking in traditional midwives, then the only available service. Health was soon seen to rest on nutrition and this got UNICEF attention early on. In the 1960s it extended its concern to the whole child, to childhood development, to education, to maternal support, realizing that a synoptic approach had to be taken. A lot of work went into creating national training for service at all levels, into strengthening and extending health and education services (health centres and schools). This was supplemented by mobile operations, mainly for mass immunization, and more and more reinforced by motivational education through radio and whatever media reached the people. In the late 1960s UNICEF tried very hard to influence decision makers, political and professional, bringing them together in orientation seminars. The object was to direct national policy and resources towards children, seen as a nation's most valuable resource, the key to a nation's prospects, so-called national development.

This led in the 1970s to the encouragement of community-based services, including primary health care services, in which the community is not just getting something from outside but is an active part of that service, a precious self-help resource. UNICEF was a full partner with the World Health Organization (WHO) in launching community-based primary health care at the 1978 international health policy conference at Alma Ata in Kazakhstan. This conference was in fact a precursor of the UN social development conferences that followed in the 1990s.

The gradual building of far-sighted social policies and rounded services is certainly the sound way to go, but it is a hard sell politically. Politicians want visible results. So when James Grant took the helm at UNICEF in the 1980s, he went about identifying goals – immunization, oral rehydration, vitamin A consumption, salt iodination, breast feeding – that, with some ingenuity, could be quantified and set in a timeframe. With a well-publicized line of attack, Grant's charisma could induce tough political leaders to throw their weight behind good works for children. To the strategic eye of Olympian planners, all this was irritatingly simplistic, but it got results.

On the political stage, Grant was UNICEF. His next move, a big one, was to try something that had never been done before – to invite all UN heads of state to a World Summit for Children to be held at the UN in New York, 29–30 September 1990. The event was meticulously planned. This turned out to be the largest gathering of world leaders up to that time, with 71 heads of state or government choreographed through the UN corridors. Altogether 159 states participated. This was not just a TV spectacle. Long before coming to the UN, participants knew why they were there: to adopt a Declaration on the Survival, Protection and Development of Children, and a ten-year Plan of Action for implementing the Declaration. These documents were remarkable in linking political commitment to technically sound and feasible action, goals to reach by the year 2000.

History seldom serves up good pudding, but this time good things were coming together. Complementing UNICEF's pragmatism was a drive to give child rights formal legal status among the several human rights conventions. International notice of child rights goes back to 1924 when, inspired by the Save the Children organizations of Sweden and the UK, the League of Nations issued its Geneva Declaration. This short and simple statement was elaborated at the UN in the 1959 Child Rights Declaration. When the International Year of the Child was celebrated in 1979, the Human Rights Commission endorsed a Polish proposal to turn child rights into law through a special convention. Ten years of hard work, with important NGO participation, yielded this convention, approved by the General Assembly in 1989. By the year 2000, 191 states had ratified the Convention.

The Convention provides a solemn and dignified frame for what UNICEF has done and adds an important dimension to its advocacy role. The generic idea is that the child is autonomous: each has a special identity, which states must recognize and affirm. Every new arrival must be registered at birth, given a name, a nationality and normally a place in its family. As the child grows and matures, it will enjoy freedom of thought, conscience and religion, and will have free access to information and ideas and be free to speak its mind. Whenever judicial or other decisions affecting the child are being made, the child has the right to be heard and its views shall be taken seriously. Built around this core idea of the child, the Convention is one integrated set of rights and obligations, derived from basic principles that underpin the whole. Chief among these principles are:

- Non-discrimination: all children enjoy all rights, no exceptions.

- The best interests of the child (not the interests of any adult power) shall govern all actions affecting the child.
- Every child has the right to life, to survival and development.
- Children have the right to free expression of their views and these views must be taken seriously in any judicial or other decision affecting any child.
- States must see that the Convention is put into practice in national laws and regulations. The only restraint may be limited resources.

When a state ratifies the Convention, it is understood that it accepts all of these basic principles because they are the ground and rationale for the technical delineations of child rights that flow from them. Chief among these are the right that children have normally to live with their parents (or, if separated, to keep in touch with both). They may be removed from their natural family only if that is in their best interests. Adoption, especially inter-country adoption, may be done with great care to see that the child, not some greedy profiteer, will benefit. A child who is 'deprived of family environment' must have special care and protection. Beyond the family, children have the right to adequate support for their growth, including access to health services (including maternal care), free education at least at the primary level and 'access' to more advanced education.

After defining the rights of children in normal conditions, the Convention addresses situations where children are especially vulnerable and where society must go out of its way to protect them. Among these, the most common is child labour. The child must be shielded from economic exploitation – as cheap labour – and from work that is dangerous or harmful to normal development. States must regulate minimum ages of employment and working conditions. The International Labour Organization (ILO) had long since done the groundwork in this field, and this was recognized in the Convention's reference to 'other international instruments'.

'Juvenile justice' – the rights of children who have fallen foul of the law – has full and careful treatment in the Convention. The whole thrust here is not simply to protect but, even more, to promote 'the child's sense of dignity and worth' and to help troubled children find their way in life.

The Convention goes on to other evils of our time – the use of children for sex, their involvement in the drugs rackets, their arbitrary arrest or torture, and their abduction and sale – a contemporary form of slavery. States are committed to strict measures against such flagrant abuse.

Then there is war – another plague of our times. Since the Geneva Conventions of 1949, states are already committed to protecting civilians in war, and this commitment is reinforced in the Child Rights Convention. The age of recruitment into soldiering, originally set at 15 years, has been raised to 18 years in a protocol adopted by the General Assembly in 1999.

The Child Rights Convention is not a sheaf of papers gathering dust. Every committed state has to report within the first year, and again every four years, on its implementation of the Convention. An expert committee reviews these reports, raises questions and suggests remedies. After three years of work the Committee concluded that war was among the worst enemies of children and that the UN should do something about it. This got to the General Assembly, which asked the Secretary-General to review and report. Thus in 1994 Graça Machel, widow of the first president of Mozambique and now the wife of Nelson Mandela, was given this critical responsibility. Her thorough on-the-ground study resulted in her 1996 report, *The Impact of War on Children*.[1] Noting that children are high among civilians targeted in war these days, the report analyses war's evils: child soldiers, children forced to flee their homes, children's sexual exploitation, children crippled by land mines; children sick, malnourished, without schools. Clear recommendations are made on what must be done by all involved: national governments, the warring parties, NGOs and international organizations. Children in war was now a hot political issue at the General Assembly and the Security Council, the latter holding extensive hearings that led to formal undertakings to support Machel, in August and September 1999. The banning of land mines under the Ottawa Convention in 1997 was certainly accelerated by Machel, and this is now being followed by formal UN advocacy of regulating small arms (a conference on illicit trade in small arms in July 2001 is a first big step). Wicked instigators of violence are being threatened as the UN War Crimes Tribunals for Yugoslavia and Rwanda have made history through their prosecutions for rape, and the Rome Statutes of the permanent International Criminal Court now recognize rape as a war crime. Child protection has penetrated UN peace operations: child protection officers are included in UN forces in Sierra Leone and the Democratic Republic of the Congo. Graça Machel did not labour in vain.

Returning now to 1990, the timing of the World Summit could not have been better, coming as it did in the year after the Convention's adoption. The Summit endorsement of the Convention led to its rapid acceptance, eventually by almost every nation. The main commitments made by heads of state at the Summit were:

- The well-being of children requires political action at the highest level. We are determined to take that action.
- We ourselves hereby make a solemn commitment to give high priority to the rights of children, to their survival and to their protection and development. This will also ensure the well-being of all societies.

The Summit Declaration then laid down these broad commitments:

- To promote ratification and implementation of the Convention on the Rights of the Child.
- To promote action to enhance children's health, to promote prenatal care and to lower infant and child mortality; to provide clean water and access to sanitation.
- To move toward eradication of hunger and malnutrition.
- To strengthen the role and status of women. To promote responsible planning of family size, child spacing, breast feeding and safe motherhood.
- To support families, parents and communities in the care and nurture of children from birth through adolescence.
- To support action to reduce illiteracy and provide education for all children.
- To help and protect children in specially difficult situations – street children, orphans, refugees, abused – and to promote abolition of child labour.
- To protect children in war, to promote peace education, and to support 'periods of tranquillity and special relief corridors' for the benefit of children during war.
- To promote 'the protection of the environment' so as to assure 'a safer and healthier future' for children.

- To work for 'a global attack on poverty'.

These broad commitments were then elaborated in a plan of action with specific goals for the decade ahead:

- Between 1990 and 2000, reduction of children dying before the age of five by approximately one-third.
- Between 1990 and 2000, reduction of maternal mortality rate by half.
- Between 1990 and 2000, reduction of severe and moderate malnutrition among children under five years of age, by half.
- Universal access to safe drinking water and to sanitary means of excreta disposal.
- By the year 2000, universal access to basic education and completion of primary education by at least 80 per cent of primary school-age children.
- Reduction of the adult illiteracy rate to at least half its 1990 level with emphasis on female literacy.
- Improved protection of children in especially difficult circumstances.

And for child health, there are six more goals:

- Global eradication of poliomyelitis by 2000.
- Elimination of neonatal tetanus by 1995.
- Reduction by 95 per cent in measles deaths and reduction by 90 per cent of measles cases compared to pre-immunization levels by 1995, as a big step towards the global eradication of measles.
- Maintenance of a high level of immunization coverage (at least 90 per cent of children under one year of age by the year 2000) against diphtheria, pertussis, tetanus, measles, poliomyelitis and tuberculosis; and against tetanus for women of child-bearing age.
- Reduction by 50 per cent in the deaths due to diarrhoea in children under the age of five years and 25 per cent reduction in the diarrhoea incidence rate.
- Reduction by one-third in the deaths due to acute respiratory infections in children under five years.[2]

All in all, in its breadth and specificity, this was a stunning global compact. Reassuring too was the fact that, with all this telescopic vision, UNICEF never dropped the E – emergency – melding the resurgent demands for emergency aid into mainstream development. Indeed the 'normal' condition of children in poverty is itself an emergency. Add to this the violent conflicts that bring such terrible suffering to millions of children.

James Grant, optimist by nature, shared the brief moment of euphoria that followed the Cold War. Introducing UNICEF's 1992 *State of the World's Children,* he wrote:

> Despite an international agenda that is crowded with pressing political, economic, and environmental problems, there is therefore more cause for hope on the human horizon than perhaps at any other time in this century. It may be that the years ahead will show optimism not to have been justified; but what is not in doubt is that a new order is emerging in our times.

The World Summit for Children, he said, presaged a new order for children:

> The emergence of this agreement, at a time when the existing world order is rapidly changing, means that there is today a better chance than ever before of finding a place on the world's political agenda for the rights of children and for meeting the minimum needs of all families.

'The world order' is indeed changing, but today we don't know where we are going. Nevertheless children remain high up on the agenda of the United Nations. The decade foreseen at the 1990 World Summit was stretched to 12 years as the successor UN Special Session on Children was held in May 2002. This was no routine affair. Nearly every state in the world was brought in through a series of preparatory gatherings. Again some 64 heads of state attended. Alongside the governments was a Children's Forum where young people (250 teenagers from 132 countries), fresh and thoughtful, challenged the political hierarchy to deliver on their commitments. Citizens' groups, 700 NGOs from 119 countries, were present and active throughout.

The 2002 Special Session was both retrospective and prospective, looking back at what had been accomplished, looking ahead at what needs to be done. 'A world fit for children', that was the mantra of this Session, reverberating through the corridors of cynicism and power. What came out of this session?

What came out was both a Declaration of general commitments, a global plan of action with goals and a commitment by participating governments to prepare national plans of action by the end of 2003. National plans are to be submitted to the UN. Compared to 1990 the Declaration has a wider outlook, taking in specific child rights from the Convention as well as UN Millennium goals. In sum, here are the 2002 commitments:

- Put children first – 'the best interests of the child'.
- Eradicate poverty, invest in children.
- Leave no child behind, girls and boys, free and equal.
- Care for every child: health, nutrition, nurture.
- Educate every child.
- Protect children from abuse, from exploitation (labour, sexual), from war.
- Combat HIV/AIDS.
- Listen to children; ensure their participation.
- Protect the earth for children.

Translated into goals, these commitments range over territory covered in 1990, while adding such concerns as social security systems, mental health, child injuries, drug abuse, gender equality, and the assured dignity and legal status of the child as established in the Convention.

Overarching goals imply overarching social and political change, change that takes time and is not easily measured. Since 1990, little can have changed in the sufferings of children from poverty, from the evils of war, labour and the sex trade. What makes for change now is the ethical and legal spotlight on such abuses. This grand Declaration points the way beyond hypocrisy.

But many goals can be put in numbers, and for these, trends since 1990 can be measured:

Changes since 1990

Under-five mortality	Down by 11 per cent, from 93 to 83 deaths per 1,000 live births globally
Malnutrition (underweight prevalence among under fives)	Down from 32 per cent to 28 per cent in developing countries
Access to safe drinking water	Up from 77 per cent to 82 per cent of world population
Primary education	Enrolment up from 80 per cent to 82 per cent globally, while doubling the proportion of girls in school
Adult literacy	Up from 20 per cent to 25 per cent worldwide
Maternal mortality (deaths in childbirth or complications of pregnancy)	No measurable change
Use of contraceptives	Up from 57 per cent to 67 per cent globally
Vitamin A deficiency	By the year 2000, over 40 countries got Vitamin A supplement to most children
Iodine deficiency (causing goitres and brain damage)	Households getting iodized salt, up from 20 per cent to 70 per cent in developing countries
Measles	Reported cases down 40 per cent globally
Neonatal tetanus	Deaths down from 470,000 to 215,000 globally. No more cases in over 100 developing countries.
Diarrhoeal disease	Down 50 per cent.
Polio	Cases down from 300,000 to under 5,000 in 2002. Eradication is in sight.
HIV/AIDS	Much worse. In 2002 around 42 million people were infected, of whom over 3 million were children under the age of 15.

Apart from maternal mortality and HIV/AIDS, here we have real progress. But there is still a long way to go. For example, more than 500,000 mothers are dying each year during childbirth for want of prenatal care. There are still 10 million preventable deaths of toddlers under five. Nearly 120 million youngsters are out of school. And remember this: the 50 million gathered up for UN humanitarian aid in 2003 are mostly children, children and their mothers.

This story is not about UNICEF, it is about the world's children. UNICEF is cast in the role of leader and catalyst. With great energy and a firm hand, Carol Bellamy, as Executive Director, now keeps UNICEF on track. She greeted the Special Session thus:

> For together we have the power and the resources to mobilise a global movement for children, a movement that will put the world on a path to end the poverty, ill health, violence and discrimination that needlessly blight and destroy so many young lives.[3]

In these days when fear feeds tragedy, when lust for power tinges compassion, young life gives back hope. So it can be in the corridors of the United Nations. A sign: UNICEF received the Nobel Peace Prize in 1965. A sign: human development pioneered by UNICEF is now the way of the UN system and the World Bank. A sign: the Security Council puts children under its tattered wings.

Far beyond UNICEF is the commitment of 191 nations to the ideals, the norms, the objectives of the Convention on the Rights of the Child. The Convention is a formidable, radical, political and moral fact. It is the giant screen on which we see good and bad, achievement and abuse. We all were children once.

CHAPTER 9

Humanitarian Rescue and On

Where are we today as we of the UN grope our way through the slaughterhouse of history? Humanitarian aid is a test. 'Humanitarian' – the word itself says something. It implies that being human is good, is kind, is compassionate. When humans torture humans, we say it is inhuman, beastly. And yet, in the UN context, humanitarian aid has become tarnished. The context is war, the homeland paroxysms around political power. 'We the peoples', invoked in the UN Charter, are made enemies of each other, manipulated, terrorized, uprooted, killed. Homeland war is total war – either you are with us or against us. No one is neutral. How can 'humanitarian aid' be neutral? Is helping people an act of war? We know that killing people is bad. How can it be that helping people is bad?

Not only is internal conflict, 'civil' war, involved. In the great wars among states there was no compunction about battering, demoralizing or starving the 'enemy' people. Even today UN sanctions when grossly applied can have devastating effects on the civilian population, as in Iraq. Further complicating the humanitarian cause, the Secretary-General used the term 'humanitarian intervention' in his historic speech to the 1999 GA, challenging the UN community to act when any government is attacking its own people (violating human rights). What he had in mind was a range of UN 'interventions' (persuasive negotiation, sanctions, force), rather than feeding people. Sovereign states shudder.

We must not be morally neutral when evil is being done. Humanitarian aid, however, cannot be the instrument for political change. It inevitably stumbles along in a political context. Maybe we should aim at impartiality rather than neutrality: impartial, even-handed aid to all in need wherever they are caught up in a divisive conflict.

The principle of impartiality is precious and should not be abandoned or obscured because of the difficulty, indeed the impossibility, of its full application in war. I speak from experience. My first UN job was directing humanitarian aid across the battle lines during China's epic civil war. That was 1946–48. My young team-mates and I were passionately committed to UN impartiality. We didn't get much aid through the battle lines but we did succeed in making a serious statement, a statement that was both applauded and resented. This statement must be repeated wherever UN humanitarian aid is deployed.

At the dawn of the United Nations (June 1945) there was already in existence the United Nations Relief and Rehabilitation Administration (UNRRA), created in 1943 by formal agreement among 44 nations, looking ahead to getting war-battered countries back on their feet. With nearly $4 billion (the equivalent of maybe $80 billion today), it did a remarkable start-up in Europe before the Cold War, while in China it was frustrated by the civil war. The UNRRA job was relief and rehabilitation, all in one package. Relief meant feeding, housing and healing. Rehabilitation was concerned with physical infrastructure, communications, industry and agriculture. R and R went together.

For the UN in social and economic affairs, the UN Charter envisages only normative functions, setting general principles and standards. The UN was not expected to get into action, either for relief or rehabilitation. In the UN's post-war lexicon relief became emergency aid and rehabilitation became development. Two little emergency operations were tacked on to the young UN: UNHCR (High Commissioner for Refugees) for Second World War refugees, and UNICEF (the Children's Fund) to finish for children what UNRRA had begun. Both were expected to be over and done with in two or three years. In 1963 along came the World Food Programme (WFP), mostly for use in emergencies. Although UNICEF quickly shifted over to helping countries help themselves – in there for the long haul – it never lost its emergency skills, and, until WFP was born, was essentially the only UN channel for 'relief' in emergencies. The UNHCR had enough on its hands, dealing with post-war refugees mainly in Europe (refugees defined as war victims outside their home countries). The enormous horde of today's refugees from civil wars (12 million), not to mention the even larger numbers uprooted at home (upwards of 50 million) was in no one's imagining. Second

World War refugees apart, up into the 1980s, emergencies covered mostly natural disasters: earthquakes, wind and water. With the Kremlin's collapse, the Cold War lid was off, and since 1989 around 50 local armed conflicts have killed over 5 million civilians and devastated many more.

The UN could not ignore what was happening but was not equipped to do much about it. In his 1991 annual report on the work of the organization, Secretary-General Pérez de Cuéllar wrote:

> International relief efforts in emergencies caused by famine or flood, earthquake or drought are mounted at the request of the affected State or States and generally create no legal or political problems. But international action with regard to situations where a population is torn by war or oppression raises sensitive political issues, calls for early warning capacity of a different character and has to be based on a determination made by a competent organ of the United Nations. It would be unwise to put the two kinds of emergencies in the same conceptual basket, even though the actual operations may on occasion assume a similar physical or logistical shape. For this reason, it would be hard to visualise a unified system of emergency relief that would be automatically triggered by situations that, between themselves, are wholly disparate.[1]

The General Assembly took up the challenge that year and created the high-level post of Emergency Relief Co-ordinator, while at the same time saying what the UN might and might not do. Not quite so timid as the Secretary-General, the GA put God and man together (natural and man-made emergencies) as humanitarian assistance. The rules of the game were that humanitarian emergency aid should be built into long-term national development and should not drain away resources from development, that more should be done to anticipate, prevent and mitigate natural disasters, and that while states are responsible for taking care of their own people, they will need outside aid: 'In this context, humanitarian assistance should be provided with the consent of the affected country.' *Consent* of the country', not request of the government – a crack in the door to let the UN in during civil conflict. For the rest, this GA resolution said that the UN should lead the world in humanitarian action, that governments should voluntarily kick in with real money, that the Secretary-General should tidy up fund raising by making 'consolidated appeals', and that an Inter-Agency Standing Committee (IASC) should pull everyone together. The Emergency Relief Co-ordinator would sit on top of the IASC, and, most importantly, should lead the political job of negotiating access, relief corridors, and zones of 'tranquillity' in war-torn countries.

So that was the legislative situation at the beginning of the 1990s. Jump to the end, and here comes the Security Council, talking 'human security' and, in February 1999, holding an open meeting on protecting civilians in war. The following September at the Security Council, Secretary-General Kofi Annan says it like it is in a comprehensive review with recommendations for action:

> Despite the adoption of the various conventions on international humanitarian and human rights law over the past 50 years, hardly a day goes by where we are not presented with evidence of the intimidation, brutalization, torture and killing of helpless civilians in situations of armed conflict. Whether it is mutilations in Sierra Leone, genocide in Rwanda, ethnic cleansing in the Balkans or disappearances in Latin America, the parties to conflicts have acted with deliberate indifference to those conventions. Rebel factions, opposition fighters and Government forces continue to target innocent civilians with alarming frequency.[2]

This is historic: given the dogged resistance of governments to facing the international mirror, the Council's response is a big gulp of reality. In two formal resolutions (September 1999 and April 2000) it looks at the whole sad spectrum of war victims, refugees, women, children, and says that, while humanitarian aid must be politically impartial, humanitarian workers must have safe and unimpeded access to civilians in armed conflict. That stand in principle was to be tested as the Council had killing fields thrust upon it.[3]

Man creates another kind of disaster, not through armed conflict, but in massive political turmoil uprooting many thousands. This was happening in the winter of 2001 in Afghanistan, where homeless thousands were starving and freezing. Then there are the so-called famines which almost always happen because people can't afford to buy food, or because food is not physically distributed to needy places. This is a political crime that has killed millions.

What about the gods, the wrath of nature? In 1990 the General Assembly declared a Decade on Natural Disasters, and serious technical work was done on how to ease and appease: stop erosion, don't live on sea-level shores, make buildings that bend but don't break. Be prepared. Here was the UN family, sharing and codifying knowledge and experience in defiance of violent nature.

But man has been busily outviolating Olympus, and in his biosphere, man has also been busily licking his self-inflicted wounds for TV voyeurs around the globe. Something like that was appearing in the Security Council showcase.

Enter Kofi Annan. It is the start-up of the 1999 General Assembly. Milošević has pushed his Serbs to the edge in Kosovo. The UN Security Council is paralysed. NATO sky bombs. Kofi speaks of the tragic charade in which virtual sovereignty shields the henchmen of slaughter, most recently in Rwanda and Kosovo. The paralysis of the Security Council, he says, 'has cast in stark relief the dilemma of what has been called humanitarian intervention'. His point is that the UN should not just sit there, it should do something. The something, he says, can take different forms, from the most pacific persuasion to armed force, from peacekeeping to humanitarian assistance, to rehabilitation.[4]

Humanitarian assistance is inexorably enmeshed in the whole complex of wars. This is not only a political problem for the Security Council, but a life-and-death problem for humanitarians. Most bloody struggles nowadays target civilians and strive to control, oust or kill whole population groups. In our headlines, the worst examples are ex-Yugoslavia and Rwanda (and Cambodia, lest we forget). These are extremes. In all wars it is almost impossible for humanitarian assistance to be regarded as impartial: you are feeding our enemies! Relief convoys are attacked, relief supplies are hijacked, humanitarian workers are harassed, captured or killed. Providing UN military escort looks even more like taking sides; and where one faction in an internal conflict is most brutal and undisciplined, the UN really ought to take a stand. Humanitarian operations may indeed be used by big powers at the UN to avoid tough political intervention. This is what happened in ex-Yugoslavia. Even worse is the Sudan, where some 2 million have died in conflict going back to its emancipation from Britain in 1960. The government in Khartoum has been reluctant to accept any outside political mediation, which has meant that humanitarian agencies have had to negotiate access and protection, a messy and inconclusive process. Both sides in the Sudan have exploited humanitarian aid to the extent that, to some degree, aid provided for civilians feeds the conflict. Without serious political mediation, there is no way out for civilian aid.

These insults have not scared off humanitarian aid. Nor should we let the imperfect obscure our vision of the good. The annual volume of humanitarian aid overall, bilateral and multilateral, has more than doubled since 1989, to the benefit of many millions. The annual level of aid, UN and bilateral, rose from around $2 billion in 1989 to over $4 billion in 1991, and, with ups and downs, has generally stayed at about that level. The ups mostly reflect concern over natural disasters such as Hurricane Mitch in Central America in 1998, aid for which exceeded $1 billion. In most years, assistance for natural disasters was a small part of total emergency aid – $200 million or less. Although the General Assembly said in 1991 that the UN should lead the world in emergency aid, only about 25 per cent of this global aid went through multilateral channels. And while UN inter-agency co-ordination got much better, the vast flow outside the UN was not at all co-ordinated, reflecting the parochial interests of donor governments and the wandering eyes of TV. Nearly 90 per cent of this global aid came from ten governments (Western Europe, Japan and North America). With all the talk about integrating humanitarian aid into basic development (the ongoing long stretch), with few exceptions governments were giving less and less to development. No doubt popular response to TV is an important reason for maintaining humanitarian aid: the emotional surge is strong but fickle. Many poor and unstable countries are in continuing agony, in endemic catastrophes that the late Jim Grant, heading UNICEF, called silent emergencies. One billion of our fellow travellers on this planet exist on something like one dollar a day. Is this not an emergency?

Where is the UN in all this? During the 1990s it was helping in 50 or more natural disasters, elsewhere in over 20 war zones. You can't be sure exactly where and when winds and wars will happen. Planning ahead is based on experience and on continuing war-zone disasters. The ideal arrangement would be a contingency fund, a special 'bank account' for use as emergencies arise. Instead, for the UN it is hand-to-mouth, an annual appeal (consolidating all UN actors) for funding foreseeable needs. As of November 2002 the UN appeal for 2003 was for $2.7 billion, in order to reach 50 million victims in more than 20 countries. Identifiable countries (some lumped together) are:

> AFRICA: Angola, Burundi, Democratic Republic of the Congo, Eritrea, Great Lakes Region and Central Africa, Guinea, Lesotho, Liberia, Malawi, Republic of the Congo, Sierra Leone, Somalia,

South African Region, Swaziland, Sudan, Uganda, West Africa, Zambia and Zimbabwe;

ASIA AND EUROPE: Afghanistan, People's Democratic Republic of Korea, Indonesia, North Caucasus, South-eastern Europe and Tajikistan.

For 50 million people in the year 2003, the UN appeal for $2.7 billion was less than the world spends on the military in one day. Experience tells us that the UN will get only a fraction of what is needed.

The UN depends on voluntary contributions by big donors. Since 1999 it has had to make do with under 60 per cent of what is required. Once more: plenty for war, pennies for peace.

CHAPTER 10

People and Poverty

Of all the goals set by world leaders at their Millennium Summit, by far the most demanding and inclusive was the halving by 2015 of the number of people (over 1 billion today) who live on something like $1 a day. This goal came out of the World Summit for Social Development in 1995. My first reaction on hearing of this was, well, it sounds good but what does it mean? One billion is one-sixth of our human siblings on this planet. I am told that if you raise the level to $2 a day, you double the number to 2 billion: two out of six is one-third. Since I don't want to believe that, I begin by assuming that it really doesn't mean anything and is just a public-relations gimmick. But then, I recall, it does have meaning. It goes back to a serious technical study by the World Bank in 1990 which defined 'absolute poverty' as 'the inability to attain a minimal standard of living', or, to paraphrase, the level below which you would be in the social morgue. This study took into account everything available from the person's whole environment. One dollar a day was a stab at expressing that survival level. Most of these desperately poor live in South Asia and Africa.

The World Bank report was in the main addressed at ways to alleviate poverty. Their line of attack is summarized in this paragraph:

> The evidence in this Report suggests that rapid and politically sustainable progress on poverty has been achieved by pursuing a strategy that has two equally important elements. The first element is to promote the productive use of the poor's most abundant asset – labour. It calls for policies that harness market incentives, social and political institutions, infrastructure, and technology to that end. The second is to provide basic social services to the poor. Primary health care, family planning, nutrition, and primary education are especially important.[1]

The report goes on to say that this strategy requires giving a larger share of national income to the poor, so that it is likely to be implemented 'in countries where the poor have a say in political and economic decision-making'. True enough, but it is also likely to be implemented in countries where there is enough to go round.

Back in 2001 I read a *New York Times* piece about the UN report on the *World Economic Situation and Prospects 2001*.[2] The reporter wrote that $1 is what a person can earn in a day. That missed the point. Most of these people are outside the cash economy and get by on whatever they can find. Think of the scavengers who live, for example, by pawing through the large mountain of Manila's garbage, a mountain called, in the heart-breaking poetry of the poor, the Promised Land. In 2000 the Promised Land collapsed and killed hundreds of its worshippers. A new flock is back every year. That is poverty.

How can anything be done about such an enormous problem? It won't be solved by handing out packets of bubble gum. It means raising the standard of living, the quality of life in the poorest countries and in the poorest communities, in slums and in villages. It means translating the words of the UN Charter ('The United Nations shall promote: higher standards of living, full employment, and conditions of economic and social progress and development') into some real process in a world profoundly changed since 1945.

What can the UN do? The UN takes in practically all nations, all governments; the Charter is their Charter, the Millennium goals are their goals. As we drift into this new century, governments are not in control of every twitch in the global economy, but they have a lot of power when they have the political drive to use it. The citizens attacking the international economic institutions – the World Bank, the International Monetary Fund (IMF) and the World Trade Organization (WTO) – may have an exaggerated notion of the influence of these bodies, but governments created these institutions and the protestors are holding governments responsible. If governments and their institutions are not in control, why aren't they?

You could stand back and say: look, it took a couple of hundred years for the core industrialized countries to rise from rags to riches. It took time. Yes, of course, it did take that time, but it took a lot more than time; it took technical progress, capital formation, trade, not to mention colonial exploitation. Today things are radically different. Mankind now has the technical means to break out of extreme poverty. The persistence of poverty is not a technical problem, it is a political problem, political between and within countries. It is a United Nations problem.

Looking back to 1945, where did the UN come in? If we stretch our definition of the UN to include the international financial institutions, the International Monetary Fund and the International Bank for Reconstruction and Development (World Bank), then the UN would be mainstream; but in practice these financial institutions were so constituted as to be run by the leading industrialized countries. Located in Washington, they were dominated by the USA. The IMF was to stabilize currencies and exchange rates; the World Bank, as its full name implies, was to invest in post-war reconstruction. The onset of the Cold War scared the USA into its enormous gift to Western Europe, the Marshall Plan, a bilateral arrangement outside the UN. The USSR created its own bloc of planned economies. This left to the UN, including the World Bank, the emerging developing countries where most of the world's people live. With the influx of emancipated colonies in the 1960s, the Non-Aligned Movement (and, within it, the Group of 77) spoke for the neglected, and at the UN led the way in 1964 to creating UNCTAD, the UN Conference on Trade and Development. With its own technical staff and triennial meetings, UNCTAD has been effectively the technical advocate for developing countries at the UN. At a Special Session of the GA in 1974, a Declaration on the Establishment of a New Economic Order, formulated by developing countries, was adopted. It called for fixing international economic relations (trade and aid) so as to give a boost to developing countries. The Declaration set the stage for many fruitless debates at the GA from then on. Why fruitless? Virtue without power, that's it. At the GA in 1993, the President of the IMF, Michel Camdessus, outlined the way the international system works: the IMF for macro-economic stabilization, the World Bank for financing projects and the UN for social development. That was a fair summation of the shape of things at that time. The WTO came two years later.

But in the 1990s things were changing, inside and outside the UN. 'Developing countries' spanned a wide range of economic achievement – many were climbing up the ladder, a few were already among the elite. The failure of centrally planned economies had taken with it the quasi-religious ideal of a fair-shares society, the welfare state. The market economy, strangely called neo-liberal, was touted as the road to riches, the latest version of trickle-down. The social logic, as I interpret it, is that the market economy will produce such a glut that the goodies will spill off the table. And now the market has gone global, both for production (cheaper = efficient) and for distribution (sales). The international *bourse* is awash with untold trillions, some for investment, some for play. The digital revolution and the instant flow of information have confirmed and accelerated the magic market. Even in China, the last big hold-out of some sort of Marxism, Deng Xiao Ping endorsed the new religion: To get rich is good. Get on board.

This new rush to wealth has been gathering momentum, speeding up since the Cold War. The North–South confrontation has blurred a bit, the debate at the General Assembly has become more nuanced, and greater attention is paid to the 'least developed countries' – the 49 left out of the mainstream international economy. But there is no fundamental change in North–South strains as the rich–poor rift keeps widening. However, worship of the globalized market was shaken by the East Asian crisis in 1997–98. It turned out that greed and myopia can derail the inevitable.

This was the setting for the GA's serious discussion of globalization in 1998. What had originally been foreseen as a consultation on how to direct the benefits of global growth to the neglected poor turned out to be an exploration both of crisis management and of fundamental restructuring of the flow of capital. Fully elaborated, the subject addressed was 'the social and economic impact of globalization and inter-dependence and their policy implications'. In these matters the GA at best has some political influence, but without really understanding what is happening that influence can be frittered away. Hard-nosed finance moguls – 'ministers' – call the shots at the IMF. At the same time everyone is in the UN which, in theory, should rule, but that isn't the way it works. All members of the family are supposed to consult, but not everyone gets to sign the cheques. Nevertheless there has been a lot more consultation between the UN and the Bretton Woods institutions (IMF and the World Bank) during recent years, especially at 'high level'.

During this discussion the human effects of the Asian glitch were aired – the vast increase in unemployment and poverty, especially in Indonesia (15,000 jobs lost every day). That was just the beginning of Indonesia's troubles. The word was that globalization is blind. The GA President's summary pretty much defined the issues.

> The general thrust of the two-day discussions may be summarised as follows. First of all, globalization is an irreversible process, not an option. It is a positive and not an evil force, but it is also blind and

therefore needs to be carefully harnessed. Secondly, national efforts to meet the challenges of globalization, in particular institution-building, are necessary but not sufficient. Action on a global scale, involving multilateral institutions as well as the world's leading economies, is imperative. Thirdly, there is a need to move beyond the status quo, in particular by reviewing the current architecture of the international financial system with a view to enhancing its transparency, accountability and participatory character. Fourthly, globalization is a multifaceted process involving many actors. In order to address effectively the issues of inclusiveness and participation, it is necessary to promote a global civil ethic to shape the rules that will ensure that globalization benefits all, including those who are currently marginalised. Fifthly, the United Nations, owing to its universality, and broad mandate, provides a unique platform for defining the principles and norms necessary to harness the potential of globalization and for promoting a comprehensive dialogue on globalization around the concept of global housekeeping.

That remains the UN platform on globalization: it doesn't feed the poor. Most of the capital flowing through the international *bourse* goes to enrich the rich, almost none to the 40-plus poorest nations. Where is the 'global civil ethic'? How can globalization be directed to serving the people, the poor? In pursuing this issue at the 1999 GA, South Africa spoke for many, saying that globalization was making things worse: adverse terms of trade, reduced prices for Africa's exports, less foreign investment, less grant aid (Official Development Assistance) and insoluble external debt. *Humane* globalization, they said, would promote human rights and eliminate poverty: 'The highest calling for all of us is to make globalization and interdependence ... a beginning of hope, redemption and enlightenment for the hungry, the poor and the wretched of the earth.'

I pause here to say something about external debt, a problem that has recently attracted serious attention. Back in the 1970s big Western banks were bloated with dollars that came from OPEC oil-rich nations. This led to reckless lending in developing countries whose governments were happy to accept what looked like easy terms. This was followed by external aid mostly as loans. As loans became due, it turned out that, for many countries, servicing of debt exceeded their net revenue from exports, but defaulting would block future access to credit. Since there was no way for many to pay off these debts, a way had to be found to adjust payments or to cancel. Thanks in part to publicity and pressure generated by the citizens' network Jubilee 2000, a good deal is being done at last to lift this debt burden, especially for the poorest countries. Debts are being cancelled on condition that the money so released be used for basic social services. This looks good, but obviously debt cancellation doesn't generate revenue.

This brings me back to the perennial debate at the GA about the relative importance of external and internal, of what impinges on a nation from the outside and what that nation does for itself. For developing countries, external factors are investment, grant aid (Official Development Assistance – ODA) and trade (commodity prices, access to markets). These factors can make all the difference: the big drop in the market value of primary products in the 1970s was a serious set-back for many countries. On the other hand, pumping external resources into a country at war with itself under a corrupt regime may do more harm than good. A taboo about mentioning bad government was breached in the Secretary-General's 1997 report to the Security Council on Africa, and that loosened things up a bit in the GA. Following the discussion of globalization, the GA in 1999 was able to shift its gaze away from macro-economic challenges to such preconditions for growth as good governance, accountability, participation and social peace. For the Group of 77, Guyana said developing countries could get ahead only if the 'North' facilitated their integration into the contemporary industrialized knowledge-based international economy. Uganda, a voice in the wilderness, called for the revival of the UN Commission and Centre on Transnational Corporations, two thorns in corporate flesh rejected by the new doctrine.

Concerning trade, at this same session many spoke of the pressing need to open 'Northern' markets to the South as a prime objective of negotiations to be launched at the WTO Ministerial meeting in Seattle in November 1999. What happened there was a remarkable citizens' protest which upset the whole conference and prevented Kofi Annan from delivering his splendid speech, although the text was passed round. He pointed out that the tariffs imposed by industrialized countries on manufactured imports from the 'South' are four times higher than on manufactured goods from advanced economies. No wonder, he said, that the South suspects that tying labour standards and the environment to rules of trade is trade protection in disguise. These concerns (labour, environment) are real, he said, but 'the industrialized world must not try to solve its own problems at the expense of the poor.' Differences among governments were such that Seattle would have failed without citizen protest. The massive demonstrations served a very useful purpose in exposing the serious social impact of trade as regulated by the WTO, and in demonstrating 'people power'. What terms of trade do to people should not be relegated to a footnote in trade treaties, adjudicated in WTO by tradesmen who have no interest or competence in social affairs.[3]

All this chatter about the macro-economy could hardly trickle down to the scavengers of Manila's Promised Land. The debates at the UN had been about how to get national economies moving, whatever that might mean. About serving the people, about helping the poor, up until the 1990s the UN had no overall strategy to sell to the big spenders, the IMF/World Bank, the big nation-to-nation bilateral organizations, not to mention the giants of commerce. Only minuscule resources were channelled through the UN and its Funds (the UN Development Programme, UNICEF, the Population Fund, the World Food Programme, the Environment Programme), and while these did serious work, there was for them no common frame, no single road map leading to that bright goal, a happy Promised Land.

But as we entered the 1990s, something surprising and dynamic happened. Blessed by the UN, government and citizens embarked on a new venture, the mapping of the many roads convergent on a better life. In this short decade, from around the world the UN brought together professionals, caregivers, government Pooh-Bahs, civic leaders and, with luck, journalists, in a sequence of conferences about the great social challenges of our time. Heads of state joined citizens in summitry throughout the decade, beginning with the World Summit for Children (New York, 1990), and going on to historic gatherings on the Environment (Rio, 1992), Human Rights (Vienna, 1993), Population (Cairo, 1994), Women (Beijing, 1995), Social Development (Copenhagen, 1995) and Human Settlements (Istanbul, 1996). These conferences worked over serious policy issues and, remarkably, produced strategies on how to tackle identified problems (e.g. in the least contentious cases, infant mortality or the provision of clean water), and plans of action with goals, sometimes both what and when. Of course conference outcomes differed a lot, depending on the issues dealt with: some gave birth to general declarations, others like the Summit on Children produced detailed plans of what to do within a period of five or ten years. I began this chapter by citing the 1995 social development goal of cutting desperate poverty in half by 2015. Overall these conferences did what the GA could not do, dealing in some depth with the human participants in development and coming up with shared ideas on how to proceed. Speaking from personal experience, I can say that this whole marshalling of social energy was anticipated in the International Conference on Primary Health Care, convened by the WHO and UNICEF at Alma Ata in 1978, a conference that yielded a radically new approach to the promotion of health worldwide.

At the UN developing countries had been pressing Secretary-General Boutros-Ghali to formulate an *Agenda for Development* to complement his *Agenda for Peace*. Prior to the 1990 conferences, there was nothing much to pour into the shell of social development. It was the GA itself that took this task in hand, and, using the broad 1990s consensus, hammered out the 1997 *Agenda for Development*.[4]

The UN had the good idea that there should be regular reviews, after five or ten years, of how things were shaping up, i.e. following conference guidelines. And as these GA review sessions came along, there was a disconcerting tendency to replay old policy battles. So far, however, original conference agreements have held. *The Agenda for Development* is not a brilliant piece of literature but it is an astonishing achievement, a road map for the world on what we now call human development. (Anyone who wishes to go a little deeper into these issues will benefit from the series of annual UNDP reports on Human Development. The 1997 report deals specifically with poverty.)[5]

Kofi Annan was a good jump ahead of the pack when, in his *Millennium Report*, he told the 'South', the developing world, to get on the digital bandwagon, to embrace the new information technology. IT has radical implications for the future growth of lagging economies. To use it, you need trained people ('intellectual capital') and an adequate electric grid. The UN Information Technology Service has just now been created to help developing countries, and a UN Task Force, combining private and public brains, will pool and share experience in applying IT in the 'South', applying IT to national growth. This is an important beginning to an open-ended journey into a virtual new world.

Where are we, the UN family, on this brave highway? Kofi Annan, speaking to the press in Geneva in June 2000 said:

During the 1990s, United Nations world conferences set major goals for economic and social development. All countries, developed and developing alike, signed on to this agenda, often at the highest political level. Since then, people have been asking whether the world has made good on these commitments. What has worked? What did not, and why? And what can we do better? ...

Poverty is an affront to our common humanity. It also makes many other problems worse. Poor countries are far more likely to be embroiled in conflicts. It is in poor countries that the worst effects of HIV/AIDS and other diseases are concentrated. And it is poor countries – especially the least developed, and those in sub-Saharan Africa – that most often lack the capacity and resources to protect the environment.

In an interdependent world, that is something that should be a concern for all of us. That is why the United Nations, the World Bank, the IMF and the OECD have joined forces. We believe a better world can be ours. We believe we can put the great new global market within reach of the poor. We believe globalization can be a positive force for all the world's people.[6]

He went on to say that poverty and what to do about it was the major challenge being presented to world leaders at the impending Millennium Summit. In the *Millennium Declaration*, coming from the Summit that September, we read:

We will spare no effort to free our fellow men, women and children from the abject and dehumanising conditions of extreme poverty, to which more than a billion of them are currently subjected. We are committed to making the right to development a reality for everyone and to freeing the entire human race from want.[7]

This sounds good, but, as Kofi Annan put it, has the world made good on its grand commitments? What is being done for the poorest of the poor? Being largely outside the global economy, these are the countries and people most dependent on external aid, grant aid (Official Development Assistance or ODA). How much grant aid is needed? I recall estimates made at the 1992 Conference on the Environment and Development (UNCED). A curious thing that happened at that Conference was that 'environment and development' by accretion came to include everything, social and economic. So the estimates of financial requirements at UNCED were *everything* estimates: annually, external ODA $125 billion, internal national funds $500 billion. These figures did not get into the official

UNCED report, but they are useful as guesstimates of ODA-related need. The official UN target for ODA from economically advanced (developed) countries is 0.7 per cent of GNP. This target had been proposed by a World Bank Commission chaired by Lester B. Pearson, the Pearson Commission, in 1969. Given the circumstances at that time, the Commission thought that ODA at that level would jolt developing countries' growth to 6 per cent a year. The 0.7 per cent target was adopted by the GA in 1970 and was subsequently accepted by most donors, though not the USA. Overall, from 1970 to 1990, ODA ran at about one-half of the target and fell even further to around one-third in the 1990s. Only five countries – Denmark, Luxembourg, the Netherlands, Norway and Sweden – are meeting the target. This means that, in any year, not much more than $50 billion ODA was available, and, of that, only about $5 billion was channelled through the UN. Do these figures mean anything to you? The US military budget is over $300 billion; the world's military expenditures runs to over $800 billion. These are annual figures.

The GA decided to convene an international conference on Financing for Development in Monterrey, Mexico, in March 2002. This Conference brought together all the stars in the drama – the UN, the World Bank, the IMF, WTO, UNCTAD, UNDP, commercial banks and even NGOs. The focus was on mobilizing international and national resources, on trade and on debt, and on putting some sort of order ('coherence and consistency') into the whole mish-mash. The Conference was a surprising advance from sterile North–South recrimination towards shared understanding of what to do. The rich and poor – developed and developing – each have their part, their responsibilities. The daunting goal of halving desperate poverty by 2015 (the main UN Millennium goal) was reaffirmed at Monterrey. Rich countries were exhorted to increase development aid up to the norm of 0.7 per cent of GNP – in effect doubling the current annual level from $50 billion to $100 billion. Relief from external debt, especially for the very poor, had to be accelerated. These actions would help the developing countries to create conditions for external investment as well as for social delivery systems. Trade tariffs must be changed so that poor countries can get their exports into rich markets. Poor countries will get ahead through clean, stable and efficient government. This is all old stuff, you say. True, but the old wine is in new flagons – it is a *consensual* brew, and the international financial institutions, including the WTO, are full participants. That is new.

What was more important and unexpected was that real money was pledged by the USA, the European Union and Canada. That President George W. Bush actually went to Monterrey was astonishing enough, but that he announced there the doubling over three years of US development aid, up to an annual $15 billion, made this show seem real. The European pledge amounted to $4 billion a year. Altogether, aid pledged at Monterrey was about $12 billion a year. President Bush said that the increased US aid would go to countries which 'respect their people, open markets, invest in better health and education'. If the President's stance is backed by the US Congress, this will be a new alignment of US policy, a return to early US commitment to boosting development.

Coming five months after Monterrey, the World Summit on Sustainable Development brought 100 heads of state and over 21,000 participants to Johannesburg, South Africa, from 2 to 11 September 2002. Attending were over 9,000 official government delegates, some 8,200 NGO representatives and a massive 4,000 voyeurs from the media. This was a follow-up to the Rio Conference on Environment and Development in 1992. Although specific environmental issues loomed large at Rio and Johannesburg, both Conferences turned out to be about basic development, about poverty and how to move on. Progress on Rio's ambitious 21-point agenda had been slow, but Johannesburg was to work out a new plan of action, where possible with targets and dates. The Conference met in a sober and litigious atmosphere. Such a huge attendance was no help.

Nevertheless substantial agreement was reached on general principles and on some specifics. Rio's Agenda 21 was reaffirmed, as was the Millennium goal of halving desperate poverty by 2015. Management of natural resources was seen as the key to attacking poverty. While no energy targets were set, much attention was paid to renewable and non-polluting sources of energy. Targets were set to restore depleted fish stocks by 2015 and to reverse the rundown in biodiversity (the rich variety of biological life) by 2010. With a glance at the wasteful rich, the Conference also agreed to promote a shift towards sustainable consumption, a ten-year study.

Although not in the official records of the Conference at Johannesburg, all major industrialized nations except the USA agreed to proceed with the Kyoto Protocol, which sets targets and dates for reducing 'greenhouse gases', the emissions from factories and automobiles that make our planet hotter.

Kofi Annan, in closing the Conference, said: 'This Summit will put us on a path that reduces poverty while protecting the environment, a path that works for all peoples, rich and poor, today and tomorrow.'

CHAPTER 11

The World Around Us: The Environment

The environment ranks with terrorism as one thing that no nation by itself can handle. Here, there is no viable alternative to the UN. However, although the environmental threats of population and industry were foreseen a century ago, 'the environment' was not in the air in June 1945 when the UN was born. There is no reference to the environment in the UN charter.

It took foresighted Swedes to initiate the first UN Conference on the Human Environment, in Stockholm in June 1972. In North America there was already a burgeoning popular concern over environmental degradation. No doubt Sweden's conscience had been pricked by the fact that thousands of their lakes had suffered from acid rain drifting over from industrial Europe. Although rich and poor were well represented at this conference, the USSR and its satellites stayed away, furnaces belching on. Already at this first Environment Conference, it was understood that protecting our environment was not just a sentimental campaign of nature lovers, but an essential basis for development, for growth towards a better life. That care of the environment translates into growth was what brought together rich and poor, North and South, in the resulting Stockholm Declaration of Principles and Plan of Action. The core principle asserts, what now seems obvious, that natural resources must be protected, shared and, where inherently feasible, renewed. This will entail pollution control, not only where people live but also in the oceans. Doing this requires deliberate action, both national and international, supported by science and technology. Popular support requires education in environmental issues. Poor countries must get help so that they can do their part. Weapons of mass destruction must be eliminated. People are entitled to a decent environment as a matter of human rights, not negotiable. This is the gist of the Stockholm Declaration, a sound and prescient base for what followed.

At the UN that same year, 1972, coming out of Stockholm, the UN Environment Programme (UNEP) was created, a small entity within the UN Secretariat with its own Executive Director and Governing Council. UNEP's job is to co-ordinate and advocate international action, including science and technology. Continuing today, UNEP says its mission is 'to provide leadership and encourage partnership in caring for the environment by inspiring, informing and enabling nations and peoples to improve their quality of life without compromising that of future generations'.[1] A tall order, but a noble one.

Besides initiating UNEP, the Stockholm Conference agreed on some specifics: a ten-year moratorium on commercial whaling, stopping oil discharges at sea within three years, and an overview of energy uses, also within three years. Many governments proceeded to enact basic legislation on the environment, and for the first time to create offices – ministries, departments – responsible for the environment.

The Stockholm Declaration was an expression of intellectual and moral concerns, not yet formalized in legally binding treaties. Stockholm launched the dynamic environment movement of our time.

In two decades, 1972–92, a groundswell of concern among governments and civil society fed by natural and man-made disasters prepared the way for the Rio Earth Summit, the UN Conference on the Environment and Development (UNCED). What happened in those 20 years?

In China the Tang Shan earthquake killed 200,000 people, and the Guatemalan quake made more than a million homeless – both in 1976. Monsoons killed 10,000 in Thailand in 1983, and drought starved millions in Africa's Sahel in 1983 and in Ethiopia in 1984. Human fallibility caused the 1979 Three Mile Island disaster in the USA, where meltdown of the nuclear power plant was narrowly avoided. Seven years later, in 1986, the Chernobyl meltdown in the Ukraine sent radioactive fallout across Europe. In 1984 an accident at the Union Carbide chemical plant in Bhopal, India, killed or maimed thousands. And in 1989 the supertanker *Exxon Valdez* spilled 50 million litres of oil into Alaska's pristine Prince William Sound. Such disasters could not be ignored.

At the same time, good work was done along the road to Rio. The decade after Stockholm saw the first steps towards co-ordinated international action. To protect endangered species, including waterfowl and their wetlands, no less than four international treaties were concluded in the 1970s (1971 Convention on Wetlands, 1972 World Heritage Convention, 1973 Convention on International Trade in Endangered Species, 1979 Convention on Migratory Wild Animals). The 1973 Convention bans or controls trade in some 25,000 plant species and 5,000 endangered animals, notably the African elephant and whales.

Major advances were made in the next decade. The threat to the ecosystem by the rapid thinning of the protective ozone layer led to the Vienna Convention (1985) and its concrete application in the Montreal Protocol (1987) on substances that deplete the ozone layer. This Protocol, which came into force in 1989, imposes strict limits on the production and trade in materials that attack the stratospheric ozone layer.

Concern over the shipping of dangerous wastes from industrialized countries to weaker countries, especially in Africa, was the impetus for the Basel Convention (1989). This Convention, which came into force in 1992, aims at cutting back the creation of hazardous wastes, and prohibits sending such material to any country that doesn't have the technical means to dispose of it.

The political and technical weight of the Law of the Sea is reflected in the time lapse between its final negotiation in 1982 and its entry into force in 1994. It took this long for governments to commit themselves formally to this treaty. The treaty mandates international co-operation to protect the marine environment, to manage marine resources and to control pollution. Vanishing fish stocks tell us today how critically important is this Law of the Sea.

We come now to Rio de Janeiro, June 1992, the spectacular Earth Summit, the UN Conference on the Environment and Development. In size and energy, this gathering was unique for its time. At Rio were 176 governments (over 100 heads of state), around 10,000 official delegates, 1,400 non-governmental organizations and 9,000 journalists. The emphasis was on *development*, advancement towards a better life, with the *environment* an organic part of that process. It was environmental concern that introduced the idea of sustainability: don't run down resources to zero. So now we think in terms of *sustainable development*. Sustainable development at Rio extended across the whole spectrum of social and economic challenges, including poverty, population, health and wasteful consumerism. This Earth Summit produced a Declaration, reaffirming Stockholm principles, and the ambitious Agenda 21, a comprehensive agreement on what has to be done. Besides social and economic issues, Agenda 21 called for careful management of the atmosphere, the oceans, fresh water, forests, agriculture and dangerous materials. To make this happen, Agenda 21 stressed the need for popular participation by citizens' groups as well as science, business and industry.

UNCED produced two formal treaties: the UN Framework Convention on Climate Change and the Convention on Biological Diversity. The Climate Convention, which has been endorsed by nearly all states, aims at stabilizing greenhouse gases, especially carbon dioxide. These are the gases that heat up the atmosphere, and industrialized countries are their main source. Specific targets for reducing emissions were worked out in the 1997 Kyoto Protocol. Most developed countries have accepted the Kyoto targets, with the USA and Russia standing aside.

The Convention on Biological Diversity became law in 1993. It aims to maintain the existing array of biological life, to ensure that resources are used in a sustainable way, and that they are shared internationally in a fair way. The Cartagena Protocol to this Convention seeks to protect biodiversity from the potential risks posed by genetically modified organisms. UNCED also began work that eventually led to treaties on other serious issues: desertification (deserts creeping into arable land, especially in Africa), fisheries, chemicals and marine pollution.

Stockholm vested UN concern for the environment in UNEP. Rio put inter-governmental follow-up in the hands of the UN Commission on Sustainable Development. The Commission has met annually and has addressed many unresolved problems (e.g. maintenance of forests), but has lacked the political support needed for a serious follow-up to Rio.

Moving on to September 2000, at the UN Millennium Summit government leaders reaffirmed their support for Agenda 21. In their Millennium Declaration, they said: 'We resolve ... to adopt in all our environmental actions a new ethic of conservation and stewardship.'[2] This set the tone for the World Summit on Sustainable Development, held in Johannesburg in September 2002. This was to take off from Rio, looking ahead. Assimilating Agenda 21 into the whole range of development issues inevitably blurred the focus on specific environmental challenges. Elaborate preparations for Johannesburg had raised hopes and expectations for big steps forward. Given the prevailing edginess among nations, such high hopes could not be realized. The big sticking point was in setting targets, already encountered in the Kyoto Protocol (reducing emissions). The complicated range of issues and the huge and disparate attendance also put consensus almost beyond reach. Nevertheless, some good came out:

- On energy, all agreed that more renewable energy must be produced, giving all people access to environmentally sound supplies of energy.
- On fresh water, the aim was to prepare efficient management plans by 2005.
- On fisheries, fish stocks were to be restored to sustainable levels, if possible by 2015. Unregulated, destructive fishing was to be stopped.
- On chemicals, a way was to be devised to manage chemicals internationally, eliminating damage to health. Common labelling was to be put in place by 2008.
- On biodiversity, the brakes were to be put on the current rate of loss by 2010.
- On forests, the current drastic rate of depletion in many countries was to be regulated.

Johannesburg tacked on two basic issues which Rio had downplayed: lavish consumption whenever income goes up, and the chequered performance of international corporations. It was agreed that a ten-year 'framework' must be built for reducing wasteful consumption and for accelerating sustainable production.

As for international corporations, UNEP has held many annual consultations with industry associations. The UN Global Compact, bringing business together with labour and civil society, pledges all to respect the environment, as well as human rights and labour standards. Reporting to Johannesburg, UNEP found that some industries were beginning to take the environment seriously, but that most have not yet seen the light.

Looking back over the 30 years since Stockholm, what do we see? Starting from zero, the record is surprisingly good, an encouraging awareness and grasp of what must be done. But huge threats lie ahead – global warming, water shortages, land erosion, pollution, skewed distribution of resources, the glamour of consumerism. It will be through the UN that humanity will succeed or fail.

CHAPTER 12

Nature's Terror: HIV/AIDS

One Friday in the early 1980s, in my New York office, my phone rang. It was Jim Grant, head of UNICEF. Next Monday, said Jim, WHO was convening in Geneva a big inter-agency meeting on HIV/AIDS. Could I go for UNICEF? Yes, of course. In one afternoon I read everything available on this strange new disease. On Monday in Geneva, the brilliant Dr Jonathan Mann, first WHO Director of the HIV/AIDS Programme, gave a frightening forecast of what lay ahead and what might be done to head off disaster. I pledged UNICEF's help in the fight, just getting under way. Up until then, only some thousands had been infected in Africa, hundreds in North America. No treatment, no vaccine. Prevention: stop transmission through sexual intercourse or infected blood.

That was 20 years ago. Dr Mann was spared the confirmation of his dire warning when his aeroplane plunged into the Atlantic in 1998. By 2002 HIV/AIDS had spread to all regions: 42 million living with the disease, 3.1 million dying in that year. At the present rate, around 45 million more will have AIDS by 2010. Since the disease was first identified, it has killed more than 20 million people. This is the worst epidemic in recorded history, and it is far from over. Although WHO and its partners, notably UNICEF, have long led the world in disease control, until now this work was regarded as largely technical, an important dimension of medicine and health. Economic and political repercussions of major diseases were clear enough in many countries, but had little place in political discourse at the UN. With HIV/AIDS, all that has changed. In 1996 UNAIDS was established as a partnership for the UN system, to ensure stronger UN response to the epidemic.

In face of the global HIV/AIDS crisis the UNAIDS resources are modest indeed, with a budget of around $60 million a year and a staff of 130 professionals. It has a largely catalytic role, to get critical actions going. The 22 governments on the UNAIDS Co-ordinating Board are joined by representatives of five citizens' organizations (NGOs), bringing people living with AIDS into the global response. This is a first at the UN: while NGOs are 'consulted' informally elsewhere, in no other UN organ do they have a formal place at the table. So far UNAIDS has been able to reach out to over 150 countries.

The General Assembly held a Special Session on HIV/AIDS in 2001, and even the Security Council has considered the radical implications of this epidemic, especially in Africa.

Although the disease was first found in Africa, it is definitely a global phenomenon. The 42 million people living with HIV/AIDS in 2002 comprise 31 million in Africa, 7.2 million in Asia, 1.5 million in Latin America, 440,000 in the Caribbean, 1.2 million in Eastern Europe, 520,000 in Western Europe and about 1 million in North America.

Africa, below the Sahara, is by far the worst affected area where, for example, in four countries HIV prevalence among adults is over 30 per cent. The disease is galloping in the Baltic states, Russia and central Asia. It is running fast in the Caribbean. India and China with their huge populations have woken up to the threat of HIV. Even in rich countries, where the disease had been stabilized, a false sense of security can mean unsafe sex and rising infection. No country is immune.

Overall, heterosexual intercourse is the main mode of transmission, followed by man-to-man sex and drug injection. Transfusion of infected blood is also a serious threat where, for example, poor people sell their blood to a lax blood supplier. In some countries, this began as a disease among men, but now as many women as men are infected. Tragically, mothers can give the disease to their babies. More than 3 million children (under 15 years) have AIDS, and millions more are orphaned because of it. Young people are particularly vulnerable, especially where drug use – needles – is common. (The world supply of heroin doubled in one year in 2002.)

People everywhere are on the move, vast migrations brought on by in-country war, natural disasters and desperate poverty. Soldiers spread the disease. Traditional prostitution – commercial sex – expands as many women sell sex just to feed their young. Ignorance about AIDS is appalling, and attempts to spread the word are often blocked by the social stigma attached to the disease. Nations' energies – farms, factories, professions, police, armies – are drained. AIDS is a global crisis.[1]

Only an enormous national and international drive can head off impending disaster. Facts must be faced. Unless people know, nothing will change. Prevention begins with information and education. Condoms must become available, as must social support: health networks, community services, especially for mothers. Ideally medical treatment of people with AIDS is not only humane and compassionate, but also cuts transmission. But the drugs regimen is complicated and exacting, requiring professional care, and these drugs are very expensive, even for rich countries. Fortunately simple and much cheaper drug treatment is available for mothers, cutting transmission to new-borns by 50 per cent.

A vaccine against HIV would be our best weapon, but the virus is elusive and volatile. Despite enormous effort, we have no vaccine. Drug treatment eases suffering and prolongs life, but its application is severely limited. A major factor is cost. In the year 2000 treating a person with AIDS for one year cost over $10,000 in drugs. Drug companies with patent protection got such bad press that prices came tumbling down so that, within two years, some drugs were offered for as little as $350 per patient per year. Prices like these were offered only to poor countries. The UN was in the lead in pressuring pharmaceuticals. As a service to the world, WHO and UNICEF produced a guide to best buys of 200 drugs worldwide, and WHO has studied 'access to quality HIV/AIDS drugs' and recently published a list of 16 drugs.

Besides costly and complicated drug treatment, the detection of individual cases remains technically difficult and relatively expensive, i.e. relative to what poor countries can afford. While much cheaper treatment can now change the picture in middle-income countries, it is still out of sight for the poor in Africa and Asia, the regions most in need.

Meeting at the UN Millennium session in 2000, world leaders adopted the goal of reversing the spread of HIV/AIDS by 2005. The next year saw the UN Special Session on AIDS, committing the full UN membership to specific actions, including the establishment of national strategies to provide care and treatment. Specific goals also included getting education and life skills to most young people (95 per cent is the target) by 2010, and reducing infant infection by a half by 2010. The funding goal was to raise up to $10 billion a year for the not-so-rich (low and middle income) countries to fight the good fight against AIDS.

Do we have the resources to do this job? What are we spending now? Leaving aside rich countries, expenditure for AIDS is running at over $2 billion a year; and if work goes ahead, this will run to over $9 billion in 2005. In response to a call by the Secretary-General, a Global Fund against HIV/AIDS, Tuberculosis and Malaria has been created. The fund has been promised $2 billion. But the money has been slow to arrive. Kofi Annan's man for AIDS in Africa is the Canadian Stephen Lewis. Returning to the UN in January 2003, Mr Lewis said, 'The Global Fund, at the end of January, can be said to be in crisis.' Challenging what he called 'a kind of pathological equanimity', he said, 'it is absolutely certain that the pandemic can be turned around with a joint and Herculean effort between the African countries themselves and the international community.'[2]

Right now, the world spends over $800 billion a year on armaments. Yes, we can attack AIDS; we can afford it and we must do it.

CHAPTER 13

'We the Peoples': Civil Society

An extra-terrestrial being fresh from vaulted skies and reading the UN Charter for the first time thinks, 'What a marvel! The myriad peoples of this Earth have come together in grand union to create one big home for the whole family, the United Nations.' But as the extra-terrestrial reads beyond the Preamble, euphoria turns to disappointment. The Charter is a compact between governments. Who are 'the Peoples' and where do they come in? By invoking 'the Peoples', is the Charter saying that all governments derive their legitimacy, their authority, from 'the people'? That all states members of the UN are, or should be, democracies? Or is this just a piece of poetry, window dressing for *Realpolitik*? True, the grand objectives in the Preamble – a world at peace, fair shares for all – are spelled out in the Charter. The Preamble then is not just poetry, but it promises more than it delivers in implying that governments and 'the Peoples' are the same. A better world ideal permeates the Charter, even as it specifies the *what* and *how* of governments, but by invoking 'the Peoples' in the Preamble it implies another voice of authority. Thus the space between national governments and their people reappears at the UN.

The interaction between people and governments is complicated enough at the national level. Citizens speak with more than one voice. How on earth can 'the Peoples' play among governments at the UN? The Charter is foresighted, it enables the play to begin. It says, in effect, that citizens' organizations that have something to contribute to the work of the UN can get a foot in the door. Here is Article 71 of the Charter:

> The Economic and Social Council may make suitable arrangements for consultation with non-governmental organizations which are concerned with matters within its competence. Such arrangements may be made with international organizations and, where

appropriate, with national organizations after consultation with the Member of the United Nations concerned.[1]

Although the choice of words here is careful – 'may', not 'must' – this is still a most unusual gesture. How many national constitutions include a formal acknowledgement that a government could actually learn something from its own people? At the UN the door was opened a crack, and practice has established a citizens' presence that cannot be ignored. As friends of the UN, they are welcome; as critics, exposing and advocating, less so. But after all, neither governments nor citizens' organizations are uniform in interest or in competence. Because this has been a living, evolving drama, the performances had to be many and mixed. Whoever wrote Article 71 certainly did not foresee the mass citizen movements that have challenged UN forums and even brought down governments.

Meanwhile, at the UN, who could come through that crack in the door? The Charter definition is loose: first, it is negative – *non-*government; and second, it is wide open, concerned with whatever ECOSOC is into, which is just about everything. By implication, this would keep citizens away from the Security Council, although, as we shall see, life at the UN began to put everyone in the same boat.

The designation 'non-government organizations' (NGOs) was initially taken up by social movements clustered around common objectives and constituencies. For access to the UN, such NGOs had to convince an inter-governmental committee that they were serious in experience and concern. NGOs that pass this test are granted consultative status with ECOSOC. This means that they may attend UN meetings on economic and social affairs, where they may say or, more often, write their piece on whatever. Their numbers grew from 41 in 1948 to 377 in 1968 and now to over 1,000. A larger group of NGOs, more than 1,500, is 'accredited' in a sort of talking relationship with the UN Department of Public Information: briefings on UN happenings and invitations to special events including a big annual NGO Conference just ahead of the GA.

The 1990s saw an historic breakthrough for NGOs, when UN rules were relaxed so as to encourage their involvement in international development conferences – on children, women, the environment, population, slums, human rights. By the thousands, informed and enthusiastic citizens found the airfare to converge on sober officialdom. NGOs met in their uncensored forums alongside the formal inter-governmental sessions. By invitation, professional and group presentations were also made at formal meetings, often enriching the formal discussions. Of course NGOs were not always in agreement among themselves, e.g. on population and family planning. But splits like these, while painful, were rare. Instead, at these conclaves NGOs most often pooled their energies to press ahead in common cause. TV coverage, and now the Internet, have brought millions more to such consultations, opening long-term political vistas.

Successive secretary-generals have been keen to engage citizens in support of the UN. In 1990, as the Cold War ended, Pérez de Cuéllar suggested in his annual report that public support for the UN could have 'important policy implications for member states. They can draw strength from the widening peace constituency which exists in all countries – and whose concerns are so well articulated by non-governmental organizations, especially in the fields of disarmament, human rights and the environment.'

As the decade rolled along, Kofi Annan arrived with a fresh new look and his 1997 comprehensive reform plans. That was the context for his overall appreciation of 'civil society' – his term – and his arrangements for taking the civils into the family, into his UN house. More broadly, his review of 'civil society' referred not only to NGOs already active at the UN, but also to 'local authorities, mass media, business and industry, professional associations, religious and cultural organizations and the intellectual and research communities'.[2] Continuing, Kofi Annan suggested that civil society has become more influential because of the push for more democratic and accountable 'governance', and also because the shift to a market economy (globalization) gave civil society more responsibility for the good of society. He noted that, in getting things done, civil organizations complemented UN programmes (e.g. for children and refugees) with knowledge and resources in the field. Internationally, civil organizations are seen 'not only as disseminators of information or providers of services but also as shapers of policy, be it in peace and security matters, in development or in humanitarian affairs'. He observed that this was evident from the involvement with the UN of NGOs, parliamentarians and business leaders. He felt it was high time to get closer to 'the business community', the World Economic Forum (the annual gathering of CEOs, usually held at Davos in Switzerland) and the International Chamber of Commerce. He would be getting together with civil and business leaders, he said, and he would open up the UN house to NGOs. Although authoritarian states are not comfortable with civil society, Kofi Annan has kept the welcome mat at his door.

It is curious that the mere existence of the UN has catalysed the NGO sprawl. Networks, sometimes closely knit, have proliferated, addressing particular issues: political, religious, economic, social, humanitarian. Initially NGOs from advanced democracies were preponderant, but more and more organizations from developing countries are coming into the mix. The full NGO story would be another book. For the UN the most broadly concerned are the 100-odd National UN Associations, now actively co-ordinated by the World Federation of UN Associations. Strongest among these UN Associations are a handful in democracies. Under 'political' I am lumping together peace, disarmament and international law, including human rights. Here NGOs are a strong presence, challenging jaded governments to bridge chasms of hatred. Pioneers among these are the International Peace Bureau, the Women's International League for Peace and Freedom (from the First World War) and The Hague Appeal for Peace (launched in 1998). Unique in authority and competence is the Swiss-based International Committee of the Red Cross (ICRC), closely connected to the Geneva protocols on war and its prisoners. The ICRC is universally regarded as the inspector-custodian of war prisoners and their rights.

As for disarmament, I cannot begin to name its many outstanding professional groups. Many bring to the UN not only enormous energy but also highly sophisticated expertise on the whole range of disarmament issues. Professional NGOs keep alive the struggle to pull back from nuclear disaster. Because the US government, in its present (2004) mode, seems ready to use nuclear weapons, the NGO 'middle powers initiative' to ban them completely is even more urgently at work. Organized scientists are at work on ways to control chemical and biological weapons. The Ottawa Land Mines Treaty and its follow-up owes much to an energetic NGO coalition, recognized by the award of the Nobel Peace Prize to its leader, Jody Williams. A successor international coalition is now hard at work on small arms.

Turning now to international law, the International Criminal Court from its inception got mighty political and technical support from a worldwide citizens' coalition, headed by William Pace of the World Federalists. UN hearings on human rights would have been muffled by many governments, reluctant to criticize each other, were it not for the testimony of NGOs, notably Amnesty International (another recipient of the Nobel Peace Prize) and Human Rights Watch. It was war's impact on women and children that opened the doors for NGOs to that inner sanctum, the Security Council. Citizens' voices have hastened the adoption of the ILO Convention on Child Labour and the UN Convention on Eliminating Discrimination against Women.

Citizens' grasp of basic issues of the environment and development came to a head at the great Rio Conference in 1992 and continues in NGOs' presence at the Commission on Sustainable Development (which tries to realize the Rio agenda). On the great debate about globalization and poverty, critical importance of 'people-centred economic growth' was advanced by NGOs in a joint policy statement to ECOSOC in July 1999. As for Third World debt, even the IMF acknowledges that Jubilee 2000 speeded up the gradual lifting of that burden.

Massive citizen protests have erupted around recent meetings of the World Trade Organization and related organizations, at Seattle in November 1999 and Genoa in 2001. These demonstrations have brought public attention to the social impact of discriminatory trade agreements. Among demonstrators, sober professional groups (e.g. organized labour) have a clear understanding and focus, but their serious participation can be lost in the media's attraction to the lunatic fringe. What these demonstrations tell us is that among citizens there is enormous and largely untapped intelligence, concern and energy.

The global compact

The UN outreach to business and labour is important and courageous. Developing countries, the Group of 77, see transnationals as a reincarnation of economic imperialism. Prominent NGOs are afraid that the UN will dirty its hands by somehow giving respectability to cruel and voracious business. But Kofi Annan has bet on long-term self-interest and good will among business leaders. In annual forays to the World Economic Forums, from 1997 onwards, he has challenged the new power elite to rise to their global responsibilities. At the Forum in January 1999 he invited big business to join the UN and civil society (yes, organized labour is there) in a Global Compact respecting human rights, labour standards and the environment. The Compact covers:

- Human rights: support and respect the protection of international human rights within their sphere of influence, and make sure their own corporations are not complicit in human rights abuses.
- Labour standards: freedom of association and the effective recognition of the right to collective bargaining, the elimination of all forms of forced and compulsory labour, the effective abolition of child labour, and the elimination of discrimination in respect of employment and occupation.
- Environment: support policies that protect the environment, undertake initiatives to promote greater environmental responsibility, and encourage the development and diffusion of environmentally friendly technologies.

As a follow-up to this challenge, in January 2000 the UN launched an interactive website (www.globalcompact.org), a unique resource centre on corporate citizenship.

What about the workers of the world, organized labour? Predating the UN, the International Labour Organization (ILO) is governed by tripartite national delegations: government, management and labour. Kofi Annan is reaching out to labour as well as management, in emulation of ILO. Following his challenge to business, the Secretary-General met international leaders of organized labour, led by Bill Jordan, head of the International Conference of Free Trade Unions (ICFTU). Jordan said that labour welcomes the Global Compact. From labour's perspective, the Compact reinforces the Universal Declaration of Human Rights and the ILO Declaration on Fundamental Principles and Rights at Work. The ICFTU is in the lead in fighting for labour rights against worldwide, often brutal, repression. Strong trade unions make for economic growth and more stable and equitable societies.

Back at the Davos Forum in January 2001 Kofi Annan renewed his challenge. When one-third of humanity is surviving on less than $2 a day, he asked, how do we explain to our young people that 'the global system of rules, at the dawn of the twenty-first century, is tougher in protecting intellectual property rights than in protecting fundamental human rights?' He went on to report on progress in the reception of the Global Compact:

> I am glad to say that many business leaders have responded positively. Equally important, they have recognised the value of working with civil society to achieve these goals.
>
> So the Global Compact now includes not only leading companies from around the world, but also the International Confederation of Free Trade Unions, and a dozen or so leading voluntary agencies which are active in upholding human rights, protecting the environment and promoting development. They are working together to identify and promote good practices, and helping, thereby, to drive out bad ones. The Compact is not a regulatory regime or a code of conduct, but a platform for learning and sharing lessons about what works and what doesn't.[3]

The Global Compact is a first serious attempt to bring the so-called 'private sector', focused on transnational corporations (TNCs), into some sort of partnership with the UN. Of course the UN would welcome more trust funds of the kind that Ted Turner contributed. But that is not the purpose of the Compact. Its stated purpose is to educate, enlighten and 'socialize' (my word) these global giants so that they behave in ways that support UN goals. The idea is good but the rules for engagement are pretty loose. There is no explicit arrangement for TNCs to report on their behaviour, nor is there any explicit arrangement for monitoring. In contrast, a number of citizens' and business organizations have launched codes of conduct for business. The danger is that the voluntary Global Compact will be used by unreformed aggressive TNCs to cover bad practice. There already are a good many constructive arrangements between the UN and business, and these are now being tied into the Compact. This is an experiment.

What will come of it? Can the wealth-making machine be tamed to direct its power towards the neglected billions?

Davos is a forum for legitimate, responsible CEOs, possible partners for the UN. Excluded from this forum are the vast international criminal networks, what Kofi Annan calls 'uncivil society'. The Security Council has shown that enormous criminal wealth can infiltrate and sometimes absorb governments. Money, guns, drugs and people are traded in this evil world market. Many wars today are made for profit – diamonds, oil, timber. The Compact served up for them is the UN Convention on Organized Crime. Its impact will be in the hands of INTERPOL and governments that sign on.

The Millennium Forum

Entering a new century in a new millennium, a great gathering of NGOs was held at the UN in May 2000. The Millennium Forum was attended by over 1,000 organizations from more than 100 countries. It delivered a detailed agenda for action, covering peace, poverty, globalization, the environment, human rights and the strengthening of the UN. The agenda was built on a common vision of a world where all can live in peace and harmony 'as envisioned in the Charter of the United Nations'. One thing I found especially encouraging was the presence of many people from the 'South', a very good sign. So often in the past, developing countries have been scantily represented at international NGO meetings. The Millennium Forum was truly a global affair.

What did the 147 heads of state have to say about all this? In their Summit Declaration they said:

> We resolve ... to give greater opportunity to the private sector, non-governmental organizations and civil society, in general, to contribute to the realization of the [UN] Organization's goals and programmes.[4]

The World Social Forum

A salutary, if untidy, citizens' reaction to the Global Economic Forum is the World Social Forum held in Porto Allegre, Brazil, in 2002 and 2003, moving to Mumbai in India in 2004. This is a huge affair, assembling many who protested against globalization and the WTO in Seattle and Genoa. While suspicious of the Global Compact, the WTO and the IMF/World Bank, the Social Forum advocates a stronger UN. Welcoming the energy and social vision at Porto Allegre, Kofi Annan invited participation in shaping social and economic policy at home and at the UN. Here is the last paragraph of his 2003 message to this Forum:

> At times it seems as if the international system will be forever held hostage by power and undermined by greed. But there are also moments when opportunities present themselves. Such a moment exists today. Now is the time when we must redouble our efforts to build up a system of rules and law, a system that is open and fair, a

system that will not tolerate poverty or injustice, a system that responds to the real needs of real people. That makes it vital for us in the United Nations and you in civil society to continue our constructive engagement. I attach the highest importance to that relationship, and to our common quest for a peaceful, safe and just world.[5]

CHAPTER 14

Mapping, Management, Money

As long as I can remember, there have been cries for UN reform. It is mostly the industrialized countries, the so-called North, who do the crying. They want the UN to be more efficient. Good. But what is the UN and who made it what it is?

The UN system is an array of inter-governmental institutions that touch on every aspect of human life. The same governments made this system.

The UN that hits the headlines, and what this book is about, is the UN that was created in San Francisco in June 1945, the UN defined in its Charter. This UN is, in the first place, the member states, now numbering 191, leaving out very few nations anywhere.

For UN purposes these national governments organized for themselves the General Assembly (all 191 members today) and the Security Council (five permanent and ten fixed-term elected members). The General Assembly is formally 'democratic' in the sense that each member has only one vote. But decisions by the 15-member Security Council are binding on all 191.

Under the General Assembly are the Trusteeship Council and the Economic and Social Council (ECOSOC). The Trusteeship Council was created to give the UN a hand in delivering colonies to independence, and since that has been done (only minuscule colonies remain) the Council now has little left to do. ECOSOC is something else. Under ECOSOC are several functional Commissions (on Development, on Human Rights, on Women, on Population, on Crime and Justice, to name the main ones). And then the General Assembly over the years has created special funds and programmes, each with its own inter-government board and its separate funding. The main ones are: the UN Development Programme (UNDP), the UN Children's Fund (UNICEF), the UN Development Fund for Women (UNIFEM), the UN Conference on Trade and Development (UNCTAD), the UN Environment Programme (UNEP), the UN

Population Fund (UNFPA), the World Food Programme (WFP), the UN Centre for Human Settlements (HABITAT), and the UN Relief and Works Agency for Palestine Refugees (UNRWA). The International Court of Justice at The Hague is also a UN Charter body, but it operates independently of the General Assembly.

The so-called UN system is even broader, comprising 14 specialized agencies that are separate and parallel to the Charter UN. They are supposed to 'co-ordinate' with the Charter UN, but they are separate in governance and funding. The International Financial Institutions (IFI), the World Bank and the International Monetary Fund are another breed of institutions with economic power analogous to the Security Council's political power. The IFI 'co-ordinates' with the UN on its own terms.

So back to the Charter UN: its many creatures must have people, 'staff', to serve meetings and to do governments' bidding. In the UN jargon, this is the Secretariat, the international civil service.

What is talk of UN reform all about? Is it about function, changing or clarifying what governments have asked themselves to do through the UN, and the consequent costs to be contributed to the UN by these governments? Is it about co-ordinating, integrating related functions? More radically, is it about amending the UN Charter, especially in updating the membership and practices of the Security Council? Obviously structural and functional reform at this level is what matters most. It is also the most difficult and the slowest to bring about. Humankind on this planet has coalesced into nation states, huge and tiny, states that struggle with problems at home and are variously groping towards international commitment. To get any agreement on common action is quite a stunt. The big states call the shots.

This is a long preamble to inter-government reform. Has anything happened? Yes, some improvements. Although there is no basic change in the Security Council, it has opened its doors to the excluded majority, it involves and consults. As for the many funds and programmes, there is better co-ordination and overseeing at ECOSOC and the GA. This means less running off on meandering paths, more sharing, more joint actions. Thus does structural reform trickle down to the Secretariat, the hired help, Kofi Annan's extended family.

So now I lead you into the United Nations house where hired help from more than 160 countries serves 191 bosses, the 191 member states that are the UN. Getting people to do things is called management, and people are called human resources. No matter what you call them, they are still people. People work for the UN. What goes on in this house?

Running the show should go like this: What? How? How much? Or, as the heading of this chapter suggests, first *mapping* where you want to go (what to do); second, *managing* the team to get there (doing it); and then *money* (getting the money, paying the bills). Simple, isn't it? It would be if your bosses knew what they wanted you to do, if they let you do it, and if they gave you enough money to do it.

Under the UN Charter, the only person hired by the 191, on the initiative of the Security Council, is the Secretary-General. He then hires and supervises everyone else in the UN house. That is the Charter arrangement. But what really happens? Kofi Annan spoke on this question at the World Economic Forum, Davos, in 1998. He began by saying that his job has been likened to that of a big firm's CEO, with UN member states as the board of directors, the world's people as shareholders, and development programmes and peacekeeping operations as the stock in trade.

> But the comparison stops there. How would you react if your board members – all 185 of them [that was the number in 1998] – micromanaged your business, gave you conflicting mandates and denied you the resources needed to do your job? What would you do as head of a club whose leading members do not pay their dues? What would you think of corporate governance that does not permit borrowing to offset this funding crisis? So if you think of me as a chief executive officer, remember that I am also equal parts juggler and mendicant.

So what is actually happening?

Mapping

The Millennium Declaration is the first ever panoramic sketch of major UN tasks and goals. Although it includes some specific time-based targets, overall it is indicative, not definitive. And not at all simple. Most of the action lies with governments; the hired help, the UN staff, have a supporting and facilitating role. Implicit in this, and clear enough to everyone in the UN house, is the fact that a lot of staff support is needed just to make the year-round meetings possible. The in-house exercises that have constituted mapping are the medium-term plan (two years ahead) and the biennial budget (two years). Gradually wearing down micro-managing resistance in the 191-member board of governors, budgeting is at last being oriented to goals, 'results based', not just slots for anonymous people. (The old 'slots' system was easier to infiltrate with political candidates. Everyone hired by the UN is sworn to political independence, never to take orders from any government.) Nevertheless the GA review of a proposed biennial budget, done in its Fifth Committee, is exhaustively intrusive. The job is often relegated to junior staff of government delegations, and the rules of the game say that everyone in the Committee has to agree on everything. Objective budgeting ('results based') in an atmosphere of trust would save time and frayed nerves, and would give to the Secretary-General the authority and flexibility he must have to run the show.

That is at the mechanical level. More important is the setting of goals. A glance at the Millennium goals will tell you that the UN is not just one homogeneous house: there are special departments (children, women, population, environment, slums, development, not to mention political affairs and peacekeeping) and surges in work, not all constant. Goal setting is fascinating – it is what the UN is all about. Here Kofi Annan's team is on a good tack, to use a sailing metaphor. This is their approach: try to set priorities for the UN (what to do), and then focus the UN's limited resources on those priorities (how to do it). The Millennium Declaration has both long-range objectives and concrete time-set goals. At least it is a 'framework', a sort of game plan for the UN. It is easy to see what are the top priorities, the big goals, for the UN: peace and security (including terrorism), humanitarian emergencies, international law (especially human rights), sustainable development (including the environment and globalization) and poverty (at the heart of development). What 'development' means was fleshed out in the human development conferences of the 1990s. Today it is essential to strengthen participation of 'civil society': NGOs, business and labour.

That is a huge agenda. Where do the foot soldiers, the Secretariat, come in? The Secretary-General's approach to all this is laid out in his paper, *Strengthening of the United Nations: An Agenda for Further Changes* (A/57/387), presented to the GA in September 2002. He recommends not so many meetings and reports, and making them more 'productive'. I don't know exactly how you define a 'meeting' – presumably a formal UN gathering – and Kofi Annan tells us that in the two years 2000–01 there were over 15,000 meetings entailing some 5,800 reports. Just a glance at the GA agenda, over 260 items, tells you that there is a lot of dead wood, uncoordinated smattering, resulting in an accretion of moribund demands to the Secretariat. A bonfire of the dead wood would help to clear the air. In his 'strengthening' paper, the Secretary-General presents a thoughtful and detailed analysis of how to align and shape-up his big family, the Secretariat.

Another demanding change for the UN staff has been the shift from headquarters-based functions towards work in the field, out there at country level. Now two-thirds of UN staff are involved in field work. This has radical implications: training, mobility, conditions of work, the family, etc. More interesting, but also more demanding and more risky. Work for the UN is not fun and games.

Management

Overall, management is leading, encouraging, watching, rewarding, scolding, hiring, firing. In a big organization where thousands toil, there have to be several tiers of managers, which means that managers have to be managed, all the way to the top. If you don't have a good manager at the top, the whole system wobbles. By great good luck, Kofi Annan by personality and experience – 30 years in the UN – is a good manager. A scion of a Ghanaian chiefdom, he leads with quiet dignity, authority and democratic outreach. Since taking over in 1997 he has brought UN management to life. At the top he has his Wednesday morning cabinet meetings with heads of department, with the video participation of UN offices in Vienna and Nairobi. He has drawn his people together into four functional groups, each with an executive committee: Peace and Security, Economic and Social Affairs, Development Co-operation and Humanitarian Affairs. Human Rights participates in all four groups. This is the structure of UN headquarters.

There is a lot of UN activity 'in the field', mostly within countries. The quadripartite grouping would not fit there. Instead, all functions, all functionaries are gathering into one UN country house – it may be real or symbolic – led by a UN Country Co-ordinator. At the country level, goal-setting appears in the form of the common UN Development Assistance Framework (UNDAF), a first ever step towards a convergent UN approach in its several development programmes. In its present form UNDAF is more procedural than substantive, more *how* than *what*; but now that there are UN goals approved at the

Millennium Summit by heads of state, the *how* can be addressed to common destinies.

Under Kofi Annan's leadership, the goal-oriented way is even radiating out into the large and loose UN system comprising the autonomous UN specialized agencies. Now Kofi Annan has coaxed agency heads to join the dance, to focus on common goals for everyone.

Good management rests on responsibility and accountability. There has to be a clear work plan against which accomplishments can be measured or, more generally, judged. In his 2000 report on accountability, addressed to the General Assembly, the Secretary-General says that accountability has been strengthened in three ways: creating a performance management plan for each department, monitoring by the Management Department and the Office of Internal Oversight Services, and a super Accountability Panel, chaired by Kofi Annan's deputy, Louise Frechette. The Panel will look over all monitoring materials and will tell the Secretary-General where things have gone wrong. I hope it will also tell him where things have gone right. Kofi Annan wants this process to apply to his top managers, not just the underlings.

There are three sets of auditors who check that the money goes where it should: the External Auditors, the Office of Internal Oversight Services (OIOS) and the Joint Inspection Unit for the whole UN system. Extant for seven years, the OIOS is tightening inspection and accountability. The first super sleuth, Karl Paschke, had a brilliant record as overall inspector of Germany's foreign service. Having completed his five-year non-renewable stint at the UN in 1999, he had found instances of poor judgement and inefficiency, but no pervasive corruption. He found less bad behaviour, he said, than he would expect to find in any big commercial corporation. His successor, Dileep Nair, brings impeccable credentials from Singapore. Nair's 2003 study of 'Human Resources Management' is a major contribution towards loosening up a moribund old department, linking management to UN goals and instituting the training of managers. This Office reports through the Secretary-General to the General Assembly and it stands in high regard.

In the midst of all this, how are the UN workers, the UN proletariat, faring? Some well, some not. Change breeds insecurity. Management needs flexibility, staff need security. Managers may just arrive by promotion, without training or aptitude. Good staff may be polluted by old-time political time-servers. The 'accountability' process is a sound way to sort this out. Inevitably, some staff are hurting, and the institution of an independent ombudsman since 2001 is an enormous improvement over the former committee-strangled grievance process.

Money

All of the above, mapping and management, rests on money: how much and when? The UN has four kinds of expenses: one is for its core functions (the regular budget), the second is for its peace operations, the third is for the War Crimes Tribunals (Yugoslavia and Rwanda), and the fourth is for assistance to countries (e.g. humanitarian emergencies and UNHCR, UNDP, UNICEF, UNFPA, UNEP). The first three are financed by member states, under their legal commitment on joining the UN. For the regular budget, the share of each state is determined by the General Assembly according to what is called 'a scale of assessments'. The scale is based essentially on GNP and population. Governments are required to pay their annual dues in the first month of the calendar year. A government that is two years behind in its contribution loses its vote in the GA. The scale of assessments is reviewed and adjusted every three years.

For peace operations, including tribunals (the 'peacekeeping budget') the scale is adjusted to assign a bigger share to the permanent members of the Security Council. Peace operations are mandated by the Security Council, and Security Council decisions are binding on all UN members.

All other UN expenses depend on voluntary contributions, mainly from governments but also from the generous public in many countries. The UN stands or falls on member governments meeting their legal obligations.

(A word about the UN specialized agencies – WHO, UNESCO, ILO, FAO and the rest. These are all creatures of the governments that created the UN itself. Each has its own governing body and each is financed by assessed government contributions. All of this is outside the financial arrangements I am discussing here.)

The wavering commitment of states to multilateralism, to the UN, is evident in the sorry history of UN funding. While adding to UN tasks, major governments, notably the USA, have kept the UN on the brink for most of its lifetime. Leaving aside voluntary contributions, the regular core budget of the UN now runs at around $1.3

billion a year. It has been frozen at that level since 1994, loosening up a little in 2003. The peacekeeping budget goes up and down, depending on what the Security Council decides to do. It was $1.4 billion in 1990, rose to $3.2 billion in 1994, dropped to $900 million in 1998 and 1999, rose again to around $2.6 billion in 2001, and dropped again to $2.3 billion in 2002. So altogether we are talking about $3 or $4 billion in a year when peace operations, themselves costing twice the core functions, have greatly increased (Sierra Leone, Democratic Republic of the Congo, Ethiopia-Eritrea). For so-called 'defence', the world still spends well over $800 billion a year. For the UN, $3 billion amounts to about 50¢ per person alive on the planet; the world's annual military budget amounts to $100 per person!

And yet there is haggling over how much it all costs, and money dribbles in late. At present the European Union carries about one-third of UN expenses, Japan nearly one-fifth. In 1946 the US share of the regular budget was 40 per cent; it was reduced to 33.3 per cent in 1954, and went down to 25 per cent in 1974. The USA now contributes 22 per cent of the regular budget, with a phased drop over four years in its peacekeeping share from 31 per cent to under 27 per cent. The US share of the regular budget is $325 million, and around twice that for peacekeeping. The US federal budget is around $1.8 trillion, of which around 17 per cent is for defence. These are political facts. Where are the strong wise voices, the visionaries, George Bush senior's 1990 euphoria? I leave it to my US friends to analyse, applaud, decry and predict the politics of this new imperial power.

Especially since the regime of President Reagan in 1982, when UN dues were left out of US appropriations for one budgetary cycle (result: US payment to the UN always comes late), the UN had been getting by hand-to-mouth. In fact it was able to keep the lights on only by internal borrowing, using money contributed for peacekeeping to pay regular bills. This bad practice was tolerated because otherwise the ship would sink. Peacekeeping money had been available because troop-contributing governments were reimbursed *after* their troops have donned Blue Helmets. This meant that, in effect, relatively poor countries – major troop contributors – had been subsidizing the delinquent rich.

To illustrate, the overall UN financial situation at the start of 2003 was as follows:

Contributions Paid and Not Paid – 31 December 2002[1]
(In millions of US dollars)

	Regular budget	Peacekeeping	Tribunals	Total
Payable 2002 and earlier	1,388.9	4,107.3	242.8	5,739.0
Received in 2002	1,084.1	2,772.0	199.4	4,055.5
Not paid	304.8	1,335.3	43.4	1,683.5

And yet the financial outlook for the UN is now the best and most predictable that it has been since the US Republican Party gained control of Congress in 1994. Right-wing hostility to the UN generated a succession of demands – conditions for the release of the US contribution. A US citizen must be in charge of the UN budget, and so Joseph Connor, former head of Price Waterhouse International, was given that thankless job. He did it well, retiring at the end of 2002. Another able US citizen, Catherine Bertini, has stepped in to that tough spot. She showed her mettle when running the World Food Programme. Then the USA demanded an Inspector General and they got it, first in the person of Karl Paschke, succeeded in 2000 by Dileep Nair.

Next, squeeze your bloated bureaucracy! The core UN staff has been cut back from over 12,000 in 1985 to under 9,000 in 2000. The last cut, from 10,000 to under 9,000, came under Kofi Annan's leadership, glossed over as promoting efficiency. There is always room for improvement in any bureaucracy, and US Congressional pressure did indeed strengthen the reforming hand of Kofi Annan.

The final demand, which took the battle into the 2000 General Assembly, was the reduction in the US share of the budgets. It was only the brilliant sleight-of-hand of retiring US Ambassador Richard Holbrooke, master of the Dayton Accords on Yugoslavia, that pulled the rabbit out of the hat in the last gasp of the Millennium Assembly – which turned out to be the last gasp of the Clinton White House. This was a $34 million rabbit; reducing the US regular share from 25 per cent to 22 per cent meant a loss of $34 million. The philanthropist Ted Turner produced $34 million, but since UN rules preclude private subvention to the core UN budget, the Turner gift had to be laundered through the US State Department. The US Congress at last was satisfied. US arrears have come way down, but at the end of

2002 still accounted for 40 per cent of all outstanding dues and, of that, 60 per cent of dues for the regular budget.

Why should the UN be in such financial jeopardy? In the global context the amount of money involved is small. Over the years several ideas have been trotted out for freeing up the UN: a tiny surcharge on international currency transfers, a levy on international arms sales, a levy on international air travel, charging interest on governments' arrears in paying their dues, commercial borrowing, an endowment fund of $1 billion. All have been turned down. The UN is hostage to its members.

Now there is a big expense looming, something out of the ordinary. The slim, elegant UN building still looks good, standing by New York's East River, but half a century has passed since it was built and it needs a major overhaul. You can't do that while all the people are in it. Another complication is that the UN building is no longer big enough to accommodate the whole range of UN work – development, women, children, population and others – so that commercial space is now rented for them. A five-year 'Capital Master Plan' is in the works, first to construct a new building adjacent to the old one, in order to accommodate UN staff while the old building is being renovated. When the staff move back, the new building will take in the UN workers now scattered in several commercial buildings. These plans have been drawn up co-operatively with the US local and federal authorities, and approved by the GA. The whole thing will cost $1.1 billion. UN start-up funds have been approved in the expectation that the USA will arrange an interest-free loan for the rest. Despite all the doom talk, it sounds as though some people expect the UN to be around at least until 2009. This great New York City certainly needs the UN – it brings in tourists and lots of money.

There is much more to this story, but enough for now. It is time to look at how all this is affecting the footsoldiers of this international corps. Let me move on by quoting Karl Paschke in his final 1999 report. Here are excepts from his preface:

> The United Nations of today, moving towards the new millennium and its global challenges, is a better Organization in many respects than, say, five years ago, and enhanced oversight has played its part in that change.
>
> However, further improvement within the United Nations is still necessary in many ways. Internal controls are not strong enough yet; accountability continues to be blurred and misunderstood; delegation

of authority must be effectively executed; and human resources management is in need of further reform. ...

Beyond these managerial challenges, some more general phenomena have been of concern to me throughout my tenure here, and remain complicating factors in the daily struggle of the Organization:

– A staff-management relationship that is characterized by antagonism rather than the spirit of co-operation;

– An overly critical attitude of many Member States towards the United Nations bureaucracy, resulting in numerous examples of micromanagement by the legislative organs;

– The constantly growing number of mandates where their reduction and a new definition of United Nations priorities would be desirable;

– The discrepancy between the expectations the world community has of the United Nations and the meagre resources it makes available to the Organization.

Having said this, I wish to express my pride and satisfaction at having been chosen to serve the world Organization whose importance is bound to grow further in this global environment of ours.[2]

With diplomatic restraint, Karl Paschke has told us that all is not well inside the UN house. How could it be? The UN flies in a chaotic political atmosphere, with plenty of turbulence and pressure, barely enough fuel in the tank, and constant crises for the pilot. The UN needs world-class staff. The Charter says, 'the paramount consideration in the employment of the staff and in the determination of the conditions of service shall be the necessity of securing the highest standards of efficiency, competence and integrity.' That is paramount, but read on: 'Due regard shall be paid to the importance of recruiting the staff on as wide a geographical base as possible.'[3] Even if you had exemplary management, making a world-class team of players from 160 countries would be quite a trick. The reality is a family which, on the whole, is truly devoted to the UN. Many departments are hard at work with high morale, others are perhaps less so. Naturally the staff is anxious about moves by the Secretary-General to tidy up the house, to open the windows, to map out where it is going, to untie people from their desks, to engage everyone in the journey. Shifting responsibility from the Human Resources Department to your own manager sounds good, but many managers have little flair and no training for their job. So everyone is to be offered training, to improve, to learn, to get ahead. A particular source of anxiety is the plan to abolish 'permanent' contracts and replace them with open-ended 'continuing' contracts.

What about grievances? The old ways of dealing with your complaint were frustrating, slow and heavy – some cases took years. The new arrangements advanced by the Secretary-General will give staff formal participation in the review of managers' performance, including decisions on new appointments. This is reassuring, as is the appointment of an ombudsman for the staff. Things are changing. With 400 retiring every year now, fresh blood will be coming in. My good friends in the Secretariat, often desperately overworked, look forward to a happier house.

The UN has an annual staff day. On that day in September 2000 Kofi Annan spoke of the 'noble tradition of international public service' and of the contributions that the staff can make in bringing UN service up to date. He said: 'I have heard many staff say that when work at the United Nations is good, there is no finer place to be. You have my pledge that I will not rest until all staff can feel that way.'

That is the ideal for any big family, an ideal that can never be fully realized. For the UN, what can best bring this polyglot team together, despite normal jealousies and jockeying, is commitment to the UN ideal – a world at peace striving towards a common good. But in a world fraught with brutal struggles over illusions of power and identity, the UN ideal is hard to keep. Staff morale at the UN is not only a reflection of what happens inside the house. In a hostile world it takes uncommon courage and commitment to stay the course.

On the firing line: what protection?

NATO took care of its military men, keeping them at 15,000 feet over Kosovo. Everywhere humanitarian workers are on the ground. At the GA in 2000, Louise Frechette said: 'UN staff have become moving targets. We all know that risk is part of the job. But a desperate irony is developing. Member states are willing to send unarmed civilians into places where they will not send well-armed troops.' Since 1 January 1992 more than 200 humanitarian workers have been killed in the service of the UN, and another 240 staff have been abducted. Others have been robbed or raped, and humanitarian convoys have been attacked. Most shocking, on 19 August 2003, 19

UN people were killed when the UN office in Baghdad was destroyed by a huge truck bomb.

In 1994 the GA adopted the Convention on the Safety of UN and Associated Personnel, and the Rome statutes of the International Criminal Court say that attacks on humanitarian workers and peacekeepers are war crimes. The Security Council has spoken. But so far these legal instruments have had very little impact on civil warriors. By the year 2002 only 22 of these killers had been brought to justice.

Louise Frechette addressed the Security Council on this issue in February 2001. In situations of great danger, she said, 'Often the United Nations has to stay because it represents the last ray of hope for suffering populations.' For our people on the spot, 'the least we can do is to make sure that they are not exposed to unnecessary danger'. Specific security measures can minimize risk. At headquarters and in the field, professional security officers with good communications equipment can advise and alert. People can be trained in how to take care of themselves, and they can be given equipment like flak jackets and satellite telephones. This has begun in the UN and its humanitarian arms, but it takes time and it costs money. The GA gave the Secretary-General just enough to get started in beefing up staff security.

Just as heads of state were gathering for the Millennium Summit, three UN workers were murdered by West Timor militia. Carlos Caseres was one of them. This is what he wrote on 6 September 2000, just before his death:

> I was in the office when the news came out that a wave of violence would soon pound Atambua. We sent most of the staff home, rushing to safety. I just heard someone on the radio saying that they are praying for us in the office. The militias are on the way, and I am sure they will do their best to demolish this office. ... These guys act without thinking and can kill a human as easily (and painlessly) as I kill mosquitoes in my room.
>
> You should see this office. Plywood on the windows, staff peering out through openings in the curtains hastily installed a few minutes ago. We are waiting for this enemy, we sit here like bait, unarmed, waiting for the wave to hit. I am glad to be leaving this island for three weeks. I just hope I will be able to leave tomorrow.
>
> As I wait for the militias to do their business, I will draft the agenda for tomorrow's meeting on Kupang. The purpose of the meeting: to discuss how we are to proceed with this operation.

CHAPTER 15

The Millennium

Only the UN could have brought 147 heads of state together to celebrate the new century and to share hopes for a better world. Meeting for three days, 6 to 8 September, this was the Millennium Summit. The presidency was shared by Sam Nujoma, President of Namibia, and Ms Tarja Halonen, President of Finland, embracing South–North, man–woman. It was, you might say, a festival of faith, an occasion to reaffirm commitment to the UN and its ideals. No fighter jets screamed overhead as all joined in launching their Millennium Declaration, a sort of road map and plan of action for the UN family of states at the start of the twenty-first century.

What good could possibly come of this big show, the largest such conclave in history? On the international stage, summitry looks like a fad, a magic ritual. Pool your problems, leaders will walk on water. There has to be summit fatigue. At a Caribbean summit in April 2000, the new President of Venezuela, Hugo Chavez, said that, in his first 73 days in office, he had already attended six summits of heads of state. 'We go from summit to summit,' he said, 'and our people go from abyss to abyss.' Six months later, caught up in the Millennium Summit, Hugo Chavez sang a different tune.

The Summit was Act One of the 55th annual General Assembly with its loosely structured encounters and discourse. Ten years back, post-*perestroika*, a rush of euphoria had stirred these waters. Since then dramatic social and humanitarian advances had been clouded over by disgrace in Srebrenica and Rwanda. Uncle Sam, the UN's paternal giant, still had not signed the cheque, keeping the UN on the verge of bankruptcy. Baffled and buffeted, the UN was in deep need of reassurance and resuscitation.

Quietly charismatic, Kofi Annan understands the power of symbols. On the common international calendar, moving from 1999 to 2000 was a powerful symbolic event, a sort of universal springtime, a time for renewal, a time for hope. The Millennium Summit was arranged for the UN to capture some of that fleeting springtime spirit.

Someone has remarked that all international meetings are a success even before they happen. Kofi Annan was well aware of what had happened only five years earlier, when the UN turned 50. At that birthday party, leaders were presented with a pre-cooked script. They signed and went home. This time, a big effort went into bringing everyone into planning the event. For governments, five regional warm-up sessions were held. In the three months before the formal event, there were global celebrations by citizens, NGOs, speakers of national parliaments and religious leaders. Kofi Annan's *Millennium Report* was launched a good five months before the Summit. His challenge had a clear historical perspective, reaching out to all people, ambitious and pragmatic.

Pulling off the Summit was quite a stunt – 147 big egos together for three days, each allowed only five minutes to speak, but then grouped informally at four round tables, an innovation that loosened things up remarkably well.

The challenge to this Summit was to set guidelines for the United Nations in the twenty-first century. Since the Summit Declaration was intended to map the way for the whole UN system, it had to be comprehensive. It begins with values and principles, and goes on to deal with major UN concerns: peace, security and disarmament; development and poverty eradication; protecting our common environment; human rights; democracy and good governance; protecting the vulnerable; the special needs of Africa; and strengthening the United Nations.[1]

Fundamental values identified include freedom, equality of all, solidarity (meaning social justice), tolerance, respect for nature and shared responsibility. These go well beyond the general principles of the 1945 Charter. There had to be some of the standard talk about national sovereignty and all that, but this Declaration has significant new elements. For example, values and principles include the affirmation that leaders 'have a collective responsibility to uphold the principles of human dignity, equality and equity at the global level. As leaders we have a duty therefore to all the world's people, especially the most vulnerable and, in particular, the children of the world, to whom the future belongs.' Here we find also that globalization is identified as 'the central challenge' to serving the poor.

Moving from principles to action, the Declaration sets specific goals for the United Nations family. The most ambitious and inclusive goal is a massive attack on poverty, to cut in half by the year 2015 the 1 billion now existing on something like $1 a day. This is not presented as a naked goal, but as something that requires both good governance at home and support from abroad: poor countries need access to rich markets, debt relief and more development aid.

What about peace and security? What about disarmament, small arms and the big bomb? These issues are addressed up front in the Declaration, right after the opening proclamation of values and principles. Regarding peacekeeping and peacebuilding, the Declaration says the summiteers will give the UN the resources needed to do the job. On mass weapons, the Declaration says that we should try to eliminate them, and that we should keep an open mind on Kofi Annan's proposal to convene an international conference on the nuclear threat. And then, it says, we must stop the black market in small arms, we should be more careful in our use of sanctions, and everyone should join the International Criminal Court.

For the rest, the Millennium Declaration is studded with development goals, some very specific, others very broad. Among specific goals are several initiated by UNICEF, and these include, by the year 2015:

- Providing full primary education to all girls and all boys everywhere.
- Reducing maternal deaths by three-quarters.
- Reducing under-five deaths by two-thirds.
- Reducing those without safe water by one-half.

Other goals which grew out of long-standing collaboration between UNICEF and WHO include, by the year 2015, stopping the spread of major diseases like HIV/AIDS and malaria, and getting essential drugs at decent prices out of the drug companies.

The Declaration goes on to capture the overarching goals that came out of those remarkable UN conferences of the 1990s – conferences on the environment, on human rights, on population, on children, on women, on slums. You will recall that these conferences defined strategies and goals that became the UN *Agenda for Development*; and that is what you find in the Millennium Declaration. In that sense, it took ten years to reach the international consensus that culminates in this Declaration.

Environmental goals are reaffirmed: the climate, forests, biological diversity, water, and (something new) access to the human genome map. Reaffirmed also are human rights in all their ramifications: political, economic, women, migrants, the media.

Special care must be given to the most vulnerable in disasters – the civilian population, and especially children and refugees.

For Africa, the Declaration pledges support for democracy, lasting peace, poverty eradication and the control of HIV/AIDS.

To strengthen the UN, the Declaration says that the General Assembly should have a central role, the Security Council should be overhauled, and the organization must get the money it needs to do its work.

So there you have the bare bones of this historic proclamation. Both its broad sweep and its concrete goals tell us why there is a UN, what states pledge to do when they join hands. The Declaration challenges us all, governments and 'the people', to do the hard work of transforming fear, hate and greed into trust, compassion and sharing.

Debating the Millennium: the General Assembly, 2000

Every year the General Assembly begins with a ten-day high-level discussion of major UN concerns. High-level usually means ministers of foreign affairs. The year 2000, the 55th GA, was different. It began with a three-day Summit of 147 heads of state of the 189 members of the UN. The usual ten-day policy discussion (called a debate) came after that. And so in September there was a two-phased debate. The two performances were not exactly the same. The second performance included many who had not attended the Summit. And while summiteers were held to five golden minutes, their underlings could carry on a good deal longer than that. I say underlings, but not all who came post-Summit were very far under. As against the 147 top dogs at the Summit, the 179 speakers who followed included three heads of state, 14 prime ministers or deputy prime ministers, and no fewer than 135 other ministers of governments. Quite a galaxy. (While I'm into numbers, I might as well point out that, among summiteers, only three were women.)

Add them up: 147 plus 179 makes 326 speeches. Compared to what goes on in national parliaments, that's not so many. Yet quite a lot to sort out, to digest. What usually happens is a fortnight of coming and going, senior statesmen, many thoughtful presentations, and then they are gone. These are the people who have a degree of authority to get things done. Among his first reform ideas in 1997, Kofi Annan said: let us harness these thoroughbreds, let us tackle one big problem at each annual debate.

So far this has been done only once, in the 1998 session on globalization. Exceptionally, the Millennium Summit gave a unique coherence to the Assembly. From year to year, developing countries, the 'South', keep insisting that the General Assembly, not the Security Council, is where UN policy should be made. In principle, they are right, but the GA is an unwieldy, uncoordinated monster. Engaging and focusing political energy at the Assembly's high-level debate might well give direction and structure to its ambling.

Of course there are variously structured alignments that give some shape to the 191 members. Some alignments are geographic/political, some functional, some cultural, some historic. Their significance was formally recognized at the Millennium Summit where heads of state listened to representatives of the European Commission, the League of Arab States, the Organization of the Islamic Conference, the Commonwealth Secretariat (the free and easy legacy of Pax Britannica), the Conference of Presiding Officers of National Parliaments, the Sovereign Military Order of Malta, the International Committee of the Red Cross, and the citizens' Millennium Forum. A curious lot, omitting all regional organizations except Europe, while welcoming the Sovereign Military Order of Malta. In practice developing countries are best represented at the GA by the Group of 77, now over 130 countries. And the mighty G7 (G8 if Russia is included) of leading techno-industrial countries have many voices. The European Union is the most tightly organized at the GA and presents one comprehensive position on current issues. Even so, the life of the Assembly displays shifting huddles as this or that issue comes to a head. Many tiny states cannot possibly deal with over 160 items on the GA agenda. Nevertheless, on basic matters, their interests are clear enough. On many issues, however, their delegates float. Probably no more than 30 or 40 states are willing and able to be seriously engaged across the board in the relentless, exhausting negotiations that go on all year. If you are serious, the UN is no picnic.

So then, at the Millennium Assembly, with 326 speeches, who said what and why? The question is important: what came out was not just a regurgitation of the Grand Declaration. There are, as always, general concerns shared by many, along with specifics of national or regional interest. It was enlightening for me to find that five minutes was enough for leaders to lay out basic policy concerns. What came after in the Assembly debate was essentially an elaboration of that. The formal proceedings at the Summit wound up with oral presentations by the chairmen of the four round tables, summarizing the informal off-the-record discussions.[2] The chairmen were Goh Chok Tong, Prime Minister of Singapore; Aleksander Kwasniewski, President of Poland; Hugo Chavez, President of Venezuela; and Abdilaziz Bouteflika, President of Algeria. The first thing that struck me was that all were enthusiastic about the round-table happening. This is what Prime Minister Goh said:

> I believe that the round-table experiment was a success. A round table for leaders deserves to be institutionalised. Since the United Nations was founded, leaders have been coming to the United Nations to give their views on global issues on a single track, that is, through speeches in the plenary. Until this round table, the United Nations process had never provided for an interactive dialogue among leaders.
>
> I suggest that we build into the United Nations process a round table for leaders every few years to allow interactive discussion among leaders in an informal setting, away from aides, officials and prepared scripts. This week's round table has shown that such a format can give rise to fresh, useful and innovative ideas. An interactive round table would also foster closer friendship and understanding between leaders and hence warmer relations between nations. We should not wait for 1,000 years to have the next round table.

Even summit-weary Chavez of Venezuela was enthusiastic: 'These round-tables should be ongoing and held frequently,' he said. 'They should be interactive and creative.'

Emanating from the round tables was also the desire, the intent to get things moving, to mobilize action through the UN. Kwasniewski put it this way:

> All in all, the discussion left me with an optimistic impression. I detected a wide-ranging meeting of minds and a determination to amplify our efforts to bring about change. This Summit is about change, and it was stressed that we should seize this opportunity to translate into action what has been agreed in principle.

Implementation is not only a job for the Secretary-General, but is first and foremost the obligation of Member States.

These round-table informal reports convey not only the substance but also the atmosphere of the Summit, an unusual insight. As for substance, dominant concerns were globalization and poverty, more than peace and security. Globalization evidently served as the catch-all for development — the progress of nations — and in that context everyone agreed that globalization must be regulated so as to serve the poor, not simply to make the rich richer. The IMF and WTO should get a handle on globalization, they said, and developing countries should have a bigger say in these institutions. Nations of the 'South' need to get their act together, and between 'North' and 'South', instead of confrontation, now is the time for open and constructive dialogue. There was strong support for a UN Economic Security Council (an idea dormant since the Nordics initiative several years ago). The Council should have regulatory powers, with authority complementing that of the Security Council.

Round-table views on poverty and Africa were linked. Poor countries must create conditions that attract investment (stability, democracy), but they will need help in doing that. The burden of external debt must be lifted, and for poor nations a much bigger infusion of development aid is essential. There were reservations about salvation through new information technology: basic needs must be met first, especially education. The calamity of HIV/AIDS needs urgent action, including access to affordable drugs. The importance of major environmental treaties, especially on the climate, was also recognized.

While there was relatively little attention in the round tables to peace and security, all agreed that the Security Council must become more inclusive, more democratic, and most felt that the veto must go. Better co-ordination with regional actors was needed, they said, and sanctions should be carefully targeted. The Brahmini proposals for strengthening UN security activities were generally endorsed. Sources of instability must be addressed: poverty, international crime and terror. Protecting human rights was seen as basic to national progress. There was strong support for the International Criminal Court. Finally all round tables agreed that the UN is indispensable and must be strengthened, with enough assured income.

There you have my summary of summaries. While I sense some nostalgia for the bad old days of South–North slugging, the turn towards dialogue gives hope. It reflects the outcome of an earlier Summit, heads of the Group of 77 states meeting in Havana in April 2000: consult, not insult. The exception was Fidel Castro, whose colourful tirades are sustained by US sanctions. But this UN Super Summit looked like a one-world gala.

This homogenized version of international discourse glosses over pervasive depths of insecurity, frustration and disillusionment. It is not surprising that not everyone sang the same tune. Looking back I have quoted US President George Bush and Soviet Foreign Minister Eduard Shevardnadze at the 1990 General Assembly. Ten years on, the younger Bush had not yet arrived on the scene. Bill Clinton was still there for the USA, saying: 'But those in my country, or elsewhere, who believe we can do without the United Nations, or impose our will upon it, misread history and misunderstand the future.'

Shevardnadze resurfaced as President of his native Georgia, having survived an attempt on his life. At the Summit he said:

> As the Cold War came to a close, we spoke a great deal about a new world and a new order. Ten years have passed. The world order we all dreamed of is still in the distance. ... Earlier we spoke of the bipolar world. Some suggest a multipolar world today. Who, then, will be able to assume responsibility for matters that cannot be shouldered by individual states? ... There is a need for a uniting and bonding force, a body with broad competence and wide duties.

The United Nations must be greatly strengthened, he said: 'There is a need for a fundamental restructuring of the United Nations and the Security Council to meet the challenges of the New Millennium.'

What do we hear from the voice of the Kremlin, Vladimir Putin? To the presidential array, he observed that 'the political term given to leaders is usually not very long' so that it behoves them 'to see at least one step ahead'. He thought that leaders had been able to endow this symbolic event, the Summit, 'with a profound meaning'. He went on to note that '[t]he twentieth century will go down in history as a century of contradictions ... of grandiose achievements and horrendous wars'. Managing to overcome the Cold War and its confrontation 'is a great achievement of the United Nations. ... There is a need to renovate and improve the United Nations, without abandoning its basic principles.'

From China, President Jiang Zemin also took a panoramic look at the schizoid twentieth century and the prospects for the twenty-first. 'The Cold War is over,' he said. 'The international situation on the whole is moving towards relaxation. ... But the unfair and irrational old international political and economic order has yet to be replaced. ... In this new century, the United Nations will shoulder a more arduous task. It should be a place where all its member states conduct international affairs through consultations and democratic means. No country or group of countries should use it when they need it, only to abandon it when they do not.'

President Obasanjo of Nigeria brought an African perspective, saying, 'Humanity has come a long way out of the ruins of the Second World War thanks to this Organization. We have emerged from the Cold War and incessant fears of global conflagrations. ... Although the world has generally become a safer place to live in, thanks to the contributions of the United Nations, we must all feel deeply worried that the message of hope which the Organization has been spreading is yet to reach the millions of mankind for whom it is intended.' Grinding poverty is their lot. Global threats now demand, more than ever, that we 'live and work together as members of one human family'. A few days later at the Assembly, Nigeria's Foreign Minister Lamido said that the UN was better represented by the work of such agencies as UNICEF, UNESCO and WHO than by Security Council resolutions.

Vice-President Maciel of Brazil joined in: 'The establishment of the United Nations is one of the great legacies of the twentieth century', but the time has come to give it new life and make it more democratic. 'No longer can we tolerate anachronistic decision-making structures that are not only selective, but fail to reflect the dynamics of world-wide transformations of the last few decades.'

Now hear the indefatigable Fidel Castro of Cuba. He began by saying that, at the Summit, 'three dozen ... wealthy nations have joined us ... to offer us more of the same recipes that have succeeded in making us ever poorer, more exploited and more dependent. There is no discussion whatsoever of a radical reform of this worn-out institution ... to transform it into a body that truly represents all the people of all the world.' The United Nations must be quick in this new century 'to save the world not only from war but also from underdevelopment, hunger, disease, poverty and the destruction of natural resources'.[3]

Prime Minister Rasmussen spoke for the Danes: 'The United Nations is what member countries make it. ... Global problems have to be tackled globally; therefore, we need a stronger United Nations.'[4]

Globalization and poverty

Globalization and poverty are not the same thing but their linkage was on everyone's mind throughout the Millennium celebrations. Here are a few representative statements: First of all, again to Obasanjo, speaking as President of the Group of 77 as well as President of Nigeria. 'Up to now,' he said, 'globalization has meant prosperity only for the chosen few in industrialized countries.' In developing countries 'globalization has to be seen to mean the eradication of poverty'. This will require 'a new system of international co-operation that will help to eliminate abject poverty throughout the world and integrate the developing countries into the globalized world economy'. He then drew attention to the shift in G77 thinking that was manifest at their first ever Summit in Havana in April 2000. At the Summit, in Obasanjo's words, 'it was resolved that a new and meaningful partnership with the industrialized nations needed to be forged in order to make this earth a better place for all of us.'[5]

Prime Minister Goh of Singapore, noting that globalization and the information revolution will widen the gap between rich and poor countries, proposed that 'the United Nations should provide the leadership within the community of multilateral organizations to help the poorer nations to profit from globalization and the knowledge revolution.'[6]

Speaking at the General Assembly, Joschka Fischer, Foreign Minister of Germany, said it was crucial to ensure that globalization benefited all people. As one measure towards poverty reduction, Germany had initiated action to lift the external debt burden of the 20 poorest countries.[7] Also at the GA, Ana Lindh, Foreign Minister of Sweden, said the world community must do all it can to integrate developing countries into the global economy.[8]

At the Millennium Summit, President Pastrana of Colombia spoke on behalf of the 33 countries in the Rio Group of nations in Latin America and the Caribbean. He said that globalization needs to be controlled and humanized: 'We need international co-operation to finance the networks of social protection and the investment in human capital ... in short, we need a new architecture for the international financial system.'[9]

Reforming the UN

Although the 1945 structures of the UN have been remarkably resilient, everyone agrees that substantial changes are needed now, especially in the Security Council and its relations with the GA. Looking ahead another 100 years, Václav Havel, the Czech President, envisaged a radical new UN with two parallel assemblies, one like the present GA and the other directly elected by everyone in the world. The two would together legislate for the world. The UN would have its own military and police. The UN would monitor and enforce security, human rights and basic social welfare. Havel felt that reforming the UN would have no meaning unless derived from 'a rediscovered sense of global responsibility'.[10]

Foreign Minister Moussa of Egypt advocated doing something now. The establishment of a new international order should involve everyone, he said. 'Egypt calls for a broad extensive debate in the framework of the General Assembly, which is a universal parliament, to draw up an international contract with the participation of representatives of various legislative bodies and civil societies.'[11]

From President Chavez of Venezuela came a call for a structural reform of the UN, specifically: 'We must democratise and expand the Security Council: ... A new world compact of the United Nations is necessary.'[12]

Human rights intervention

This is a deeply divisive issue: should the UN intervene, by various forms of pressure, ultimately by force, in a country where there are gross violations of human rights?

Jiang Zemin of China, says no: human rights are an internal matter. China's Foreign Minister, Tang Jiaxuan, at the GA, was explicit: 'To interfere in other countries' internal affairs in the name of protecting human rights in order to advance one's own political agenda is simply a blasphemy and betrayal of the human rights cause.'[13]

At the GA, Nigeria's Foreign Minister Lamido suggested that humanitarian intervention should be considered not only where conflict was killing people, but where people were dying from other causes such as HIV/AIDS, natural disasters, or sanctions.[14]

Spain's Foreign Minister Piqué was typical of Europe when he said, at the GA, that the UN could not stand aside when there were massive violations of human rights. National sovereignty must not imply impunity for trampling on human rights.[15] President Clinton said, 'There are times when the UN must take a side, not merely stand between the sides or only on the sidelines.'[16] Canada's Foreign Minister, Lloyd Axworthy, observed that the UN needs new ways to deter violations of human rights. To consider what to do, what is feasible, Canada had created an independent International Commission on Intervention and State Sovereignty, to share ideas and suggestions with the UN.[17]

Any thanks to the UN?

Ongoing UN peacekeeping and development assistance seldom evoke expressions of gratitude at the GA. There are, however, some countries exceptionally benefiting. Here are a few.

Guatemala's President Portillo spoke of his country's 'profound identification with the United Nations. ... We have been direct beneficiaries of the activities of the Organization, particularly in the establishment of peace. ... Guatemala provides an example of how the United Nations can assist in consolidating peace and respect for human rights, without any improper intrusion into the internal affairs of a nation.'[18]

President Chissano of Mozambique, among leaders at the Summit, had this to say: 'Mozambique has, to a large extent, experienced the positive impact of an effective and co-ordinated action by the United Nations and the international community at large, in times both of peace and of conflict.' He went on to express thanks for all the aid received from the international community during the recent devastating floods.[19]

From tragic Sierra Leone, President Kabbah observed that his country will be 'hosting' more than 16,000 UN peacekeepers, one of the largest UN peace operations. He said: 'May I, on behalf of all the people of Sierra Leone ... express my profound gratitude to the Security Council for giving the UN Mission in Sierra Leone additional responsibilities. ... Our thanks go also to those countries that have contributed troops and other resources. ... Their efforts have given true meaning to the term collective security.'[20]

The Security Council Summit at the Millennium, 2000

In 1992 the first Security Council Summit met in an atmosphere of euphoria. The 2000 Summit (7 September) was a lot more sober, closer to what had happened, both good and bad. You could say that this second Summit was a symbolic affair – it lasted only a couple of hours, there was no debate but only a series of general statements by heads of government. The meeting began solemnly with a minute of silent tribute to the three UN humanitarian workers murdered by Indonesian militia in refugee camps in West Timor.

We have heard the PERM 5 and Canada in 1992. But what were they saying in the year 2000?[21]

President William Clinton, USA: 'We will be forced increasingly to define security more broadly. ... Until we confront the link between deprivation, disease and war, we will never be able to create the peace that founders of the UN dreamed of.' He spoke of malaria, tuberculosis and AIDS, especially in Africa. 'We must do more to equip the United Nations to do what we ask it to do.' Bill Clinton, soon to leave the White House, could make no promises: 'I hope the United States will always be willing to do its part.'

President Jiang Zemin, China: We must find better ways for the UN to promote peace in this world where conflicts have increased. UN peacekeeping helps, but it is no cure. 'The success of the United Nations peacekeeping operations depends on the observance of the purposes and principles of the Charter, particularly the principles of respect for State sovereignty, non-interference in the internal affairs of recipient countries.' Africa needs more assistance.

President Jacques Chirac, France: Despite its increased activities in the past ten years, the Council's record is flawed. We must adapt our ways to deal with domestic conflict, tackling crises, promoting democracy and human rights. The illegal trade in diamonds, drugs and small arms must be stopped. We must strengthen the UN hand, as Brahmini proposes, and bring more developing countries into the Council. France supports UN long-term building of peace.

President Vladimir Putin, Russia: The UN Charter has stood the test of time, and the Security Council has gone all out 'to safeguard the world from a new global military catastrophe'. Law is the most important principle of the UN Charter; only the Security Council has the authority to sanction military interventions. National reconciliation can be mediated, with UN participation, as in Cambodia, Central America, Mozambique and Tajikistan. Russia is participating in ten of the 15 current UN peace operations. More summit meetings would help.

Prime Minister Tony Blair, UK: Peacekeeping is much tougher now, but it is even more needed. It can stand between anarchy and stability, as in Bosnia, East Timor and Sierra Leone. We must address causes of conflict: poverty, debt, disease and poor governance. The world is changing, and we need an orderly transition.

Prime Minister Jean Chrétien, Canada: Canada joins in this Summit's affirmation of support for strengthened UN peacemaking. 'In the twenty-first century, peace depends no longer solely on securing borders, but also on securing people.' During its two years (1999–2000) on the Security Council, Canada has 'tried to make the Council a more effective instrument for ensuring human security and more open and democratic'. The UN hand needs strengthening, as proposed in the Brahmini Study.

Entering the Millennium: The Security Council

There is a Christian sect, the Millenarians, who believe that all will be well after Doomsday when Christ will reign on earth for 1,000 years. So many sects pin their hopes on destruction, the end. Despair is their ultimate hope, but it isn't of much use to us as we try to patch things up and get on with the living United Nations. By the year 2000, where had the UN, the Security Council, arrived?

The first thing that strikes me is the deeper understanding of security. Instead of balancing power between states, the Security Council speaks of human security, social and individual security. From this it follows that the UN, the Security Council, must try to protect the civilian population from the disasters of war. Since 1998 the Council has held many sessions on protection of civilians, children, women, refugees and humanitarian workers. Concerned organizations (UNICEF, UNHCR, ICRC) have participated. This is new. The Security Council has also faced up to the shameful fact that humanitarian aid has often become a substitute for effective political action to end conflict. Examples are in the Sudan, Somalia and Yugoslavia. Humanitarian aid gets caught up in conflict.

The Security Council, supported by the Secretary-General and his staff (the Department of Political Affairs) must be more active in foreseeing and preventing conflict. In the short run this means better information, more fact-finding missions, more diplomatic mediation. In the long run, it means creating the conditions for stable societies (reducing poverty and providing basic services).

For the first time the Security Council has addressed transnational disease as a source of insecurity. In January 2000 it held a special meeting on HIV/AIDS in Africa, the cause of even more deaths than the epidemic of violent conflict.

Concerning UN intervention, there is still no bridge between the sovereigntists and the universalists, i.e. between those opposing any forceful intervention within a sovereign state, and those favouring forceful intervention not only to stop fighting but also to stop egregious violations of human rights. Kofi Annan put the issue clearly before the General Assembly in September 1999, and although his *Millennium Report* makes no recommendation specifically on intervention (wisely – only governments can sort this out among themselves), he does say, 'But surely no legal principle – not even sovereignty – can ever shield crimes against humanity.'[22]

Sanctions, a form of intervention, must be carefully designed to target the responsible elite and to spare the common folk. Peace operations must include stronger support for nation-building and protection of human rights. This poses a problem for the General Assembly which has maintained that national development is its responsibility. I have noticed, however, that the GA is not unanimous on this, as shown in its 2000 discussion of the Security Council's report.[23] India and Pakistan said: Hands off, this is GA territory, but Nigeria and South Africa supported the Security Council.

On Security Council reform, no solution is in sight for increasing its membership, but a great deal has been done to open up the Council to the wider UN membership, including regular information on agendas and plans, open meetings and consultation with concerned governments.

Politics can be lethal. How many present would survive? Shekh Hasina, Prime Minister of Bangladesh, reminded the Millennium Summit that her father, after leading the country to independence, was assassinated along with most of his family in 1975. Although not present at the UN, the President of Democratic Congo, Laurent Kabila, was soon to meet his end, shot down by his own. Fujimori would flee the Peruvian presidency to find refuge in Japan. Scandal would bring down Estrada in the Philippines. The electoral process in one way or another would shuffle away Barak in Israel, Clinton in the USA and Zedillo in Mexico. Leaders come and go; national policies are slow to change.

Looking back at the Millennium celebrations, the UN told itself not to forget. The Assembly was thinking of the whole UN system, the financial institutions and the specialized agencies; but what about the governments themselves?

Looking ahead, in just over two years, how have terrorists and Iraq changed the UN?

CHAPTER 16

Into the Twenty-First Century

Rituals embrace and give dignity. On 10 September 2002, at the UN in New York City, the 57th session of the General Assembly was convened. The President of the Assembly, Jan Kavan of the Czech Republic, opened the session with the traditional one minute of silent prayer or meditation. One minute isn't much, but it is at least a nod towards something above and beyond. This is how the annual 'general debate' gets started, the occasion for senior officials to speak, mixing global issues with parochial concerns. Nearly all 191 governments come to the podium to present themselves within their allotted 15 minutes. Two weeks of speeches – the 'general debate' – is hard to take; and since nothing happens, no decisions, no winners or losers, this so-called 'debate' is ignored by press and TV. But this show is unique. Reading and decoding the transcripts takes time and patience, but from it you can get a feel for worldwide concerns, tensions and actors.

The 2002 debate got under way on the first anniversary of the terrorist attacks on New York and Washington. Eulogies and sympathy came from many. Typical was the statement of Prime Minister Bondevik of Norway:

> Yesterday we stood united in remembrance of all those who lost their lives a year ago. The terrorist attacks of 11 September 2001 were an attack on us all. ... Today we stand united in unwavering determination in the struggle against international terrorism and in the fight for the values, ideals and human rights that this great organization is founded upon.[1]

Beyond sympathy, there was a sense in this Assembly that the terrorist attacks on the USA had repercussions for the whole fragile international order. The attacks had brought all together in common cause, while at the same time tempting the USA to strike back, to go it alone.

A legacy of the Cold War is the Non-Aligned Movement (the NAM), where 115 developing countries, the 'South', cling together. Malaysia chaired NAM; and speaking for NAM at the GA, Deputy Prime Minister Badawi said 'the need to strengthen the multilateral process is now more urgent than ever. ... Malaysia will work together with other NAM members to ensure the contained centrality of this process, including the promotion of their development agenda.'[2]

Prime Minister Rasmussen of Denmark spoke for the European Union. After an eloquent tribute to the 9/11 victims, he said:

> The key role played by the United Nations in the fight against terrorism is a reminder of the fact that the United Nations itself was born out of hope grounded on the ashes of the Second World War – a war which defeated tyranny and terror. With the adoption of the Millennium Declaration, the United Nations has been given renewed impetus to deal globally with conflict prevention, crisis management, humanitarian assistance, post-conflict rehabilitation and development, and disarmament and arms control.[3]

He went on to say that the European Union supports the integration of human rights into all UN activities, opposes the death penalty and supports the International Criminal Court 'as an important historic milestone'.

Why the UN? From their behaviour, this welter of nations seems anything but united. Yet here, together in the GA, faced with urgent transnational problems, all agreed that no nation can live alone, that the UN is essential. Egypt's Foreign Minister, concerned about a 'trend' to unilateral action, said this would lead to deadlock. 'We must therefore break this deadlock,' he said, 'by renewing our commitment to the Charter and reaffirming our determination to work together to strengthen the United Nations.'[4] In that same vein, Mexico's Foreign Minister said: 'Mexico is convinced that, at this time, the only legitimate path of action is that based on a multilateral approach that favours agreement and collective action.'[5] Nevertheless many said it was high time for structural reform, time to update the Security Council, to add new members so as to bring the Council closer to the General Assembly. Among states at this session, Poland was the most outspoken advocate of reform, proposing a radical revision of the whole system.

Meanwhile, despite its shortcomings, the UN got thanks for its helping hand from Croatia, Guatemala, Ethiopia-Eritrea and Sierra Leone. Afghanistan said thanks, but this is only a beginning, please stay with us. Diplomatic politeness notwithstanding, bitter disputes flared: India and Pakistan, Armenia and Azerbaijan, Georgia and Russia, Israel and the Palestinians. The GA can't negotiate, but it can listen.

What I have written is only a glimpse of issues and attitudes in this 2002 General Assembly. Yet in these years, 2002 and 2003, it was not just more of the same. A violent storm was brewing.

Another final conflict?

There is plenty of crisis talk as the UN teeters from brink to brink. So once more, in 2003, the UN faces imminent death. About nothing and everything, we used to say: It's dead but it won't lie down.

Why is it dying again now? Not blessed by the Security Council, the USA/UK 'invade' Iraq. Did the USA consult the UN before invading Vietnam? Did the USSR consult the UN before invading Afghanistan? Did Iraq consult the UN before invading Iran? No. So why now this impending doom? Is it because this time the UN was consulted, precipitating an unprecedented global debate?

It was terrorism that galvanized the UN in 2001. It was Iraq that galvanized the UN in 2002. Or was it the new face of Washington, lit up by terror and Iraq? Even so, why Iraq? The 1991 Gulf War was a UN war, led by the US army. It was won, but not finished. The Security Council, in meticulously detailed resolutions, told Saddam Hussein that he must give up all weapons of mass destruction, and that the UN would make sure that he did so by sending in weapons inspectors. For more than a decade, UN inspection was on again, off again, while UN sanctions squeezed civilian Iraq with little impact on their rough government. Saddam Hussein's envoys taunted the UN. But Iraq was not the only place where Security Council decisions, offering terms for conflict resolution, had been ignored: there was (and is) India and Pakistan, Israel and Palestine, and little Cyprus. Except for Israel/Palestine, in these situations, a small UN presence, observers in the main, had helped to cool hot heads, but no one was crazy enough to suggest that the UN could solve those political stand-offs by mounting massive military intervention.

For Israel/Palestine, Kofi Annan was not alone in saying that, if ever truce happened, there must be an international presence to hold the line. Truce first, then talk about peace. So what was different about Iraq?

Two things made it different. One was that it seemed soluble, something the UN could do. And yet Saddam Hussein kept teasing the Security Council. This kept the issue alive. The other thing was the new Washington outlook, under President George W. Bush.

UN veterans are inured to US ambivalence about joining the world, about taking the multilateral road. But now came alarming signs of imperial hubris. In September 2002 a US policy paper, finding its way into the public domain, announced that the USA henceforth would hit first before being hit. This is called a pre-emptive strategy. The USA would decide where threat lies and then strike. The public was also treated to a Pentagon strategy paper that implied that nuclear weapons are central to US security, that tactical nuclear weapons may actually be used, and that big new ones – blockbusters, to penetrate into hidden depths – may be developed. In the Byzantine labyrinths of Washington, it is hard to know whether such 'think pieces' are firm policy, but that they exist at all is troubling. This way of looking at the world is consistent with what the USA has been doing internationally: its opposition to the Kyoto Protocol aimed at holding back global warming, its attack on the International Criminal Court, the weakening of the 2001 UN Small Arms Conference, refusal to commit to banning tests of nuclear weapons, ending the Anti-Ballistic Missiles Treaty and reactivating Missile Defence ('Star Wars'). Just as troubling has been Washington's handling of international trade – for example, steel, wheat and lumber – shaking up even the conservative World Trade Organization. And then, in the midst of all this, along came the terrorists on 9/11 2001, bringing international violence to New York and Washington.

Stung by this outrage, Washington looked for nests of terror, flexing America's enormous military muscle. After calling on the UN, all nations, to make an all-out attack on terrorists, Washington turned its eye on *perceived* haunts of terror, the incubators: first Afghanistan, and then Iraq. Getting the UN Security Council engaged in Afghanistan was no big problem. Only two states – Pakistan and Saudi Arabia – had recognized the Taliban regime in Kabul, and there was ample evidence of Al-Qaeda masterminding, with the elusive Osama bin Laden, terrorist activities in Afghanistan. While the USA took the military lead, this was a UN operation, with broad international participation in getting a more democratic government in place in

Kabul. Although Operation Afghanistan was far from finished, Washington soon turned to Iraq.

Back at the UN, with the beating of muffled drums, President Bush addressed the General Assembly on 12 September 2002, a year and a day after 9/11. Beginning with a reference to this anniversary and Afghanistan, he said: 'The United Nations was born in the hope that survived a world war – the hope of a world moving towards justice, escaping old patterns of conflict and fear.' An improvement over the League of Nations, he said, was the UN Security Council, empowered to act. Indicative of US commitment to human dignity, he said, was its humanitarian aid, while 'joining the world ... to extend trade and the prosperity it brings'. In the Middle East, he said, 'America stands committed to an independent and democratic Palestine, living side by side with Israel in peace and security.' Moving on to terrorism he said: 'Above all, our principles and security are challenged today by outlaw groups and regimes that accept no law of morality and have no limit to their violent ambitions.' He said that terrorists in many countries, including the USA, 'are building new bases for their war against civilization'.

The great fear is that 'an outlaw regime' one day may give the terrorists the means to wreak mass destruction. 'In one place, one regime, we find all these dangers' – Iraq. His speech then went on to review Iraq's intransigence and duplicity in resisting the UN demand to disarm. If the Iraqi regime wants peace, he said, it will *immediately* (my emphasis) destroy all weapons of mass destruction, will end all support for terrorism, will stop persecuting its own people, and 'open the prospect of the UN helping to build a Government that represents all Iraqis'. If these demands, backed by the Security Council, are not met, 'the world must move deliberately and decisively. ... But the purposes of the United States should not be doubted. The Security Council resolutions will be enforced ... or action will be unavoidable, and a regime that has lost its legitimacy will also lose its power.' Leading up to all this, he said: 'Will the United Nations serve the purpose of its founding, or will it be irrelevant?' The message was clear. The USA soon began amassing troops within striking distance of Iraq.[6]

You can be sure that the Assembly hall was packed when President Bush spoke. This was how the 'debate' began, and indeed how it ended. The basic precepts of the UN seemed to be in question. Was this a challenge or a threat? Predating the 9/11 terror, the Security

Council's case against Iraq was that, having gone against its Charter commitment in attacking sovereign Kuwait, it must forswear the means to do such a thing again, it must give up its weapons of mass destruction. That was at the core of President Bush's statement, but around that core he introduced two new elements: one, that Iraq was fomenting terrorism; and two, its government should be brought down and a new one installed ('regime change').

Neither of these two elements had come into the Security Council's decisions. UN intervention (sanctions and inspection) was based exclusively on eliminating mass weapons. The first phase of UN inspections ended in 1998 when frustrated inspectors were withdrawn and the USA and UK bombed Baghdad. Iraq then refused to let inspectors return. Would it now let them back in? Would it help, not hinder them? If UN inspectors were to certify that Iraq had no weapons of mass destruction (WMD), UN sanctions would be lifted and that would be the end of it. (WMD include nuclear, chemical and biological agents and the means to deliver them.) If, for whatever reason, Iraq was not given a clean bill, certified no WMD, the Security Council would consider what next, it being understood that military force would be the last resort.

UN inspection had already enforced destruction of some WMD capacity. Now in 2002 with the US military, later joined by the UK, poised to strike, Saddam Hussein opened his gates to unconditional UN inspection. The original UN inspectorate had made a good beginning, although tainted with alleged collusion with national intelligence networks. It had been four years since that inspection had come to a halt. In the dawn of 2003 a brand-new UN team, headed by distinguished Hans Blix (former director of the International Atomic Energy Agency (IAEA)) set to work. The team also included Mohammed El Baradei, the current head of the IAEA. This team was able to go anywhere, even into Saddam Hussein's palaces, and in its first weeks found nothing much (especially no nuclear weapons capacity), except for SCUD missiles with a range beyond the limit set by the Security Council. Iraq began to destroy these missiles, as required. Hans Blix told the Security Council that, with time, some months, his team could finish the job of inspection.

In outline, this was the setting for the historic debate: to invade or not to invade. Although the formal responsibility for Iraq lay with the Security Council, the fundamental challenge – UN or USA – affected all. President Bush knew this. He spoke to the GA, not the Security Council.

All eyes turned to Iraq and terror. Saddam Hussein's Baath Party, originating in Syria during the Second World War, was secular, suppressing religious groups in its hold on political power. As such it was anathema to the Al-Qaeda network and its brand of extreme Islam. It was well known that Saddam Hussein encouraged Palestinian suicide attacks on Israelis, giving cash rewards to suicide families. This was a way to play with the anti-Israeli Islamic rage in the region. The brutal regime of Saddam Hussein certainly used terror at home. He exported terror to his neighbours, Iran and Kuwait, with his army. Did his investment in terror go beyond WMD?

Then there is 'regime change', ousting a sovereign national government. There is nothing in UN doctrine (the Charter) or in practice (the Security Council) that opens that door. The UN is an odd mix of states, of governments, variously fragile, and in this UN club you don't talk about killing some obnoxious member. You may have the courage to criticize bad behaviour – this is what occasionally happens among governments at the Human Rights Commission – but even there the UN club can't agree on going much beyond publicity to chastise brutal governments. Of brutal tyrannies there are more than a few. In no case has the Security Council mounted an operation to overthrow a brutal government for its violation of the human rights of its own people. This was not even contemplated in Security Council resolutions on Iraq. The Security Council would cut Saddam Hussein down to size, but not kill him. That is politics, not justice. If you want justice, there is now the International Criminal Court, where individuals, not governments, may be put on trial.

To recapitulate: what grounds were there, practical or legal, for an immediate invasion of Iraq before UN inspection was completed? And always stalking in the wings was the blood feud between Israel and Palestine. That was at the heart of this drama.

This was a drama in three acts. Act One was in the General Assembly. Act Two was in the Security Council, October–November 2002. Act Three was again the Security Council, February–March 2003. This play – fraught with life, death, hate, fear and tragedy – would not sell on Broadway. Every act was essentially the same, the outcome was left hanging, the drama ended off stage.

Since all three acts had essentially the same script, I am bundling them into one. Who were the actors? In the General Assembly, all governments. In the Security Council it is usually resident ambassadors who represent their governments. In this case, ministers of foreign affairs came all the way from national capitals to three Council meetings, absolutely unprecedented; furthermore, besides the 15 Council members (PERM 5 plus the elected ten), many more nations attended as non-voting participants in this historic debate: open sessions of the Council in October 2002 and again in February–March 2003. The number of extra-Council states attending rose to over 60 in February. And then, invisible but audible, some 15 million citizens worldwide protesting against war were acknowledged when the Council met in February.

The debate revolved around two things, two related aspects of the same thing: the *what* (substance) and the *how* (process, what to do and how to do it). Both came together in international law. On the 'what', there was no disagreement over the fact that Saddam's Iraq had not come clean on WMD, as required by the Security Council. The government of Iraq was therefore 'in breach' – it had not done what the UN told it to do.

The US add-on, terror, was not part of the Security Council package, but could not be ignored. After all, terrorism is real, not only for the USA. How far was Iraq into this deadly game? Would attacking Iraq help? Many delegates warned that illicit unilateral war against any Arab state would breed, not inhibit terrorists. Already Palestine with its myriad frustrated youth was sprouting terrorists like dragon's teeth. To equate Islam with terror was false, they said. At the General Assembly on 13 September 2002, Egypt's Foreign Minister, Maher El Sayed, said: 'I would like here to reiterate what everybody knows: no religion – Islam, Christianity, Judaism or Buddhism – preaches terrorism.'[7]

The other add-on, implied in President Bush's address, was 'regime change', ousting a national government. Although this is one of the things that imperial powers do, the very idea is taboo at the UN; and so was deflected towards Iraq and possibly the other two countries in President Bush's 'axis of evil', Iran and North Korea.

Rising above China's imperial past, on 13 September 2002 Foreign Minister Tang Jiaxuan admonished the General Assembly, saying:

> The indiscriminate use of force can only lead to greater trouble in our world ... countries should rise above their differing ideologies and social systems, abandon the cold-war mentality and the power

politics mindset, and refrain from harbouring suspicion and hostility towards each other.[8]

Addressing the Security Council on 19 February 2003, Malaysia said that every effort must be made to reach a peaceful solution to this problem, 'and not to legitimize war against Iraq to effect regime change'.[9] Remembering the past can be a nuisance. An irony in this sovereign assembly is that many states, notably Iraq, are creatures of imperial fiat.

So now to the UN case against Saddam Hussein: that he had not abandoned his WMD, and instead had prevented UN inspectors from finding such weapons, and seeing to their destruction.

In retrospect, what followed was a desperate attempt to hold back the American juggernaut. At stake, it seemed, was the UN itself. This is why ministers of foreign affairs came from afar and why so many from the GA infiltrated the Security Council. Kofi Annan saw this as a test of multilateral cohesion: could the PERM 5, the Security Council, hang together? At first, when the Council met in October, this seemed possible with the unanimous approval of resolution 1441. This resolution in effect said: Saddam Hussein, we give you one last chance to come clean on your WMD. Do it, or else. Unanimous approval was achieved by omitting a deadline and by not defining 'or else'.[10]

All eyes then turned to the outcome of the UN inspections. With the Pentagon breathing down his neck, Saddam Hussein beckoned the UN back. This time great care was taken to ensure the professional independence and integrity of the UN team. While Saddam Hussein did not grovel in abject confession, the inspectors were well received and could go anywhere at any time. Systematic inspection was proceeding. However, on 5 February 2003 US Secretary of State Colin Powell made a detailed presentation to the Security Council of US intelligence interceptions that seemed to indicate Iraqi cover-up of WMD. The USA considered that there were already grounds for 'or else'. Then came UN inspectors with their reports to the Security Council on 14 February 2003. There is no evidence that nuclear weapons exist or are being made, said El Baradei. There is nothing conclusive yet about chemical and biological weapons, said Hans Blix, but tracking them down for sure will take some months.[11] On 7 March Dr Blix told the Council that his inspectors had found missiles that could travel beyond the 150-kilometre limit set by the Security Council, and that Iraq had set about destroying them.

The line-up now was clear: in favour of immediate action were the USA, UK, Spain and a few others; in favour of more time for inspection were France, Germany, Russia, China and many more. Nevertheless serious efforts continued to avoid an impasse. France and Germany proposed strengthening the UN team. Canada proposed setting specific steps for inspection so as to have a base for assessing progress. All to no avail. Colin Powell floated a draft Security Council resolution authorizing immediate invasion. The PERM 5 was split: USA and UK in favour; China, France and Russia opposed. The issue was not so much *whether* as *when*. President Bush said now. Leading the opposition moderates, President Chirac said that France would veto. Colin Powell withdrew his draft. The show was over. US and UK forces entered Iraq.

Where does this leave the UN? At what could be a turning point in its very existence, Kofi Annan has pointed out that the core UN concept of collective security was challenged by the unilateral action of the US-led coalition. In Iraq, the USA has found that military victory was easy but that peacebuilding is extremely difficult. Iraqi resistance forces, well organized and sophisticated, continue to frustrate the US-led coalition. Military victory is a shaky way to introduce democracy.

Nevertheless, in the wake of the military victory, the UN at first maintained and even accelerated its humanitarian assistance. Along with that, it sent its highly respected Sergio Vieira de Mello as an informal UN presence to facilitate the process of peacebuilding. Although the US had not formally asked the UN to take over responsibility for peacebuilding, it was inevitable that, in the eyes of Iraqi resistance, all external presence was in some way complicit in the military occupation of their country. Hence the UN office in Baghdad was bombed on 19 August 2003. Sergio de Mello and more than 20 others were killed. There followed attacks on other humanitarian and diplomatic missions. Most international staff were ordered out of the country, leaving emergency aid largely in the hands of local staff.

As I am writing, updating this story at the end of 2003, the USA has announced that governing authority will be transferred to an interim Iraqi government in June 2004. The way in which this interim authority will be installed remains in dispute. The USA has assumed that, by June 2004, there will be adequate Iraqi military and police in place (along with a continuing coalition force) to provide security. This will not happen without a great deal of help from the international community.

And that, in turn, will depend on the extent to which the United Nations is given authority to lead in restoring national government to civil institutions.

And now, just as we go to press, the US military has captured Saddam Hussein. Whether this has more than symbolic political importance, time will tell.

CHAPTER 17

Yes, We Can

Seventy years have passed since Albert Einstein and Sigmund Freud exchanged letters on the causes of war, 'Why War'. Both saw in mankind a lethal struggle between love and hate, life and death. It is easy to whip up war hysteria. War gives licence to murder. Instead of prison, we get medals. What about love, that much prostituted word? What about compassion? Compassion is work, it begins with ourselves, it begins in humility, it leads to trust, to sharing, to the security of friends.

Right now we are lost in a fog of violence, of cynicism, of despair. We need a touch of old-fashioned Utopianism to grow again the Garden of Eden in this bitter Promised Land. Desperate fanatics dream that death is the gateway to beatitude. Where is our hope? It surely is not in neo-liberal unconstrained greed. Is there a better starting point than the UN Charter? Read again the relevant parts of the Preamble:

> We the peoples of the United Nations determined:
>
> To save succeeding generations from the scourge of war …
>
> To reaffirm faith in fundamental human rights, in the dignity and worth of the human person, in the equal rights of men and women, and of nations large and small.
>
> To establish conditions … under which international law can be maintained.
>
> To practice tolerance, and live together in peace with one another as good neighbours.
>
> To ensure … that armed force shall not be used save in the common interest.
>
> Have resolved to combine our efforts to accomplish these ends …

And do hereby establish an international organization to be known as the United Nations.

It took a bloody war and 50 million lives to give us this Charter. Must there be another? The future is inevitable after it happens.

Notes

Sources

United Nations official papers are the primary documentary base for this book. These documents are available on the UN website.

Among these papers, a major source is the annual report of the Secretary-General, always number one in the year's series of documents (e.g. A/55/1 – A means Assembly, 55 is the 55th session).

Official statements in plenary meetings of the General Assembly and in open meetings of the Security Council are recorded in the PV (Provisional Verbatim) series (e.g. A/45/PV is a statement at the 45th session of the General Assembly, and S/PV/4644 is a statement at the Security Council). Major official documents (reports, etc.) addressed to the General Assembly, are in the A/ series. Each UN Fund or Programme (e.g. UNDP, UNICEF) has its distinct document series.

PV sources of speeches are identified in these notes, as well as major official reports (at the UN, nearly all official papers are called 'reports').

Contextual interpretation and sequencing come from the experience of the author and his colleagues in and around the UN.

Terminology

A resolution is a formal decision by a UN body. Only decisions of the Security Council are legally binding on member states. Other resolutions represent the majority view of UN members. A declaration is a formal statement of principles approved by a majority of the UN members. It is a political statement and is not legally binding. Treaties, sometimes called covenants or conventions, are formal legal instruments that constitute international law. A state may sign a treaty, indicating its intention to make a legal commitment to it. A state is formally committed when it ratifies a treaty, following its approval by its national legislative authority. A protocol is a formal addendum or supplement to an existing treaty. States parties are the states (the nations) that have ratified a treaty.

Introduction
[1] Secretary-General's statement at the 2002 General Assembly, A/57/PV.2.

Chapter 1. The Great Thaw?
[1] A/45/PV.14.
[2] A/45/PV.6.
[3] A/45/PV.8.
[4] A/45/PV.4.
[5] A/45/PV.12.
[6] A/45/PV.9.
[7] A/45/PV.14.

Chapter 2. Human Insecurity: Ten Years and More
[1] Summit Meeting of the Security Council in 1992, S/PV/3046.
[2] *Agenda for Peace*, A/47/277 – S/24111.
[3] Supplement to the *Agenda for Peace*, A/50/60 – S/1995.1.
[4] *Report of the Independent Inquiry into the Actions of the UN during the 1994 Genocide in Rwanda*, 15 December 1999, S/1999/1257. Srebrenica Report: *Report of the Secretary-General Pursuant to General Assembly Resolution 53/55*, A/54/549.
[5] *The Brahmini Report*, A/55/305 – S/2000/809.
[6] Secretary-General's *Millennium Report* published by the UN Department of Public Information, New York, 2000.

Chapter 3. Disarm: Life or Death?
[1] A/C.1/55/PV.3.
[2] *Stockholm International Peace Research Institute (SIPRI) Yearbook, 2002*.

Chapter 4. Who Owns Terror?
[1] Press Release SG/SM/7945.

Chapter 5. No Hiding Place: War Criminals
[1] Robert Jackson, 'Opening statement at Nuremberg by Chief US Prosecutor, Justice Robert H. Jackson', 1945.

Chapter 6. Human Rights, Human Wrecks
[1] Vienna Declaration and Programme of Action, A/Conf.157123, 12 July 1993, World Conference on Human Rights, Vienna 14–25 June 1993.
[2] Annual Report of the UN High Commissioner for Human Rights, addressed to the General Assembly. The report for 2002 is A/57/36.
[3] Report of the UN High Commissioner for Human Rights to the UN Commission of Human Rights, E/CN.4/2002/, 18 February 2002.

Chapter 7. Women: The Whole World in Their Hands?

[1] Beijing Conference and Plan of Action 1995, A/CONF.177/2C/Rev.1.
[2] Cairo Conference on Population and Development 1994, A/CONF.171/13/Rev.1.
[3] General Assembly Special Session follow-up to Beijing, 5–9 June 2000, A/Res/S-23/2-3.

Chapter 8. Children: The Future is Now

[1] Graça Machel, *The Impact of War on Children* (London: C. Hurst & Co., 2001).
[2] Declaration at the World Summit for Children, 29–30 September 1990, A/C.3/45/SR.42.
[3] United Nations Children's Fund Executive Director Address at the Special Session for Children, 8–10 May 2002.

Chapter 9. Humanitarian Rescue and On

[1] Javier Pérez de Cuéllar, Annual Report on the Work of the Organization, A/46/1.
[2] Report of the Secretary-General to the Security Council on the Protection of Civilians in Armed Conflict, 8 September 1999, S/1999/957.
[3] Security Council Resolution 1265 (1999) adopted by the Security Council at its 4046th meeting on 17 September 1999, S/1999/957 (1999). Security Council Resolution 1296 (2000) adopted by the Security Council at its 4130th meeting on 19 April 2000, S/RES/1296 (2000).
[4] Secretary-General's annual report to the General Assembly, 20 September 1999, SG/SM/7136/GA/9596.

Chapter 10. People and Poverty

[1] World Bank, *World Development Report 1990: Poverty* (Washington DC: World Bank, 1990), p 3.
[2] UN Department of Economic and Social Affairs and United Nations Conference on Trade and Development, *World Economic Situation and Prospects (2001)* (New York: United Nations, 2001).
[3] Secretary-General's address at an event sponsored by the Rotary Club of Seattle, Washington, 30 November 1999, Press Release SG/SM/7245.
[4] United Nations Ad Hoc Working Group on an Agenda for Development, *Draft of Agenda for Development*, June 1997, A/AC.250.
[5] UNDP, *Human Development Report 1997: Human Development to Eradicate Poverty* (New York: Oxford University Press, 1997).
[6] Secretary-General's address at the Palais des Nations, Geneva, 26 June 2000, UNIS/SG/2601.
[7] UN Millennium Development Summit, *Millennium Declaration*, A/RES/55/2.

Chapter 11. The World Around Us: The Environment

[1] UNEP, *Global Environment Outlook 3*, p 4.
[2] UN Millennium Development Summit, *Millennium Declaration*, A/RES/55/2.

Chapter 12. Nature's Terror: HIV/AIDS

[1] AIDS Epidemic Update, December 2002, UNAIDS/02.46E.
[2] Stephen Lewis's statement as reported in UN Press Release DH/3805, 8 January 2003.

Chapter 13. 'We the Peoples': Civil Society

[1] UN Charter, Article 71.
[2] *Renewing the United Nations: A Programme for Reform*, A/51/950, 14 July 1997.
[3] Kofi Annan's address to the World Economic Forum, Davos, Switzerland, 28 January 2001, SG/SM/7692.
[4] Millennium Summit Declaration, A/RES/55/2.
[5] Message to the World Social Forum delivered by Mr Nitin Desai, Under-Secretary-General for Economic and Social Affairs, Porto Allegre, Brazil, 27 January 2003.

Chapter 14. Mapping, Management, Money

[1] Contributions Paid and Not Paid – 31 December 2002: Note from the Secretariat (unpublished).
[2] Karl Paschke, final report 1999: excerpts from preface, A/54/393.
[3] UN Charter, Article 101.

Chapter 15. The Millennium

[1] *Millennium Declaration*, adopted by the General Assembly, September 2000, A/RES/55/2.
[2] UN round-table discussions at the Millennium Summit, September 2000, A/55/PV.8.
[3] A/55/PV.4.
[4] A/55/PV.7.
[5] A/55/PV.7.
[6] A/55/PV.5.
[7] A/55/PV.14.
[8] A/55/PV.14.
[9] A/55/PV.4.
[10] A/55/PV.8.
[11] A/55/PV.5.
[12] A/55/PV.5.
[13] A/55/PV.12.

14 A/55/PV.22.
15 A/55/PV.15.
16 A/55/PV.3.
17 A/55/PV.15.
18 A/55/PV.3.
19 A/55/PV.4.
20 A/55/PV.5.
21 Security Council Summit Meeting, 7 September 2000, S/PV.4194.
22 Secretary-General's statement at the opening of the General Assembly, September 1999, A/54/PV.4.
23 UN Security Council 55th Annual Report to the General Assembly, covering the period 16 June 1999 to 15 June 2000.

Chapter 16. Into the Twenty-First Century

1 A/57/PV.3.
2 A/57/PV.7.
3 A/57/PV.2.
4 A/57/PV.5.
5 A/57/PV.5.
6 President Bush's address to the General Assembly, 12 September 2002, A/57/PV.2.
7 A/57/PV.3.
8 A/57/PV.5.
9 S/PV/4709.
10 Resolution 1441, S/PV/4644.
11 UNMOVIC report by Hans Blix to the Security Council, 14 February 2003, S/2003/580.

Bibliography

I. General interest and historical origins of the United Nations

Alger, Chadwick F., *The Future of the United Nations System: Potential for the Twenty-First Century* (United Nations University Press, 1998)

Ayton-Shenker, Diana (ed), *A Global Agenda: Current Issues before the General Assembly of the United Nations* (Rowman & Littlefield/UNA-USA, 2002)

Bailey, Sydney Dawson, *The United Nations: A Concise Political Guide* (Barnes & Noble Books, 1995)

Diehl, Paul F., *The Politics of Global Governance: International Organizations in an Interdependent World* (Lynne Reinner Publishers, 2001)

English, John, Andrew Cooper and Ramesh Thakur, *Enhancing Global Governance: Toward a New Diplomacy* (UNU Press, 2003)

Hoopes, Townsend and Douglas Brinkley, *FDR and the Creation of the UN* (Yale University Press, 1997)

International Commission on Intervention and State Sovereignty, *The Responsibility to Protect*, 2 volumes (International Development Research Center (IDRC), 2001)

Knight, W. Andy, *A Changing United Nations, Multilateral Evolution and the Quest for Global Governance* (Palgrave, 2000)

Krasner, Stephen D., *Sovereignty, Organized Hypocrisy* (Princeton University Press, 1999)

Meissler, Stanley, *United Nations: The First Fifty Years* (Atlantic Monthly Press, 1997)

Roberts, Adam and Benedict Kingsbury, *United Nations, Divided World: The UN's Roles in International Relations* (Oxford University Press, 1994)

Russell, Ruth, *A History of the United Nations Charter* (The Brookings Institute, 1958)

Schlesinger, Stephen C., *Act of Creation: The Founding of the United Nations* (Westview Press, 2003)

Simmons, P.J. and Chantal de Jonge Oudraat, *Managing Global Issues: Lessons Learned* (Carnegie Endowment for International Peace, 2001)

Weiss, Thomas G., David P. Forsythe and Roger A. Coate, *The United Nations and Changing World Politics* (Westview Press, 2000)

A. THE GREAT THAW

Clark, Ian, *The Post-Cold War Order: The Spoils of Peace* (Oxford University Press, 2002)

Gaddis, John Lewis, *We Now Know: Rethinking Cold War History* (Oxford University Press, 1998)

Lebow, Richard and Janice Stein. *We All Lost the Cold War* (Princeton University Press, 1994)

Mingst, Karen A., Margaret Karns and George A. Lopez, *The United Nations in the Post-Cold War Era (Dilemmas in World Politics)* (Westview Press, 1995)

B. SECRETARIAT AND SECRETARY-GENERAL

Boutros-Ghali, Boutros, *Unvanquished, A US–UN Saga* (Random House, 1999)

Childers, Erskine and Brian Urquhart, *Renewing the United Nations System* (Hammarskjöld Foundation, 1994)

Commission on Global Governance, *Our Global Neighborhood* (Oxford University Press, 1995)

Glassner, Martin I., *The United Nations at Work* (Praeger, 1998)

Rivlin, Benjamin, *Ralph Bunche: The Man and His Times* (Holmes and Meier, 1990)

Urquhart, Brian, *Hammarskjöld* (Knopf, 1972)

C. MILLENNIUM

Cooper, Richard N. and Richard Layard, *What the Future Holds: Insights from Social Science* (MIT Press, 2003)

Mandelbaum, Michael, *The Ideas That Conquered the World: Peace, Democracy, and Free Markets in the Twenty-First Century* (Public Affairs, 2002)

Nye, Joseph S., *Governance in a Globalizing World* (Brookings Institute Press, 2000)

II. Security

Boulden, Jane, *Peace Enforcement* (Praeger, 2001)

Boutros-Ghali, Boutros, *An Agenda for Peace* (United Nations, 1995)

Brown, Michael E. and Richard N. Rosecrane (eds), *The Costs of Conflict: Prevention and Cure in the Global Arena* (Carnegie Commission on Preventing Deadly Conflict, 1999)

Cousens, Elizabeth, Chetan Kumar and Karin Wermester, *Peacebuilding As Politics: Cultivating Peace in Fragile Societies* (Lynne Reinner, 2000)

Fahey, Joseph and Richard A. Armstrong, *Peace Reader: Essential Readings on War, Justice, Non-Violence and World Order* (Paulist Press, 1987)

Hillen, John F. and Robert B. Oakley, *Blue Helmets: The Strategy of UN Military Operations* (Brassey's Inc., 1998)

Kaldor, M., *New and Old Wars: Organized Violence in a Global Era* (Stanford University Press, 2001)

Krasno, Jean E. and James S. Sutterlin, *The United Nations and Iraq: Defanging the Viper* (Praeger, 2003)

Langholz, Harvey J., *The Psychology of Peacekeeping* (Praeger, 1998)

Otunnu, Olara A. and Michael W. Doyle *Peacemaking and Peacekeeping for the New Century* (Rowman & Littlefield Publishers, 1998)

Ratner, Steven R., *The New United Nations Peacekeeping: Building Peace in Lands of Conflict after the Cold War* (St Martin's Press/Council on Foreign Relations, 1995)

Rogers, Paul, *Losing Control: Global Security in the Twenty-First Century* (Pluto Press, 2000)

Russett, O'Neill and James Sutterlin, *The Once and Future Security Council* (St Martin's Press, 1996)

Shawcross, William, *Deliver Us from Evil: Peacekeepers, Warlords, and a World of Endless Conflict* (Simon and Schuster, 2000)

Walzer, Michael, *Just and Unjust Wars* (Basic Books, 1977)

A. TERRORISM AND 9/11

Friedman, Thomas L., *Longitudes and Attitudes: Exploring the World after September 11* (Farrar, Strauss, Giroux, 2002)

Lewis, Bernard, *The Crisis of Islam: Holy War and Unholy Terror* (Modern Library, 2003)

Reich, Walter and Walter Lacquer, *Origins of Terrorism: Psychologies, Ideologies, Theologies, States of Mind* (Woodrow Wilson Center Press, 1998)

Rose, Gideon and James F. Hoge, Jr., *How Did This Happen? Terrorism and the New War* (Public Affairs, 2001)

Zinn, Howard and Anthony Arnove, *Terrorism and War* (Seven Stories Press, 2002)

B. DISARMAMENT

Cirincione, Joseph, Jon B. Wolfsthal and Miriam Rajkumar, *Deadly Arsenals: Tracking Weapons of Mass Destruction* (Carnegie Endowment for International Peace, 2002)

Graham, Thomas J., *Disarmament Sketches: Three Decades of Arms Control and International Law* (University of Washington, 2002)

Lennon, Alexander T.J., *Contemporary Nuclear Debates: Missile Defenses, Arms Control, and Arms Races in the Twenty-First Century* (MIT Press, 2002)

SIPRI Yearbook 2002: Armaments, Disarmament and International Security (Stockholm International Peace Research Institute/Oxford University Press, 2002)

III. War crimes

Bass, Gary Jonathan, *Stay the Hand of Vengeance: The Politics of War Crimes Tribunals* (Princeton University Press, 2000)

Goldstone, Richard J., *For Humanity: Reflections of a War Crimes Investigator* (Yale University Press, 2000)

Hayner, Priscilla B., *Unspeakable Truths: Confronting State Terror and Atrocities* (Routledge, 2002)

Ratner, Steven R. and Jason S. Abrams, *Accountability for Human Rights Atrocities in International Law: Beyond the Nuremberg Legacy*, 2nd edition (Oxford University Press, 2001)

Robertson, Geoffrey and Kenneth Roth, *Crimes against Humanity: The Struggle for Global Justice* (New Press, 2003)

Schabas, William A., *An Introduction to the International Criminal Court* (Cambridge University Press, 2001)

IV. Human rights

Alston, Philip, et al, *International Human Rights in Context: Law, Politics, Morals* (Oxford University Press, 1996)

Amnesty International, *Amnesty International Annual Report* (Amnesty International, 2002)

An-Na'Im, Abdullahi Ahmed, *Human Rights in Cross-Cultural Perspectives: A Quest for Consensus* (University of Pennsylvania Press, 1995)

Brysk, Alison, *Globalization and Human Rights* (University of California Press, 2002)
Buergenthal, Thomas, et al, *International Human Rights in a Nutshell* (West Law School, 2002)
Flood, Patrick J. *The Effectiveness of UN Human Rights Institutions* (Praeger, 1999)
Laber, Jeri, *The Courage of Strangers: Coming of Age with the Human Rights Movement* (Public Affairs, 2002)
Neier, Aryeh, *Taking Liberties: Four Decades in the Struggle for Rights* (Public Affairs, 2003)

A. WOMEN

Agosin, Marjorie, *Women, Gender, and Human Rights: A Global Perspective* (Rutgers University Press, 2001)
Cook, Rebecca J., *Human Rights of Women: National and International Perspectives* (University of Pennsylvania Press, 1994)
Goldstein, Joshua S., *War and Gender* (Cambridge University Press, 2001)
Peterson, V. Spike and Anne Sisson Runyan, *Global Gender Issues* (Westview Press, 1999)
Pietila, Hilkka, *Making Women Matter: The Role of the United Nations* (Zed Books, 1994)
Snyder, Margaret, *Transforming Development: Women, Poverty and Politics* (Women's Ink, 1995)
Winslow, Anne, *Women, Politics, and the United Nations* (Greenwood Press, 1995)

B. CHILDREN

Alston, Philip, *The Best Interests of the Child: Reconciling Culture and Human Rights* (Clarendon Press, 1997)
Andrews, Arlene Bowers and Natalie Hevener Kaufman, *Implementing the UN Convention on the Rights of the Child* (Praeger, 1999)
Beigbeder, Yves, *New Challenges for UNICEF: Children, Women, and Human Rights* (Palgrave Macmillan, 2002)
Goodwin-Gill, Guy and S. Ilene Cohn, *Child Soldiers: A Study on Behalf of the Henry Dunant Institute* (Oxford University Press, 1994)
Haspels, Nelien and Michele Jankanish, International Labour Organization, *Action against Child Labour* (Brookings Institute, 2000)
Machel, Graça, *The Impact of War on Children* (C. Hurst & Co., 2001)

Mower, A. Glenn, *The Convention on the Rights of the Child: International Law Support for Children (Studies in Human Rights)* (Greenwood Publishing Group, 1997)

Smith, Anne, Kate Marshall and Karen Nairn, *Advocating for Children: International Perspectives on Children's Rights* (University of Otago Press, 2000)

UNICEF, *The State of the World's Children* (annual publication)

V. Humanitarian aid

Commission on Global Governance, *Our Global Neighborhood* (Oxford University Press, 1995)

Helton, Arthur C., *The Price of Indifference: Refugees and Humanitarian Action in the New Century* (Oxford University Press, 2002)

Loescher, Gil, *Beyond Charity: International Cooperation and the Global Refugee Crisis* (Oxford University Press, 1993)

Macrae, J., *Aiding Recovery?: The Crisis of Aid in Chronic Political Emergencies.* (Zed Books, 2001)

Minear, Larry, et al, *The Humanitarian Enterprise: Dilemmas and Discoveries* (Kumarian Press, 2002)

O'Hanlon, Michael, *Saving Lives with Force: Military Criteria for Humanitarian Intervention* (Brookings Institute, 1997)

Rieff, David, *A Bed for the Night: Humanitarianism in Crisis* (Simon and Schuster, 2002)

Terry, Fiona, *Condemned to Repeat?: The Paradox of Humanitarian Action* (Cornell University Press, 2002)

Wheeler, Nicholas J., *Saving Strangers: Humanitarian Intervention in International Society* (Oxford University Press, 2003)

VI. Globalization and poverty

Emmerij, Louis, Richard Jolly and Thomas Weiss, *Ahead of the Curve?: UN Ideas and Global Challenges* (Indiana, 2001)

Friedman, Thomas L., *The Lexus and the Olive Tree: Understanding Globalization* (Anchor Books, 2000)

Gardner, G. and Brian Halweil, *Underfed and Overfed: The Global Epidemic of Malnutrition* (World Watch Institute, 2000)

Gilpin, Robert and Jean M. Gilpin, *Global Political Economy: Understanding the International Economic Order* (Princeton University Press, 2001)

Harrison, Paul, *Inside the Third World: The Anatomy of Poverty* (Penguin Books, 1993)
Kaul, Inge, *Providing Global Public Goods: Managing Globalization* (Oxford University Press, 2003)
Sen, Amartya, *Development as Freedom* (Oxford University Press, 2001)
Stiglitz, Joseph E., *Globalization and its Discontents* (W.W. Norton & Company, 2002)
UNDP, *Human Development Report* (annual publication)
World Bank, *World Development Report 2003: Sustainable Development in a Dynamic World: Transforming Institutions, Growth, and Quality of Life* (World Bank, 2003) (annual publication)
World Watch, *Vital Signs 2002: The Trends That Are Shaping Our Future* (W.W. Norton, 2002)

VII. Health and HIV/AIDS

Garrett, Laurie, *The Coming Plague: Newly Emerging Diseases in a World Out of Balance* (Penguin, 1995)
Irwin, Alexander, Joyce Millen and Dorothy Fallows. *Global AIDS: Myths & Facts* (Southend Press, 2003)
Mann, Jonathan, et al, *Health and Human Rights: A Reader* (Routledge, 1999)
Stine, Gerald, J. *AIDS Update 2003* (Benjamin/Cummings, 2002)

VIII. Environment

Bertell, Rosalie, *Planet Earth: The Latest Weapon of War* (Black Rose Books, 2003)
Brown, Lester R., *Eco-Economy: Building an Economy for the Earth* (W.W. Norton & Company 2001)
Guha, Ramachandra, *Environmentalism: A Global History* (Addison-Wesley, 1999)
Middleton, Nick, *The Global Casino: An Introduction to Environmental Issues*, 2nd edition (Edward Arnold, 1999)
Panjabi, Ranee K.L. and Arthur Campeau, *The Earth Summit at Rio: Politics, Economics, and the Environment* (Northeastern, 1997)
World Watch, *State of the World 2003* (W.W. Norton & Company, 2003) (annual publication)
World Watch, *Vital Signs 2001: Environmental Trends That Are Shaping Our Future* (W.W. Norton & Company, 2001)

IX. Civil society

Civicus, *Civil Society at the Millennium* (Kumarian, 1999)

Hudock, Ann C., *NGOs and Civil Society: Democracy by Proxy?* (Blackwell, 1999)

Kaldor, Mary, *Global Civil Society: An Answer to War* (Polity Press, 2003)

Keane, John, *Global Civil Society?* (Cambridge University Press, 2003)

Laxer, Gordon and Sandra Halperin, *Global Civil Society and its Limits* (Palgrave Macmillan, 2003)

Paolini, Albert J., et al, *Between Sovereignty and Global Governance: The United Nations, the State and Civil Society* (Palgrave Macmillan, 1998)

Salamon, Lester M., et al, *Global Civil Society: Dimensions of the Nonprofit Sector* (Center for Civil Society Studies, 1999)

Walzer, Michael, *Toward a Global Civil Society* (Berghahn Books, 1998)

Index

abbreviations and acronyms for UN agencies, programmes, etc., vi
access to markets to fight poverty, 143
accountability of
    governance, demanded by civil society, 121
    governments, precondition for economic growth, 102
    international financial institutions, 98, 101
    UN functions and activities, 133, 134, 137
Accountability Panel, 133
accredited NGOs, 120
Ad Hoc Tribunals on war crimes *see* war crimes tribunals
Addams, Jane, WILPF, 68
Advisory Board in Disarmament, 26
Afghanistan, xxi, 23, 48, 159, 160
    emergency aid to, 96
    human rights in, 63, 66
    nation-building and social reconstruction in, 18, 160–161
    peacekeeping in, 15
    sanctions in, 9
    Security Council role in (1988), 6
    UN–US military operations in, 17–18
    use of chemical weapons in, by Russia, 31
Africa
    HIV/AIDS, 115, 116, 155
    nuclear-free zone, 36
    poverty in, 97, 144, 147
Africa, Great Lakes and Central Africa: emergency aid to, 95
Africa, South, Region: emergency aid to, 96
Africa, West, 30, 96
Agenda 21, Earth Summit, 112
Agenda for Development (1997), xx
    road map for human development, 104
Agenda for Peace, 7, 9, 10, 104
    supplement, 7–9, 8, 30
Aidid, Mohammed, 12
Al-Qaeda, 17, 160, 163
Alaska oil spill, 110
Albania, 30
Albright, Madeleine, 16
Algeria, 61
Amnesty International, xix, 65, 66, 123
Angola, 5, 9, 15, 16, 95
Annan, Kofi, Secretary-General (1997–), xx, 65, 66, 166
    Africa, report on, 16, 30, 102
    civil society, 121–122, 126–127
    global responsibilities of new power elite, 123
    human development, 104, 105
    humanitarian assistance, 93, 94
    Iraq, 165
    Millennium Summit, 141–142
    role of Secretary-General 'equal parts juggler and mendicant',

130
social impact of trade on developing countries, 102–103
Strengthening of the United Nations: An Agenda for Further Changes, 131–132
terrorism, 41
uncivil society, 125
anthrax, 32
Anti-Ballistic Missile Treaty (ABM), ended by USA, 36, 37, 160
apartheid, 58, 59
Arbour, Louise, Prosecutor, 49
Argentina, 36, 38
armaments, spending on, 118, 135
see also defence spending
armed conflict
children in, 58, 63, 77, 82, 83
local, 92
prevention of, *Agenda for Peace*, 7
protection of women and girls, 75
see also war
armed force
use of, 25
use of, only in common interest: UN Charter, 168
armed forces, as weapons, 27
Armenia/Azerbaijan conflict, 159
arms control, 25–26
against terrorism, 41
arms industry, 28, 55
globalization of, 27
arms race, 24, 25
arrears in UN dues, USA, 136–137
Asia
HIV/AIDS, 116
poverty in southern, 97
assassinations, political, 155
Assembly of States Parties, 46
assessments, member countries, 134
see also contributions of member countries to UN

atomic bomb *see* nuclear weapons
atrocities committed by ordinary citizens, 53–54
Auditors, external: for UN functions and activities, 133
Australia, 17
axis of evil, 164
Axworthy, Lloyd, Foreign Minister, Canada, 152
Ayola-Lasso, José, UN High Commissioner for Human Rights, 62
Azerbaijan/Armenia conflict, 159

Baath party, Iraq, 163
Badawi, Deputy Prime Minister, Malaysia, 158
Baghdad, bombing of UN headquarters (19 August 2003), 40, 140, 166
banks
International Conference on Financing for Development, Mexico (2002), 106
see also international financial system and institutions; World Bank
El Baradei, Mohammed, weapons inspector, 162, 165, 166
Barak, Israel, 156
Basel Convention: dangerous wastes, shipping of, 111
Bellamy, Carol, Executive Director, UNICEF, 89
Bendevik, Prime Minister, Norway, 157
Bertini, Catherine, 136
Bhopal chemical accident, 110
bio-security, 32
biodiversity, 107, 113
convention, 112
biological weapons, 28, 32, 165
NGOs working to control, 122
see also weapons of mass destruction
birthrate, decline in, xvii

black market
  in small arms and firearms, 30, 31
  weapons and terrorism, 40
Blair, Tony, Prime Minister, UK, 154
Blix, Hans, chief weapons inspector, 162, 165, 166
Blue Helmets, 135
  education on human rights, 65
  humanitarian aid, Yugoslavia, 13
bombing of UN headquarters: Baghdad (19 August 2003), xxi, 40, 140, 166
Bosnia, 63
Bosnia-Herzegovina, 13, 51
Bouteflika, Abdilaziz, President, Algeria, 146
Boutros-Ghali, Boutros, Secretary-General, 9–10, 30, 104
  Agenda for Peace, 7
Brahmini, Lakhdar, review of UN peace operations, 5, 19, 147, 153, 154
Brazil, 36
Bretton Woods financial institutions (IMF and World Bank), 61, 100
  see also international financial institutions
Brooks, Angie, President of the General Assembly (1969), 68
budgeting, UN *see* UN Secretariat, budgeting
Burundi, 63, 95
Bush, George Herbert Walker, President, USA, xvi, 1, 3, 6
Bush, George W., President, USA, 107, 160
  nuclear arms reduction, 34
  on invasion of Iraq, xv, *161*
  unsigned Rome Statute for ICJ, 47

Cambodia, 9, 54, 63

civilian targets, 38, 94
  national reconciliation, 153
  role of UN in, 6, 15, 18
Camdessus, Michel, President, IMF, 99
Canada, 107
capital flow, restructuring of, 100, 101
Caribbean: HIV/AIDS, 116
Carlsson, Ingvar: study of UN failure in Rwanda, 19
Cartagena Protocol, 112
Carter, Jimmy, President, USA: human rights in US foreign policy, 62
Caseres, Carlos, 140
Castro, Fidel, President, Cuba: radical reform of UN required to save the world, 149
Central America
  common approach to political stability, economic growth (1987), 6
  national reconciliation, 153
Charter, 4, 10, 67, 119–120, 168–169
Chavez, Hugo, President, Venezuela, 146, 151
Chechnya, 64
chemical accident, Bhopal, India, 110, 113
chemical weapons, 28, 31, 165
  convention, 31, 32
  NGOs working to control, 122
  see also weapons of mass destruction
chemicals as environmental threat, 112, 113
Chernobyl nuclear accident, Ukraine, 110
child as autonomous being, Convention on the Rights of the Child, 81–83
child labour, 82, 84, 123
child mortality, 77, 88
child pornography, prostitution, 63

Child Rights Convention, xix, 58, 64, 81, 88
    Protocol to prohibit sale or prostitution of children, 64
Child Rights Declaration, 81
child soldiers, 64, 77, 83
children
    and HIV/AIDS, 116, 117
    criminal trade in, 55, 58, 77
    health and development, xv, 77, 80, 88
    humanitarian aid to, 88
    in disasters, 144
    in poverty, 77
    in war, 58, 63, 77, 82, 83
    protection of, 81, 83–84, 154
    sexual exploitation of, 63, 64, 82, 83
Children's Forum, 85, 86
Children's Fund *see* UNICEF
China, 23, 29, 38
    expenditures on weapons, 27
    HIV/AIDS, 116
    human rights violations and reforms, 61–62
    humanitarian aid, 91
    nuclear arms and testing, 33, 36
Chirac, Jacques, President, France, 153
Chissano, President, Mozambique, 152
Chrétien, Jean, Prime Minister, Canada, 154
Churchill, Winston, 43
citizen movements and protests, 6, 98, 120, 123
    against US invasion of Iraq, 164
    WTO Ministerial meeting, Seattle (1999), 102–103
    see also NGOs; women's movement
citizen participation, 121
    in Millennium Forum, 145
    see also NGOs
civil society
    demands accountability of governance, 121
    human rights, 60
    in Global Compact, 123
    participation in human development, 130
    precondition for economic growth, 102
    role in World Social Forum, 126–127
    support for International Criminal Court, 44
civilian police in peacekeeping, 19
civilians
    as targets in civil wars, xvii, 5, 9, 21, 45, 93, 154
    in peacekeeping, 16, 20–21
    protection of, 42, 154
    protection of, report on, 62
    see also children, in war
Clark, Helen, New Zealand, 75
Clark, Joe, Foreign Minister, Canada, 3
climate change, 112, 147
Clinton, William, President, USA, 148, 152, 156
    Africa, visit to, 16, 153
    link between deprivation, disease and war, 153
    nuclear arms reduction, 34
    plan to stabilize Yugoslavia, 12–13
Coalition to Ban Land Mines, 29
codes of conduct for scientists, 31
Cold War, 1, 2, 3, 23, 24
    conflict within and among its proxies, 11
    Security Council hobbled during, 6
collateral damage, 8
    see also sanctions
collective security: challenge to, by invasion of Iraq, 166
Commission
    and Centre on Transnational Corporations, 102

on Crime Prevention and
Criminal Justice (ECOSOC),
30, 128
on Development (ECOSOC),
128
on Human Rights (CHR)
(ECOSOC), xix, 56, 58, 65, 66,
128; annual meetings, 59–60;
criticism of violations, 163;
Subcommission to examine
complaints, 65
on Population (ECOSOC), 128
on Sustainable Development,
112, 123
on the Status of Women (CSW)
(1946), 68–70, 128
Commission on Human Rights,
xix, 56, 58, 65, 66, 128
Committee of Experts: to monitor
implementation of Convention
against Racism, 58
Commonwealth of Independent
States (CIS), Treaty on Combating Terrorism, 40, 49
Commonwealth Secretariat, 145
community-based health services,
80
community-building, UNICEF, 78
Comprehensive Test Ban Treaty
(CTBT), 35–36
USA refusal to ratify, 37
Conference
on Disarmament, 26, 35, 36
on Environment and Development (UNCED), 105–106,
107, 110, 111, 123
on the Human Environment,
Stockholm (1972), 109
on Human Rights, xix, 59, 60–61
on Population and Development, Cairo (1994), 73
on Racism, 64
on Security and Cooperation in
Europe, 62
on small arms, illicit trade in,
29, 30–31, 160
on Trade and Development
(UNCTAD), 99, 106, 128
on Women, 70–73
Conference of Presiding Officers
of National Parliaments, 145
conflict prevention, Security
Council, 154
Connor, Joseph, 136
conservation ethic for environmental management, 113
consumerism, 111–112, 114
contingency fund for emergency
aid, 95
contributions of member countries
to UN, 134–136
Convention
against Torture, 58, 64
against Transnational Organized Crime, 30, 55, 126
for the Prevention and Punishment of Terrorism,
International (1937), 38
on Biological Diversity (1993),
112
on Chemical Weapons, 31
on Climate Change, UN
Framework, 112
on Elimination of All Forms of
Discrimination Against
Women, 57–58, 64, 69, 74, 123
on Elimination of All Forms of
Racial Discrimination, 57–58,
64, 69
on International Trade in
Endangered Species (1973),
111
on Migratory Wild Animals
(1979), 111
on Political Rights of Women
(1952), 69
on Prohibitions or Restrictions
on the Use of Inhumane
Weapons, 28–29
on the Prevention and Punishment of the Crime of

Genocide (1948), 44, 57, 58, 64
   on the Protection of the Rights of All Migrant Workers (1990), 58
   on the Rights of the Child, xix, 58, 64, 77, 81; Protocol to prohibit sale or prostitution of children, 64; Protocol to raise age for military service, 64
   on the Safety of UN and Associated Personnel, 140
   on the shipping of dangerous wastes, Basel, 111
   on Wetlands (1971), 111
   to Control Biological Weapons (1975), 32
conventional weapons, SSOD I, 27
   see also firearms; illicit arms; inhumane weapons; small arms
convergence
   government and citizen agendas, 103–104
   in UN development programmes (UNDAF), 132–133
   of women's rights, development, the environment, 73
co-operative security, 3
core function expenses, UN, 134, 136
Corell, Hans, UN Legal Counsel, 44–45
corporate citizenship, 124
Country Co-ordinator, 132
Covenant
   on Civil and Political Rights, 57, 64
   on Civil and Political Rights, Protocols, 58, 64
   on Economic, Social and Cultural Rights, 57
Crime and Justice Commission, 128
crimes against humanity, 45
   Nuremberg Tribunal, 43
criminal wealth, 125
Croatia, 12, 63, 158

CTBT see Comprehensive Test Ban Treaty
Cyprus, 15, 23, 159
Czechoslovakia, 1

Dallaire, Romeo, Gen., 14
dangerous wastes, 111, 112
   see also toxic wastes
Davos Forum see World Economic Forum
Dayton Accords, 13
death penalty, 45, 58, 158
debt burden, 101–102, 106, 123, 147, 150, 154
   move by Germany to lift, 150
debt relief
   to attack poverty, 143
   see also Jubilee 2000
Decade for Women (1976–1985), 70
Decade on Natural Disasters, 93
Declaration
   Beijing Conference on Women, and Platform for Action, 72–73, 75
   of the Establishment of a New Economic Order, 99
   on Human Rights Defenders, 64
   of Measures to Eliminate International Terrorism, 38
   on the Right to Development ('the right to get rich'), 59
   on the Survival, Protection and Development of Children, 81
defence spending, 118, 135
Del Ponte, Carla, 49, 52
   role of the tribunals in bringing justice, 53–54
Democratic Republic of the Congo (DRC), 14, 16–17, 63, 83–84, 95, 135
   Security Council mission to, 5
   UN mediation in, 15
Deng Xiao Ping, 59, 100
Desert Storm, 11

desertification, 112
developing countries, 99
development
    and environment, 105, 109, 111
    and peace interrelated, 9
    and poverty, 76, 143
    based on human rights, 65
    Commission on, 128
    involvement of NGOs, 120
    'right to get rich', 59
development aid, to attack poverty, 147
Development Co-operation, functional grouping within UN, 132
Dhanapala, Jayantha, Director, Department of Disarmament Affairs, 26
    NPT Review Conference (1995), 35
diamond trade, 16, 17, 18, 125, 153
diplomacy as road to peace, xiv
diplomacy, preventive, 7, 8
disabled persons, human rights abuses, 63
disarmament, xviii, 6,
    Conference, 26, 35, 36
    conventions and treaties, 28–29, 29
    role of General Assembly, 25–26
    role of NGOs, 122
    SSOD I (1978), 27
    structures, 25–27
disarmament centres, regional, 26
Disarmament Commission, 26
disaster relief outside UN, 95
discrimination
    against: migrants, 58; women, 69
    Subcommission of Experts on Prevention of Discrimination and Protection of Minorities, 59
discriminatory trade agreements, 123

disease
    childhood, xv, 77, 80, 88
    transnational, 155
    underlying cause of conflict, 154
displaced persons, 63, 93
domestic conflict
    not foreseen in UN Charter, 10
    UN efforts to end, 5
    see also civilians, as targets
donations to UN
    by Ted Turner, 125, 136
    for humanitarian causes, 95, 96
    see also contributions of member countries to UN
drinking water, 85
drug trade, 153
    criminal wealth, 125
    exploitation of children in, 82
    related to terrorism, 40
drugs, 55
    access to affordable, 143, 147
    AIDS treatment, 117

Earth Summit, Rio de Janeiro, 110, 111
earthquakes, 110
East Timor, xviii, 17
    see also Timor-Leste
East Timor/Indonesia, Security Council mission to, 5
Economic and Social Affairs, functional grouping within UN administration, 132
Economic and Social Council (ECOSOC), 56, 128
    consultation with NGOs, 119–120
    subcommission on Minorities, 59
    see also Commissions
economic contribution of women, 70
economic growth
    people-centred, advocated by NGOs, 123

preconditions for, 102
Economic Security Council, 147
education, 84, 85
    basic development need, 97, 147
    equal access for boys and girls, 77
    as human right, 66
    HIV/AIDS, 117
    right of children to, 82
    UNICEF, 79, 80
education, environmental, 109
education, primary, 77, 85
    Millennium Declaration, 143
    Special Session on Children, 87, 88
Egypt, 4, 23, 32
El Salvador, 6
elections in troubled countries, 6, 15, 17
emergencies, silent: poor and unstable countries, 95
emergency relief aid, 91, 92
    UNICEF, 86
Emergency Relief Coordinator, 92–93
endangered species, 111
energy sources, 110
    renewable, 107, 112, 113
environment
    as basic human right, 109
    conservation ethic, 112
    disasters, 110
    goals, Millennium Declaration, 144
    human, conference, 109
    problems worst in poor countries, 105
    protection of, for children, 84, 85, 87
    respect for, by international corporations, 113, 124
environment and development: conferences (UNCED), 105–106, 107, 123
environmentally friendly technologies, 124
equality, treatment of children, 85
Equatorial Guinea, 63
Eritrea, 15, 95
erosion, land, 114
Estrada, President, Philippines, 155
Ethiopia, 15
Ethiopia-Eritrea, 135, 158
ethnic cleansing, 13
Europe, 91, 96
    HIV/AIDS, 116
European Commission, 145
European Union, 145
    financial support for the UN, 135
    funding, promise of: International Conference on Financing for Development, Mexico (2002), 107
expenditures on weapons, 27
Exxon Valdez oil spill, 110

family environment, right of children to, 82
family planning, 84, 97
famine, as a political crime, 93
FAO (Food and Agricultural Organization), 134
Federal Yugoslavia (Serbia), 63
    see also Serbia
financial support for terrorism, 40
firearms, 30
    see also small arms
First Committee, 35
    disarmament, 25–26
Fischer, Joschka, Foreign Minister, Germany, 150
fish stocks and fisheries, 107, 111, 112, 113
food and nutrition, 80, 85, 88
    to fight poverty, 97
food as a human right, 66
foreign debt, 66
forests, maintenance of, 112, 113
France, 23, 168

expenditures on weapons, 27
nuclear arms, 33, 36
support of Iraq, 11
Frechette, Louise, Deputy Secretary-General, xx, 75, 133
    safety of UN workers as 'moving targets', 139, 140
Fujimori, President, Peru, 155
fund-raising for emergency aid, 95
funding of UN activities
    by member countries, 107, 134–136
    fight against HIV/AIDS, 117–118
    proposals for UN, 137

G7, 145
General Assembly, 92–93, 128, 157
    children at war, 83
    debate about external assistance, 102
    disarmament structures, treaties and conferences, 25–27
    Nuremberg principles, endorsement of, 43
    establishment of international criminal court, by treaty, 44
    Millennium Summit (2000), 144–152
    programmes and funds, 128–129
    terrorism, action against, 41
    weapons of mass destruction, elimination of, 33, 161
genetically-modified organisms, 112
Geneva Conference on Disarmament, 29
Geneva Conventions, 42
Geneva Declaration, 81
Genoa peace marches, xv, 123
genocide, 44
    Bosnia, 12
    Convention on, 44, 57, 58, 64
    Rwanda, 14

war crimes tribunals, 75
Georgia, 15
Georgia/Russia conflict, 159
Germany, 150
global civil ethic, 101
Global Compact, 66, 113, 123–127
    website: www.globalcompact.org, 124
Global Fund against HIV/AIDS, Tuberculosis and Malaria, 118
global warming, 114
globalization, 100–101
    arms industry, 27
    central challenge to serving the poor, 142
    humanization of, 150
    and poverty, 123, 126, 147, 149, 150
    UN priority, 131
Goh Chok Tong, Prime Minister, Singapore, 146, 150
Goldstone, Richard, Prosecutor, 49
Gorbachev, Mikhail, USSR, 62
governance
    good, precondition for economic growth, 102
    poor, underlying cause of conflict, 154
governments
    accountability of, demanded by civil society, 121
    infiltration by criminal wealth, 125
grant aid (Official Development Assistance, ODA), 102, 105
Grant, James (Jim), UNICEF, 80, 85, 86, 95, 115
greenhouse gas emissions, 107–108, 112
Group of 77, 99, 102, 123, 145
Group of Experts, ad hoc: to examine complaints of torture against South Africa, 58–59
Guatemala, 6, 15, 158
Guinea, 95

Gulf War (1991), 159
gun lobby, 31
guns, criminal wealth from illicit trade in, 125

The Hague Appeal for Peace (1998), 122
The Hague Peace Conference (1902), 66, 67
The Hague, world courts, 46
Haiti, 9, 15, 63
Halonen, Tarja, President, Finland, 75, 141
Hasina, Shekh, Prime Minister, Bangladesh, 155
Havel, Václav, President, Czechoslovakia: proposed UN with 2 parallel assemblies, 151
health promotion, 104
health services, 80
    for children, 82
    to fight poverty, 97
    see also immunizations
Heyzer, Norleen, UNIFEM, 69–70, 71
High Commissioner for Human Rights (HCHR), 61, 62
High Commissioner for Refugees (UNHCR), 91, 134
Hiroshima, US bombing of, 24
HIV/AIDS, 115, 117, 118, 147
    and children, 77, 87, 88
    humanitarian intervention by UN, 151
    prevention, 117, 143
    as source of insecurity, 155
    worst in poor countries, 105
Holbrooke, Richard, xx, 13, 136
housing as human right, 66
human development, xx, 59, 65, 105–106, 107
    Agenda for Development (1997), 104
    Annan, Kofi, 104, 105
Human Development Report (2000), UNDP, 65

human genome map, access to, 144
human insecurity, 5–6
Human Resources Management, Nair, Dileep, 133
human rights, 11, 21, 23, 24, 65, 113, 158, 168
    advocacy linked to action, 63
    conventions and treaties, ratification of, 64
    Global Compact, 124
    monitoring, xix, 65
    reporting overload, 64–65
    UN peace operations, 19, 63
    UN priority, 131, 132, 144
    violations of, 23–24, 61, 63, 151–152, 155; annual review by US State Department, 62; not grounds for overthrow of brutal government, 163; reported at annual meeting of CHR, 60
    see also child rights; Commission on; migrant workers; NGOs; women's rights; Universal Declaration; World Conference
human rights defenders, 66
    declaration, 64
Human Rights Watch, xix, 123
human security, 21, 93, 154
human security and cooperation, conference, 62
Humanitarian Affairs: functional grouping within UN administration, 132
humanitarian aid, 13, 24, 91, 134, 152
    Agenda for Peace, 7
    exploitation of, 94
    for children and mothers, 88
    impartiality of, 91, 94
    in peacekeeping operations, 9, 19
    as substitute for political action, 154
humanitarian emergency aid
    part of long-term national

development, 92, 95
  UN priority, 131
humanitarian intervention
  in civil war, 21
  in internal affairs of countries, 3, 151
  in internal conflict, 90, 94, 102, 104
  for natural disasters, sanctions, HIV/AIDS, 151
humanitarian reconstruction, Afghanistan, 17–18
  see also Kosovo; nation building; Sierra Leone; Timor-Leste
humanitarian workers
  murder of, in West Timor, 153
  security of, 94, 139–140, 154
Humphrey, John, Director, Division of Human Rights, 56, 68–70
Hungary, 1
hunger and malnutrition
  World Summit for Children, 84, 87
  see also food as a human right
Hurd, Douglas, UK Foreign Secretary, 2
Hussein, Saddam, Iraq, 1, 11, 159, 160, 163, 167
Hutu (Rwanda), 14, 51

illicit arms
  conference, 83
  trade in, 29–30
illiteracy, 69, 84, 85
immunizations, 77, 80, 85
  child health, xv, 84, 85
The Impact of War on Children (Machel, Graça), 83
India, 15, 23
  Comprehensive Test Ban Treaty, 36
  HIV/AIDS, 116
  nuclear capability, 34, 37
India/Pakistan conflict, 159
indigenous people, UN Forum for, 64
individual appeal to UN: Covenant on Civil and Political Rights, Protocol, 58
Indonesia, 17, 96, 100
industrial accidents, 110
infant and child mortality, 84, 85, 143
  caused by preventable diseases, xvii
information technology, 104, 150
inhumane weapons: convention on Prohibitions or Restrictions on the Use of, 28–29
inspections for WMD *see* weapons inspections
Inter-Agency Standing Committee (IASC)
  humanitarian action and fund-raising, 92
international aid, 18
International Atomic Energy Agency (IAEA), 162
International Bank for Reconstruction and Development *see* World Bank
International Chamber of Commerce, 121
International Commission on Intervention and State Sovereignty, 152
International Committee of the Red Cross (ICRC), 42, 122, 145, 154
International Confederation of Free Trade Unions (ICFTU), 125
International Conference
  of Free Trade Unions (ICFTU), 124
  on Financing for Development, Mexico (2002), 106, 107
  on Primary Health Care, WHO and UNICEF, Alma Ata (1978), 104
International Court of Justice

(ICJ), 46, 129
  disputes between states, xiv
  opinion on use of nuclear
    weapons, 36
  opposition by USA, 47–48
International Criminal Court
    (ICC), 14, 42, 58
  creation of, by treaty, 44–45
  human rights, xix–xx, 66, 143,
    147, 163
  illicit arms trade, 31
  jurisdiction, 45–46
  opposition to, by USA, 48, 160
  support from: European
    Union, 158; International Law
    Commission, 44; World Federalists, 122
International Criminal Police
    Organization *see* INTERPOL
International Financial Institutions
    (IFI), 129
international financial system and
    institutions, 99, 101, 107, 150
  accountability of, 97
international fraud, 55
International Labour Organization
    (ILO), 82
  Convention on Child Labour,
    123
  Fundamental Principles and
    Rights at Work, 124
international law and judicial
    system, 42, 131
  UN Charter, 168
  see also International Court of
    Justice; International Criminal
    Court
International Law Commission, 44
International Monetary Fund
    (IMF), 61, 98, 99, 105, 106,
    123, 129, 147
  sanctions, 8
international morality, xiv
International Peace Bureau, 122
International Research and Training Institute for the
    Advancement of Women, 70,
    71
international security, xxi, xxii
international trade, USA, 160
INTERPOL, 31, 126
  black market trade in illicit
    arms, 31
intervention in internal affairs of
    sovereign country *see* humanitarian intervention; sovereignty,
    national
Intrahamwe (Rwanda), 51, 52
investment, external, 102, 106
Iran, 23, 164
  chemical weapons used by Iraq,
    32
  human rights, 63
  invasion by Iraq, 11
  Security Council role (1988), 6
Iraq, xxi, 23, 24
  Gulf War (1991), 159
  human rights, 63
  invasion by USA and allies
    (2003), xiv–xv, 160, 162–167
  invasion of Iran, 11; Kuwait, 1–
    2
  overthrow of government not
    contemplated by Security
    Council, 163
  sanctions, 9, 90
  Security Council role (1988), 6
  transfer of authority, 166
  UN role in, xv
  use of chemical weapons, 32
  weapons inspections (1991–
    1998), 11–12
  weapons inspections (2002),
    162
Israel, 4, 23, 48
  nuclear arms, 34
  road map to peace, 15
  withdrawal from Lebanon, 15
Israel/Palestine conflict, xxi, 159

Jackson, Robert, 43
Japan, 135

Jewish underground, use of terror by, 39
Jiang Zemin, President, China, 151, 153
  UN where member states should conduct international relations, 148–149
Joint Inspection Unit, UN system, 133
Jorda, Claude, France, ICC, 47
Jordan, Bill, ICFTU, 124
Jubilee 2000 (citizen's network), 102, 123
judges, International Court of Justice, 46–47
juvenile justice, 82

Kabbah, President, Sierra Leone, 152
Kabila, Laurent, President, Democratic Congo, 155
Kambanda, Jean, President, Rwanda, 52
Kashmir, 15, 23
Kavan, Jan, President, Czech Republic, 157
Kirsch, Philippe, ICC, 44, 47
knowledge revolution, 150
Korea, 23
Korea, People's Democratic Republic of, 96
Kosovo, 13, 65
  nation-building and social reconstruction, xviii, 13, 18
  Security Council, 5, 17
  suppression of, by Milošović, 17
  war crimes tribunal, 49
Kouchner, Bernard, Dr, 18
Krasno, Jean E., *The United Nations and Iraq*, 11
Kuwait, 1–2, 11
Kwasniewski, Aleksander, President, Poland, 146
Kyoto Protocol, 107–108, 112, 113
  opposition by USA, 160

labour
  productive use of, to fight poverty, 97
  rights: fundamental principles and rights at work, ILO Declaration, 124
  standards, 113, 124
bin Laden, Osama, 160
Lamido, President, Nigeria, 149
land mines, xix, 8, 28, 29
  children victims of, 83
Land Mines Treaty, 83, 122
Latin America, 116
Law of the Sea, 111
League of Arab States, 145
League of Nations, xvi, 22, 38, 81
Lebanon, 15
legal status of children, 81–82
Lesotho, 95
Lewis, Stephen, Global Fund against HIV/AIDS, Tuberculosis and Malaria, 118
Li Peng, Premier, China, 6
Liberia, 9, 17, 95
Libya, 9
Lindh, Ana, Foreign Minister, Sweden: developing countries integrated into global economy, 150
literacy, adult, 88
Luxembourg, 106

Macedonia, 14
Machel, Graça, *The Impact of War on Children*, 83
Maciel, Vice-President, Brazil, 149
Major, John, Prime Minister, UK, 6
malaria, stopping spread of, 118, 143
Malawi, 95
Mali, 8, 30
mandate for peace operations, 19–20
Mann, Dr Jonathan, Director for AIDS, WHO, 115

marine environment, 111, 112
marine resources: management of, 111
market economy, 121
    benefit of, 99–100
markets, Northern: opening of, 102
Marshall Plan, 99
mass murder: mass complicity in, 11
maternal mortality, 88, 143
media and the internet in human rights, 60
mediation: in national conflict, 8, 15
mental health: children, 87
Middle East
    outside controls on biological weapons, 32
    weapon-free zone in, urged by 1995 NPT Review Conference, 36
midwife training, 78, 80
migrant workers, protection of the rights of all: Convention, 58
migrants: criminal trade in, 55
migrations of people: AIDS, 116
migratory wild animals: convention, 111
military intervention in Serbia, by NATO, 13
military spending, 96, 106, 118, 135
    annual reporting, 27, 28
Millennium celebrations, xiii
Millennium Declaration, 41, 77, 96, 105, 130, 142–144
Millennium Forum, 126
Millennium Report, 104, 142
Millennium Summit, xx–xxi, 141–142, 144–156
    goal to reverse spread of HIV/AIDS, 117
    HIV/AIDS, reverse spread of, 117
    participation of women, 75
    poverty, eradication of, 96, 105
    support for *Agenda 21*, 112
Milošević, Slobodan, President, Serbia, 12, 50, 53
    war crimes, 13, 17
minorities: Subcommission on Protection of, 59
missile defence, 37
    Star Wars, reactivated by USA, 160
Mitterrand, François President, France, 2, 6
money
    criminal wealth, 55, 125 (*see also* transnational crime)
    flow of, related to terrorism, 40
monitoring
    implementation of Convention against Racism, 58
    of biological weapons, 32
    of women's rights, 69
    prevention of discrimination and protection of minorities, Subcommission of Experts, 59
Montreal Protocol (ozone depletion), 111
mortality rates
    children, 77, 79, 88
    maternal, 79
Moussa, Prime Minister, Egypt: international contract, participation of countries and civil society, 151
Mozambique, 18, 153
multilateralism, xiv–xv, 158
Muslims, Bosnia, 12
Myanmar (Burma), 61, 63

Nair, Dileep, Inspector General, 133, 136
NAM (Non-Aligned Movement), 57, 59, 99, 158
Namibia, 6, 18
nation-building, xviii, 24, 155
    Afghanistan, 17–18; through peace missions, 20
    Kosovo, 13

Sierra Leone, xviii
Timor-Leste, 18, 66
national/War Crimes Tribunal: Sierra Leone, 18
national behaviour, xiv
national elections: UN presence in, 6, 15, 17
national reconciliation, 15, 153
  see also truth and reconciliation
NATO, 2, 34
  bombing of Serbia, 13, 17
natural disasters, 110, 116
  humanitarian intervention by UN, 151
  relief for victims of, 92, 95
natural resources management: key to development, 107, 109, 140
Netherlands, 106
NGO Coalition to Ban Land Mines, 29
NGOs, 106, 120, 121, 122
  against nuclear weapons, 34
  against small arms, 31
  complement to UN programmes, 119, 121–122
  for children's rights, 86
  for disarmament, 26
  human rights monitoring, xix, 60
  impact in humanitarian negotiations, 29
  Millennium Forum, 126
  on UNAIDS coordinating board, 116
  part of Global Compact, 124
  sustainable development, 107
  women's rights, 71
Nicaragua, 6
Nobel Peace Prize
  Addams, Jane, WILPF, 68
  Amnesty International, 66, 123
  NGO Coalition to Ban Land Mines, 29
  Pearson, Lester B., 4
  UN peacekeepers, 6
  UNICEF, 89

Williams, Jody, Ottawa Land Mines Treaty, 122
Non Proliferation Treaty Review Conference (1995), 35
Non-Aligned Movement (NAM), 57, 59, 99, 158
non-governmental organizations see NGOs
Non-Proliferation Treaty (NPT), xviii, 34–36
  Review Conferences, 35, 36
non-state entities (guerrillas and terrorists)
  in black market arms trade, 31
North Korea, 23, 164
North/South dialogue, 100, 147–148
Norway, 106
NPT see Non Proliferation Treaty
nuclear disasters, 110
nuclear scares and accidents, 33
nuclear threat, 142, 160
nuclear weapons, 24, 28, 33
  as deterrents, 34
  Iraq, 165
  opinion of ICJ on use of, 36
  SSOD I, 27
  US position on, xviii–xix, 160
  see also disarmament; weapons of mass destruction
nuclear-free zones, 35
Nujoma, Sam, President, Namibia, 141
Nuremberg Tribunal, 43
nutrition see food and nutrition

OAS treaty: controls on small arms in the Americas, 30
Obasanjo, President of Nigeria, 149, 150
Ocampo, Moreno, Prosecutor, ICC, 47
OECD, 105
Office of Internal Oversight (OIOS)
  monitoring of UN functions,

activities, 133
Official Development Assistance (ODA), 102, 106
   external aid for poorest countries, 105–106
oil resources, 11
   war for profit, 125
oil spills, 110
ombudsman for UN staff, 132, 133–134, 139
Operation Afghanistan, 161
Organization of Africa Unity (OAU)
   terrorism convention, 40
Organization of American States (OAS)
   Inter-American Convention on the Granting of Rights to Women (1948), 69
Organization of the Islamic Conference (OIC), 145
   terrorism convention, 40
organized crime
   Convention on, 126
   see also transnational crime
Ottawa Treaty to Abolish Land Mines, xix, 29, 83, 122
outlaw regimes, 161
outreach programme: by War Crimes Tribunals, 50, 52
oversight body for treaty implementation: Committee of Experts, 58
ozone layer: threat to, 111
   see also greenhouse gas emissions

Pace, William, World Federalists, 122
Pakistan, 15, 23
   nuclear capacity, 34, 37
   recognition of Taliban regime, 160
Pakistan/India conflict, 159
Palestine, 15, 39, 63
Palestine/Israel conflict, 159
Pandit, Vijaya Lakshmi, President of the General Assembly (1953), 68
Paschke, Karl, Inspector General, 133, 136, 137–138
Pastrana, President, Colombia: humanization of globalization, 150
peace
   and development interrelated, 9
   goal of UN, xvi, 4, 131, 132, 168
Peace and Security: functional grouping within UN administration, 132
peace building, 19–20, 20, 75, 142, 166
   Agenda for Peace, 7
   need for clear mandate, resources, 20
peace marches, xv
   see also citizen movements and protests
peace operations, xviii, 4, 5, 8, 14–17, 23, 75, 142
   budget, xvii, 7, 134–136
   child protection officers in, 83
   human rights experts in, 65
   humanitarian aid, 9
   mandate of, 19–20
   organization and personnel, 20
   reimbursement of participating countries, 21
   support for nation-building and protection of human rights, 63, 155
peacekeepers, xviii
   killed in peace missions, 15
   military and civilian, 15–16
   Nobel prize, 6
   training of, 9
peacekeeping vs peace enforcement, 8
peacemaking
   for human rather than state security, 16

Millennium Report, 20–21
Pearson Commission, 106
Pearson, Lester B., 106
    Nobel Peace Prize, 4
people smuggling, 55
people's courts, Rwanda, 52–53
People's Democratic Republic of Korea, 96
People's Liberation Army (PLA), 27
Pérez de Cuéllar, Secretary-General, 92, 121
PERM 5, Security Council, xvi, 22, 128
    action in Iraq, 166
    members' share of peacekeeping budget, 134
    support for *Agenda for Peace*, 9
    support for war crimes tribunals, 49
Pillay, Nawanathem, South Africa, judge, ICC, 47, 49
Piqué, Foreign Minister, Spain, 151–152
Pol Pot, 38
Poland, 1, 158
polio, xvii
political assassinations, 155
political life: women in, 70, 71, 75, 76
political scandal, 155–156
pollution control, 109, 114
    marine environment, 111
population, xvii
    and family planning, 73
    Commission on, 128
    conferences in Budapest (1974), Mexico (1980), Cairo (1994), 73
Population Fund, 103
Portillo, President, Guatemala, 152
post-war reconstruction: investment by World Bank, 99
poverty, 131
    absolute, 97
    affront to our common humanity (Kofi Annan), 105
    as a political problem, 98
    children, 77, World Summit, 84, 85
    conflict, underlying cause of, 147, 154
    eradication of, 6–7, 21, 63, 66, 85, 108; Africa, 144; International Conference on Financing for Development, Mexico (2002), 106; Millennium Declaration, Summit, 142, 143, 147; UN strategy for world financial institutions, 103; UNDP reports on Human Development (1997), 104
    globalization, cause of, 150
    women in, 70, 71, 72, 75
Powell, Colin, Secretary of State, USA, 165, 166
pre-emption, US doctrine of, 37, 160
preventable diseases, 88
    of children, 77
    World Summit for Children, 84, 85
preventive diplomacy, 8
preventive UN troop deployment, 7
primary education *see* education, primary
primary health care *see* health services
prisoners, treatment of: Geneva Conventions, 42
Promised Land, Manila, 98
prostitution, 116
protocol, 170
public health
    goals for children, 85
    role of UNICEF, 79–80
public life, women in, 71
Putin, Vladimir, President, Russia, 148
    Security Council authority to

sanction military intervention, 153

Quan Quichen, Foreign Minister, China: intervention in internal affairs of countries, 2–3

racism and xenophobia, 63
rape
    as genocide, 74
    as war crime, 49, 52, 83
Rasmussen, Prime Minister, Denmark, 149, 158
reconciliation: national, mediation of, by UN, 153
reform
    of Security Council, 22, 158
    of UN, 128, 148, 151
refugees, 91–92, 134
    Millennium Declaration, 144
    protection of, 154
regime change, 163, 164, 165
rehabilitation: as development aid, 78, 91, 95, 99
relief: as emergency aid, 91
relief corridors for children during war, 84
religious intolerance, 63
renewable energy, 107
    see energy sources, renewable
resources distribution, 114
Rhodesia, 8
Rio Conference on Environment and Development *see* Conference on Environment and Development
road map to peace: Israel and Palestine, 15
Robinson, Mary, UN High Commissioner for Human Rights, 62, 66
Romania, 1
Rome Statute, 47
    attacks on humanitarian workers and peacekeepers considered war crimes, 140
    setting up the International Criminal Court, 44, 46–48
Roosevelt, Eleanor, 68
    chairman, Commission on Human Rights, 56
Roosevelt, Franklin Delano, xvi
Roosevelt, Theodore, 43
root causes of war, 24
rules of engagement, 19
Russia, 27
    chemical weapons in Afghanistan, 32
    devastation of civilian Chechnya, 64
    expenditures on weapons, 27
    Kyoto Protocol, 112
    nuclear weapons, 34, 37
Russia/Georgia conflict, 159
Rwanda, xviii, 5, 9
    atrocities in civil war, 14, 51, 63
    civilian targets, 94
    peacekeeping, 7–8
    Security Council intervention, 14

safe haven
    for terrorists, 40
    Srebrenica, 13
sale, prostitution of children: Convention on Rights of the Child, 64
sanctions, 16, 21, 90, 143, 155
    cause of suffering, 9
    humanitarian intervention by UN, 151
    Iraq, 159, 162
    to target running wars, 8–9
Sarajevo, 13
Saudi Arabia, 160
Save the Children organizations, 81
Savimbi, Jonas, 15, 16
scale of assessments of member countries, 134
scandal, political, 155–156
SCUD missiles, 162, 165

Seattle peace marches, xv, 123
Secretariat, UN *see* UN Secretariat
Secretary-General
role: 'equal parts juggler and mendicant', 130
see also names of Secretary-Generals
Security Council, 22–24, 154–156, 162, 170
Agenda for Peace, 10
children at war, 83
condemnation for attack on World Trade Centre, 11 September 2001, 40
deliberations on Iraq, 165–166
failure to act in Rwanda, 14
mediator in domestic conflicts, 23–24
membership, 22, 128, 155
missions, 5
NATO bombing of Serbia challenge to authority of, 17
nuclear arms reduction, 33
open meetings on Women, Peace and Security, 75
peacekeeping, 5–10, 19, 153, 154, 155
peacemaking for human rather than state security, 16, 93, 154
PERM 5, xvi
reaction to invasion of Kuwait, 1, 2
reform, 151, 158
Special Committee on Terrorism, 40
summit (1992), 5–6
veto, 147
war crimes tribunals, 14, 48–55
Sen, Amartya, *Development as Freedom*, 65
September 11, 2001, xxi, 39–40, 157
Serbia, 12
Shevardnadze, Eduard, xvi, 2, 148
Sierra Leone, 9, 64, 65, 135, 158–159

child protection in peacekeeping, 83–84
diamond trade, 17, 18
emergency aid to, 95
nation-building in, xviii
national/international war crimes tribunal, 18, 54
peace and reconciliation, 15, 18, 66
Security Council mission to, 5
slavery, child, 83
small arms, 25, 26, 28, 125
black market in, xix, 16, 31, 142, 143
civilian casualties of, 29–30, 31
controls on, 26, 30, 83
limit on sales to non-state entities, opposed by USA, 31
trade in, 8, 29, 30, 125, 153
see also firearms
Snyder, Margaret, International Research and Training Institute for the Advancement of Women, 70
social delivery systems, 106
social development, 97
role of UNICEF in, 78
see also human development; rehabilitation
social impact of trade on poor countries, 102–103
social peace: precondition for economic growth, 102
social planning, 78–79
social reconstruction, 18
Somalia, 9, 24, 63
emergency aid to, 95
humanitarian aid, as substitute for political action, 154
humanitarian crisis, 12
peacekeeping, 7–8; US retreat from UN operations, 12
South Africa, 6, 8–9
South America, 36
South Pacific, 36
Southern Africa Development

Community, 70
Sovereign Military Order of Malta, 145
sovereignty, national
　limits to, UN membership, 11
　rationale for intervention: threat to international peace, human rights, 23–24
　respect for, 3, 21, 151, 153, 155
Special Rapporteurs (expert inspectors)
　apartheid, 59
　human rights, 63, 64
Special Session
　on AIDS (2001), 116, 117
　on Children (2002), 86
　on Disarmament, (SSOD 1, 1978), 27
species loss, 113
Srebrenica, xviii, 13, 19
Sri Lanka, 39
SSOD1 (1978), 27
Stalin, Josef, 38, 43
stand-by peacekeepers, 8
standard of living, 98
START I, 33
State of the World's Children, UNICEF (1992), 86
state sovereignty: respect for, 151, 153, 155
stateless terrorism, 11
states parties, 170
Steiner, Michael, 18
stewardship ethic, 112
Stockholm Declaration of Principles and Plan of Action, 109
Strategic Arms Reduction Treaty (START I), 33
Strengthening of the United Nations: An Agenda for Further Changes: Annan, Kofi, 131–132
Subcommission of Experts on Prevention of Discrimination and Protection of Minorities, 59
Sudan, 9, 63, 96

humanitarian aid, as substitute for political action, 154
humanitarian intervention, exploitation of, 94
Suez crisis, 4, 6, 23
suicide attacks, 163
summitry, 6
　heads of state and citizens, 1990s, 103
survival agenda, 37
sustainable consumption, 107, 112, 113
sustainable development, 109, 111–112
　Commission on, 123
　UN priority, 131
sustainable production, 113
Sutterlin, James S., xi–xii
　The United Nations and Iraq, 11
Swaziland, 96
Sweden, 106
Syria, 61

tactical nuclear weapons, 34
Tajikistan, 15, 153
　emergency aid to, 96
Taliban regime, 17, 160
Tang Jiaxuan, Minister of Foreign Affairs, China, 164–165
　intervention by UN, in internal affairs of countries, betrayal of human rights cause, 151
Taylor, Charles, 16, 18
Taylor, Telford, 43
terror, use of, by contemporary totalitarian regimes, 38–39
terrorism, xxi–xxii, 66, 131, 158, 159, 161
　as a source of instability, 147
　financial support for, 40
　incubators of, 160
　international convention (1937), 38
　no religion preaches terrorism, 164
　Security Council focus, 24

September 11, 2001, 15, 38–39, 160
  suicide attacks, 163
  UN conventions, 38, 39, 40
  used to justify invasion of Iraq, 164
Terrorism, Special Committee on, 40
terrorism, stateless, 11
third world debt *see* debt burden
Three Mile Island nuclear disaster, USA, 110
timber: war for profit, 125
Timor-Leste, xviii, 17, 48, 64, 65
  social reconstruction, 18, 66
TNCs *see* transnational corporations
Tokyo war criminals trials, 43
torture, 58–59, 83
toxic wastes, illicit moving and dumping, 63
trade
  agreements, discriminatory, 123
  in people, 125
  social impact of, 103
trade and aid, 102
  to boost developing nations, 99
trade in drugs, small arms, diamond: *see* drugs, trade in; small arms, trade in; diamonds, trade in
trade tariffs, 102–103, 106
transnational corporations, 102, 125
  as reincarnation of economic imperialism, 123
  environmental protection, 113
transnational crime, 30, 55
  as a source of instability, 147
  organized, convention against, 55
  related to terrorism, 40
transnational disease, 155
transnational trade, small arms, 30
Treaty
  Anti-Ballistic Missile (ABM), 36, 37
  on Combating Terrorism, Commonwealth of Independent States (CIS), 40
treaty, 170
Trusteeship Council, 128
truth and reconciliation, 153
  Sierra Leone, 18, 54
  South Africa, 54
Turkey, 61
Turner, Ted, 136
  donation to UN, 125
Tutsi, 51

Uganda, 96
UK
  expenditures on weapons, 27
  invasion of Iraq, 159
  nuclear arms, 33
  Suez crisis, 23
Ukraine, Chernobyl nuclear accident, 110
The United Nations and Iraq, 11
UN
  administration: functional groupings, 132
  diplomatic missions, 16
  failure in Rwanda and Srebrenica, 19
  members and membership: legal commitment related to use of force, 21–22
  personnel: intelligence, planning and support staff, 18–19; safety of, 140; senior diplomats, back-up field staff, 8
UN Advisory Board in Disarmament, 26
UN Centre for Human Settlements (HABITAT), 129
UN Development Assistance Framework (UNDAF), 132–133
UN Development Fund for Women (UNIFEM), 69–70, 71, 128

UN Development Program
(UNDP), 70, 103, 106, 128, 134
reports on Human Development, 104
UN Environment Programme
(UNEP), 103, 110, 112, 113, 128, 134
UN Forum for Indigenous People
(2000), 64
UN High Commissioner for
Refugees (UNHCR), 91, 134
human security, 154
UN Information Technology
Service, 104
UN Institute for Disarmament
Research, 26, 30
UN Population Fund (UNFPA)
(1969), 129, 134
UN Register of Conventional
Weapons, xix, 27, 28
UN Relief and Works Agency for
Palestine Refugees (UNRWA), 129
UN Secretariat, 129–134
Accountability Panel, 133
budgeting, 129, 130, 131, 133, 134–139 (*see also* assessments, by member countries)
Departments: Disarmament Affairs, 26; Management, monitoring UN functions and activities, 133; Public Information, 120
Division for the Advancement of Women, 70
goal setting, 131, 132, 133
human resources management, xvii, 129–130, 132, 133–134, 137, 138–139, 140; gender equality, 75–76; ombudsman for UN staff, 134, 139
Office of Internal Oversight (OIOS), 133
reform and strengthening of, 128, 129, 131, 144, 147, 148, 151

UN Special Session
on AIDS, 117
on Children (2002), 86–87
UN specialized agencies (WHO, UNESCO, ILO, FAO, etc.), 134, 149
UNAIDS, 115–116
UNCED, 105–106, 107, 110, 111, 123
UNCTAD, 99, 106, 128
UNEP, 103, 110, 112, 113, 128, 134
UNESCO, 149
UNFPA, 134
UNICEF (UN Children's Fund), 91, 103, 128, 134, 149
emergency relief, 91
founded to continue emergency assistance to children, 78
HIV/AIDS, 115; guide, 117
human security, 154
International Conference on Primary Health Care, Alma Ata (1978), 104
Nobel Peace Prize (1965), 89
primary health services, 80
State of the World's Children (1992), 86
UNIFEM (UN Development Fund for Women), 69, 70, 71, 128
United Nations Inter-Agency Task Force for Child Survival and Development, xv
United Nations Relief and Rehabilitation Administration (UNRRA), 91
UN associations, national, 122
UN building, New York, in need of overhaul, 137
UN involvement in individual countries *see* name of country
UN viewed by world leaders (1990), 1–3
UN-European Union plan: to set borders in Yugoslavia, 12–13

uncivil society, 125
unilateral action, USA, 41, 160
Universal Declaration of Human
    Rights, 44, 56–57
    reinforced by Global Compact,
    124
    see also Covenant on Economic,
    Social and Cultural Rights,
    Covenant on Civil and Political
    Rights
USA, 23
    Anti-Ballistic Missile Treaty
    (ABM), scrapping of, 36, 37
    arms trade, 31
    chemical weapons, 32
    expenditures on weapons, 27
    financial support for UN, 107,
    135
    in Iraq, 11; invasion of (2003),
    159, 161, 162–167
    in Somalia, 12
    Kyoto Protocol, opposition to,
    112, 160
    land mines, 29
    nuclear weapons, 33, 34, 160
    opposition to ICC, 47–48
    State Department, annual
    review of human rights viola-
    tions, 62
    unilateral action against terror-
    ism, 41, 160
use of force, 25
    legal commitment of member
    nations, 21–22
    situations in which force may
    be used, 19–20
USSR, 23
    collapse of, xvi
    nuclear arms left after, 33
    see also Russia

Versailles Treaty, 43
veto
    PERM 5, xvi
    Security Council, 147
Vieira de Mello, Sergio, xxi, 18, 40,
62, 166
Vienna Convention (1985), 111
Vienna Declaration: human rights,
    60–61
Vietnam, 23
    use of chemical weapons in, by
    USA, 32
Vike-Freiberga, Vaira, Latvia, 75
violence against women, 63, 69, 74,
    76
virtual sovereignty, shields hench-
    men of slaughter, 94
voluntary contributions to UN,
    134–136
vulnerable children, 81–82, 84, 85

war
    for profit, 125
    fuelled by dirty commerce, 21
    impact on children, 58, 63, 77,
    81–82, 83
    the UN charter, 168
    victims, 91, 93
war crimes, 12, 13, 14, 45
    against women, 74, 75
    attacks on humanitarian work-
    ers considered as, 140
    genocide, 74, 75
    justice for, 53–54
    rape, 49, 52, 83
war crimes tribunals, xix, 13, 14,
    48–55, 134, 136
    deterrent effect of, 50
    joint national-international
    court, Sierra Leone, 18, 54
    Nuremberg, 43
    prosecution of major criminals,
    50
    Rwanda, 48, 51–53, 52–53
    Tokyo, 43
    Yugoslavia, 14, 48, 49–51
Warsaw Pact, 1
water shortages, 114
water, safe, xvii, 113
    goal of Millennium Declara-
    tion, 143

wealth, creation of, in developing countries, 100
weaponization of space, xix, 37
weapons inspections: Iraq, 11–12, 159
weapons of mass destruction (WMD), 26, 28, 33, 37, 109, 161
    elimination of, by USA, 162
    Iraq, 11, 12, 164, 165
    SSOD I, 27
    see also biological, chemical weapons
weapons trade, xix
weapons, inhuman, 28–29
wetlands, 111
    convention, 111
WFP *see* World Food Programme
WHO (World Health Organization), 80, 149
    guide to AIDS drugs, 117
    HIV/AIDS, 115
    International Conference on Primary Health Care, Alma Ata (1978), 104
Williams, Jody: Nobel Peace Prize, 122
WILPF *see* Women's International League for Peace and Freedom
WMD *see* weapons of mass destruction
women
    and girls, protection of, 75, 154
    criminal trade in, 55
    discrimination against, convention, 57–58, 64, 69, 123
    empowerment of, 73, 76
    health issues for, 74
    in power establishments, 72
    legal status and treatment of, annual survey, 69
    participation in government, 75
    peace, promotion of, 72
    role and status, World Summit for Children, 84
    violence against, 63, 69, 74, 76

Women's International League for Peace and Freedom (WILPF), 67, 122
women's movement, 67
women's rights, 67, 69, 123
    Beijing Conference on Women, Declaration and Platform for Action, 72–73, 75
    Commission on the Status of Women (CSW) (1946), 68–70, 128
    denial of, 71–72
    equality of, explicitly affirmed in UN charter, 67
    monitoring of, 69, 70
    political, in international law, 69
    The Hague Peace Conference (1902), 67
Women, Decade for (1976–1985), 70
World Bank, 61, 70, 105, 106, 129
    report on alleviating poverty, 97
    sanctions, 8
World Bank Commission, 106
World Conference
    against Racism, Racial Discrimination, Xenophobia and Related Intolerance (2001), 64
    on Human Rights, Vienna (1993), xix, 59, 60–61
    on Women, 70–73
World Customs Union: criminalization of black market trade in illicit arms, 31
World Economic Forum, 121, 123, 124–126
World Federalists: support for International Criminal Court, 122
World Federation of UN Associations, 122
World Food Programme (WFP), 91, 103, 129
World Health Organization *see*

WHO
World Heritage Convention (1972), 111
World Plan of Action for UN Decade for Women: as participants in public and political life, 71
World Social Forum, Porto Allegre, Brazil (2002, 2003), 126
World Summit
   for Children, New York (1990), 81, 84–86, 103, 104
   for Social Development (1995), 97
   on Human Rights, Vienna (1993), 103
   on Human Settlements, Istanbul (1996), 103
   on Population, Cairo (1994), 103
   on Social Development, Copenhagen (1995), 103
   on Sustainable Development, Johannesburg (2002), 112–114
   on the Environment, Rio (1992), 103
   on Women, Beijing (1995), 103
World Trade Organization, 98, 106, 123, 147, 160
   Ministerial meeting, Seattle (1999), 102–103
World Trade Towers, New York: 11 September 2001, xxi
WTO *see* World Trade Organization

Year of the Child, International (1979), 81
Year of the Woman (1970), 70
Yeltsin, Boris, Russia, 6, 34
Yemen, 32
Yugoslavia, 9, 12–13
   civilian targets, 94
   humanitarian aid, as substitute for political action, 154
   peacekeeping, 7–8
   war crimes tribunal, xix

Zambia, 96
Zedillo, President, Mexico, 156
Zimbabwe, 96